ALAN CONNOR

The Joy of Quiz

PARTICULAR BOOKS

an imprint of

PENGUIN BOOKS

PARTICULAR BOOKS

UK | USA | Canada | Ireland | Australia
India | New Zealand | South Africa

Particular Books is part of the Penguin Random House group of companies
whose addresses can be found at global.penguinrandomhouse.com.

First published 2016
002

Copyright © Alan Connor, 2016

The moral right of the author has been asserted

Set in 10.5/14.5 pt ITC Galliard Pro
Typeset by Jouve (UK), Milton Keynes
Printed in Great Britain by Clays Ltd, St Ives plc

A CIP catalogue record for this book is available from the British Library

ISBN: 978–1–846–14868–2

www.greenpenguin.co.uk

For Lucy

Contents

Continuity
announcement

Introduction

Here's a question:

Why do we spend our childhoods in fear of exams, then quite willingly put ourselves through pretty much the same tests as adults?

It's not a good quiz question – good quiz questions never start with 'How?' or 'Why?' – but it is a good question.

The short answer is: fun. The joy of quiz is in making a gratifying game out of all that knowledge sploshing around in our heads – fascinating information, but information for which our jobs and our personal lives stubbornly refuse to find any use. This information started as a trickle, with widespread literacy; then newspapers were joined by the twin floods of radio and television – and by the internet. As a bonus, if it's a certain kind of quiz, you might win something.

Not that a quiz need offer a prize. In this book, 'quiz' means competing to answer factual questions for enjoyment. Questions themselves aren't enough. We've had questions for ages.

When the Sphinx asked, **What is it that walks on four legs in the morning, on two at noon and on three at the close of the day?,**[1] that was not a quiz. Even if one measly question were enough, this one is not factual. And crucially, the Sphinx's questionees were *not* taking part for the fun of it: they were

---

[1] According to Sophocles, the answer is 'Man' (accept: a woman, people, human beings, etc.), since a person typically begins life crawling and may end it using a cane.

simply trying to get to Thebes – and it hardly counts as a prize to escape being strangled and eaten by the thing asking the questions. So not quiz.

The same goes for the schoolroom. If, dangling overhead, there's a detention (or, in the case of Sunday school and its question-and-answer catechisms, eternal hellfire), answering questions is not a game. Exams are not quiz, although quiz as we know it would not exist without them.

In fact, quiz as we know it in the UK only really kicked off with a radio programme on a regional BBC station as recently as 1938 – though there were a few false starts.

Despite the Victorians' extraordinary ability to find new ways of entertaining each other in a parlour of an evening, the answering of questions was not among their fads. Now, this is not as surprising as it may seem. If you've ever tried to put together a quiz, you'll remember that it takes much longer than you'd hoped to concoct decent questions which cover a satisfying range and which have answers that are unarguably correct. With Charades, by contrast, Victorians could be up and at it with no preparation, and for Pass the Slipper, they needed only a solitary slipper.

No, it was radio that gave birth to quiz. And quiz redefined radio, here and in America: in the 1930s, everything else on air had been adapted from some real-world event (the talk, the play, the concert) or the written word (the newspaper, the essay). Quiz was new. During the Second World War, one in four programmes on American radio was a quiz and, by the time television arrived in 1941, an evening without quiz was inconceivable. Quiz created 'interactivity' and put ordinary people on the airwaves for the first time.

And then ungrateful TV very nearly killed quiz off. The prizes got a little too big, and the corporations funding the prizes wanted everything rigged, so the first era of quiz ended with the indignity of American congressional hearings. Over here, the effect was felt, too: TV had to clean up its act and so evolved higher-minded programmes, beginning with ITV's *University Challenge* and then the BBC's *Mastermind*. In time, there was a quiz for pretty much everyone. In a poll I commissioned in 2016, 81 per cent of British adults said they watch, listen to or take part in quizzes, with 44 per cent doing so at least once a week (with more women among the more ardent devotees of quiz – and Chapter 17 has some sobering stats on how we cheat).

And so, while the shows mentioned above and their hosts will feature in this book, so, I hope, will you. Not just in answering the questions throughout; I'd also hope that the experience is like that of a good quiz: alternately comforting, startling and illuminating; some things you knew and some things you didn't about quizzes on TV and radio, in pubs and homes. Chapter 8 provides reassurance that you *can* revise for an exam which might be on anything at all, though Chapter 9 looks at how knowing facts is barely half the battle. And, along the way, I'll give you some tips on how to get lucky, and let you know what happens when you're unlucky enough to forget everything you once knew. Naturally, there will also be space for the major and the cough, the *Mastermind* cabbie-contender and other heroes and villains of quiz.

'Quiz', by the way, is the word I'll be using for the activity itself. Understand it as you might 'judo' or 'chess'. 'Quizzing' feels pitifully vague: after all, who is quizzing – the person asking or the person answering? I'll use 'setters' for those who write the questions, 'hosts' for those who ask them and 'contestants' for the willing victims trying to answer.

And it's 'a quiz' for an individual set of questions – like the ones peppered in **bold type** throughout this book. In the answers, the words you must say to win the point are <u>under-lined</u>, like on the cards held by TV-quiz hosts. If, for example, you were asked who has a prerogative over all the swans in England and Wales, you really need not answer with HM's full title, 'Elizabeth II, by the Grace of God, of the United Kingdom of Great Britain and Northern Ireland and of Her other Realms and Territories Queen, Head of the Commonwealth, Defender of the Faith', or even with 'Queen Elizabeth II'. 'The <u>Queen</u>' will do. But as you encounter the questions, you may of course award points to yourselves and others in whichever way you fancy. It's your book now.

I'll begin with the story of a quiz from the 1980s which got the world excited all over again about the prospect of asking each other questions. The tale of Trivial Pursuit raises a lot of questions about how quiz works and what makes it such fun. The rest of the book, I hope, gives the answers.

Title theme

1. Mighty contests rise

The timely arrival of Trivial Pursuit

'We were the world's largest game publisher,' recalled a rueful executive at Milton Bradley, makers of Twister and Yahtzee. 'We knew it all. First, we knew adults didn't play games. We also knew no one would pay $29.95 to $39.99 retail.'

So it was that, in 1982, MB graciously declined to take and make Trivial Pursuit, a game which, in 1984, sold 22 million boxes costing up to sixty dollars a pop. As for America's other games behemoth, Parker Brothers (Monopoly, Risk), they returned the copy of the game they had been sent. It was unopened.

Tales of corporate klutzing are irresistible and common: take the record label **Decca, who in 1962 turned down the chance to sign which group, formerly known as Johnny and the Moondogs, on the basis that 'guitar groups are on the way out'?**[1] or **the BBC comedy editor who in 1974 wrote of which programme: 'I'm afraid I thought this one as dire as its title. It's a kind of "Prince of Denmark" of the hotel world'?**[2] These

[1] The Beatles.
[2] Fawlty Towers.

tales evoke **that delight in another's misfortune which the Germans denote using what single word?**[3]

But perhaps we can forgive the suits their caution about the idea that adults might enjoy asking each other general-knowledge questions. It wasn't just that the whole point of a board game was generally accepted to be occupying the time of bored children. (The typical board-game box may have depicted an unreal world of smiling über-children, but at least it was jolly. The packaging of Trivial Pursuit looked more like a presentation case for a set of fish knives.)

No, the game itself was also suspect. *Quiz?*

American quiz had not yet recovered from the 1950s Congressional Committee on Legislative Oversight, which revealed that the outcomes of all the big shows were fixed. When quiz fell off the schedules, game shows filled much of the gap, and even America's smartest quiz – that warhorse *Jeopardy!* – spluttered in and out of consciousness throughout the 1970s, disappearing from TV screens for years at a time and coming off the air in March 1979 – for all anyone knew then, permanently.

And even if quiz had been in its heyday, at least on quiz programmes, you might win some money, or a set of fish knives. Who on earth would *pay* for the privilege of answering questions? Without any sort of prize, the business of factual Q-and-As was, like Ker-Plunk or Hungry Hungry Hippos, for schoolchildren – students, at best. But the age recommended on the Trivial Pursuit box was 'Adult'.

At this point, quiz had existed for barely more than fifty years. How it all started is something we'll get to, just as soon as we've seen how the men who devised Trivial Pursuit persuaded themselves and each other that the world needed home

[3] Schadenfreude.

quizzing and went on to own golf courses and suchlike as their reward.

> It is highly recommended that players keep the plastic trees on which the tokens and scoring wedges come. They make excellent swizzle sticks.
>
> – from the Rules of Play in the 1981
> edition of Trivial Pursuit

For a game that is so evocative of the rainy days of the 1980s, it's perhaps a surprise to learn that Trivial Pursuit was developed on a Spanish beach. And that its inventors resembled a family of drunken walruses.

Chris 'The Horn' Haney and Scott 'Spunky' Abbott were Canadian, and a certain kind of hippy: the kind that likes money but doesn't have any. They had concocted a chain-letter scheme in the late 1970s which yielded a couple of thousand (Canadian) dollars but, as the 1980s approached, times were tight.

Abbott was a moustachioed sportswriter for the Canadian Press news agency and Haney a moustachioed photo editor at the offices of the *Montreal Gazette*, across the road from which was a bar called the American Tavern. At the Tavern, Abbott's near-infallible memory for sporting facts and figures became a little local legend. You only had to ask him . . .

The pair would spend their evenings there and then retire to Haney's, where Abbott's rent as a lodger was helping Haney and his wife, Sarah, pay the bills. How, they pondered, could a couple of guys like them make their fortune?

What they lacked in spendable capital they made up for in 'cultural capital' – in their case, lots of little facts – and their penny-drop moment was deciding to turn those facts not into journalism, or even a book, but a game. If they could only come up with a game which, like Scrabble, in Haney's words, 'everyone has stashed away in their closets . . .'

So they mocked up a board on a piece of bent cardboard, then returned to the bars of Montreal to tap up the other barflies for investment: $200 per share with a minimum purchase of five. This seed capital funded a 1980 boat trip (Haney wouldn't fly, despite or perhaps because of his wife having a pilot's licence) to the sunny counter-cultural hangout of Nerja in Andalucía.

They packed mainly reference books (including a couple which they might later have wished they'd forgotten to stow in their duffel bags) and set up camp at the El Capistrano resort, where they had wangled rent-free accommodation in Haney's parents' villa.

Each day for several months they took some books and some beer to the beach and continued to assemble the volume of questions they guessed they would need (which also gave them their underwhelming working title 'Six Thousand Questions'). They favoured, said Haney, 'the kind of things we knew from being in the news business, being attuned to small details', and tested them on passing American and British beach bums to see which questions 'got people going'.

They also took the opportunity, in the bars after hours, to see whether any of those beach bums had a thousand dollars which they could turn into a share of a million. Unfortunately, in the words of a local, the Canadians' 'main investment seemed to be in San Miguel, so everybody laughed and called for another round'. Fortunately, one barman, who prefers to remain prosperously anonymous, took them up on it.

Six thousand questions later, they were back in Canada, ready to tackle the tricky bits: making the thing and selling it. Abbott's brother John, a hockey player who was getting a little old for the game, had joined the team, along with Ed Werner, a former team mate turned lawyer. For the company name, they combined Chris

'The Horn' Haney's nickname (minus 'the') with Abbott (minus one 't'), and their logo was . . . a horny abbot. For the game itself, they dabbled with the name 'Trivia Pursuit' until Sarah added an 'l' to the 'Trivia' because 'it sounded better'; many players would later add an 's' to the 'Pursuit' and an 'i' in the middle of the 'Genus', the name of the first 'edition'.

Giving themselves 'a crash course in capitalism' by using their yellowing press passes to sneak into Montreal's Canadian Toy Fair, Haney and Abbott pointed a camera at games manufacturers and retailers and asked them to explain to the viewers how to make the leap from idea to hit product. There was no film in the camera.

The answer to that question, it turned out, was: expensively and exhaustingly. They painstakingly assembled prototypes of Trivial Pursuit, on their first attempt printing the question cards at their local post office. Once they had 1,100 sets, the next hurdle was to get some sales momentum going: they wanted to shift each set for $29.95 retail and $16 wholesale. It escaped nobody's notice that it cost *them* $60 to make each one. Sarah just about made enough to pay the bills by sewing lavender sachets and recycling for pennies the many beer bottles which were accumulating.

Abbott sums up the period like this: 'I had hangovers all the time and I was dreaming in Q-and-A.' And, of the pair, he was the healthier. It was Haney who 'really carried the ball', recalls Sarah.

'He'd be gone from 7.30 a.m. to 8 p.m.' Then he would relax with a bartender who, as he phrased it, 'really enjoyed giving me triple scotches at night'. He kept the food bills down by switching from eating to going through five packets of Camels a day. After two nervous collapses in the space of a fortnight, he went to Sarah's parents' farm for a few weeks to chop wood and be silent. And the horny abbot lost money with every sale.

They were saved by the boredom of Glenn Close.

Close had come across a copy of Trivial Pursuit – by then being manufactured by the company Selchow & Righter in goodlier quantities, although more were pining on shop shelves than were stashed in home closets – and took it on to the California set of *The Big Chill*. The fit was perfect: the stars of an ensemble film about baby boomers, with time on their hands, confronted with a quiz containing thousands of boomer-friendly questions.

Time magazine told the nation how Kevin Kline, Jeff Goldblum, Meg Tilley and the rest were filling the hours of waiting around that come with movie-making: 'In Hollywood, where game playing is sometimes the most exigent art form, Trivial Pursuit [is a] monster [hit]. During the filming of *The Big Chill*, the entire cast became addicted to the game, playing it night and day'; and the stars found themselves inadvertent ambassadors for the game. A set was presented to every journalist at the movie's New York screening. And that was that: Abbott and Haney's aspirations to make quiz aspirational were fulfilled by celebrity endorsement and found their way into the yuppie market.

It wasn't just luck, though, which made Trivial Pursuit a monster. The game not only provided players with more questions than they could have made up themselves, it also had a great structure – and quiz needs a structure to be enjoyable. The game offers the tense ebb and flow of advantage, a clear endpoint and a range of material – not to mention the satisfaction of knowing the answers to the questions. (It has to be said, however, that the first edition was not 100 per cent accurate: one card, for example, claimed that Aldous Huxley was **the person who coined the phrase 'brave new world'.**[4])

Buying a copy of Trivial Pursuit let you stage a quiz show in

---

[4] William Shakespeare. (Huxley borrowed it from *The Tempest*'s 'O brave new world / That has such people in't!'.)

your own home, with no need to expend any toil or imagination in coming up with the questions. You took it in turns to be the 'host', you had a fair idea of how long the game was going to last and you had intriguing items in front of you, like the player counters which double as score cards (and, if you match the position of your 'wedges' to the 'category headquarters' on the board, a handy map showing where you need to go next). There was no jackpot at the end of it, but the game was relentlessly sociable.

Selchow & Righter's interest was born of a hope that the explosion of single-player video games (like the one in the excellently gettable Trivial Pursuit question about **the games character which was inspired by the shape of a pizza with a slice removed**[5]) might, rather than crush the board game, remind people of what they loved about social gaming.

The company, which years before had declined Monopoly so as not to be seen to promote gambling, persuaded Abbott and Haney to make the experience less 'adult', removing the occasional question to which there was a sweary answer, and other family-unfriendly posers such as **how many months pregnant was Nancy Davis when she walked down the aisle with Ronald Reagan?**[6]

They left in, though: 'Who invented the brassiere?', the given answer to which was 'Otto Titzling'. It was both vaguely rude and wholly wrong, having been taken from a spoof history of the bra. This one might have had Science & Nature as its category on the card but, for Haney and Abbott, it was a 'snapper': a short, punchy question with a kick.

The pair didn't just divide the questions by category, they had their own terminology to describe the effect they thought various questions might have in the course of a game. Along

[6] Two and a half (which a player can only be expected to guess).
[5] Pac-Man (though this may be a tidied-up creation myth).

15

with the 'snappers' were the occasional 'stoppers', which would limit the chances of a trivia buff spoiling the game by collecting all the wedges before anyone else had so much as rolled the die. Abbott's example: 'We asked what hospital-room number Ed Norton of *The Honeymooners* stayed in after being injured in a sewer explosion. Nobody in his right mind would know that,' he said, adding hopefully: 'but somebody will.'

At the other end of the scale were those questions Haney – regrettably – termed 'mongies': 'for people who are brain-dead at one in the morning, and they'll still get them right'.

The snappers reflect Abbott and Haney's understanding of the deliberation gone through when trying to answer a question and the players' response to its answer are as important to quiz as the questions themselves. You might fail to give the right answer to **who is the only US President to have worn a Nazi uniform?**,[7] but you will surely slap your forehead when you hear it.

The snappers did much to give Trivial Pursuit its quiz personality. So did the stoppers, though if you made it back to the hexagonal hub with six wedges only to be asked for something as arcane as a fictional hospital-room number, you'd be rightly aggrieved.

One of the stoppers irritated one customer so much – though for very different reasons – that he launched a $300 million lawsuit.

Fred L. Worth was a good air-traffic controller but an excellent amasser of trivia. In the 1970s, Worth spent his off-time jotting down pieces of cultural information on three-by-five-inch cards.

The cards listed the names of film and television characters, along with their addresses, social-security numbers, car registration plates . . . Others noted which actors had appeared in which

7 Ronald Reagan, in the 1942 film *Desperate Journey*.

programmes or appeared on the covers of which magazines. These disparate micro-facts, garnered from hundreds of thousands of sources, he indexed, sorted and then published in 1974 as *The Trivia Encyclopedia*. It was a kind of analogue version of what would later be known as a 'fan website' – except that Worth was a fan of pretty much the entire noösphere of pop culture.

Other volumes followed, and the questions on their covers give a sense of Worth's interests. **What was written on the Mad Hatter's hat?**[8] **Who was Miss Hungary of 1936?**[9] **For how long is a US patent in effect?**[10]

Worth was gathering this information from scratch, noting down data as the late-night TV played. If pop minutiae is a field, he was a pioneer in it. But what was to stop anyone else reproducing in a moment this information which he had so long toiled to amass? Worth used a trick long deployed by many others who compile reference works: he included one little lie.

No one calls them 'lies', of course; they tend to be referred to as 'mountweazels', after an entry on page 1,850 of the *New Columbia Encyclopedia* (1975 edition), which gives the sad biographical details of photographer Lillian Virginia Mountweazel, who died 'at 31 in an explosion while on assignment for *Combustibles* magazine'. Mountweazel never existed; she was in the book, said one of its editors, because '[i]f someone copied Lillian, then we'd know they'd stolen from us'.

Likewise Bartlett Place, which the most assiduous search of the Isle of Dogs will never ferret out, as it is one of the hundred or so fictional streets which have been planted in the London *A–Z*. And if the existence and explosion of Ms Mountweazel seems more obviously fictitious than the location of

[8] In John Tenniel's illustration, 'In this style 10/'.
[9] Zsa Zsa Gabor (accept Gábor Sári), who was later disqualified for being under age.
[10] Twenty years.

Bartlett Place, the mountweazel inserted by Fred L. Worth was tiny, inconspicuous and eminently plausible. In the entry for the character Columbo in the detective series of the same name, Worth added a line: 'First name: Philip.'

In fact, Columbo has no first name; he is, simply, 'Columbo'. Worth's was a wonderful choice of bogus fact. Even if you were a diehard fan of **Columbo's lead actor**[11] and had watched dozens of episodes, it's perfectly plausible that you'd missed the lead character's first name, or that it had cropped up in one of the episodes you had missed. In 1974, the 'fact' was effectively unverifiable, unless you waited for re-runs and spent every episode glued to the screen.

'Philip' waited.

Come 1984, and Worth was out of work. He had joined an air-traffic strike, and he and his fellow strikers were permanently debarred from holding any federal post, at the insistence of Ronald Reagan. He had published more trivia books, but trivia hadn't made him rich. And this was certainly not because there was no appetite for the stuff of trivia. You only had to look at Trivial Pursuit: in 1984, people shelled out $400 million for much the same material.

Very much the same material.

Worth was working on a book entitled *Questions* and had been advised to keep away from anything in a question-and-answer format while he was writing it. 'When I turned in my manuscript,' he remembers, 'the first [game] I picked up was Trivial Pursuit. I said, "Boy, this stuff sure looks familiar."'

The game had misprints where Worth's books had misprints, errors where they had errors. In one answer, **the colours**

11 Peter Falk.

of the five Olympic rings[12] were listed in the same random and non-alphabetical order as in Worth's *Encyclopedia*. In other words, there were all the basic clues you look for when you suspect that someone might have 'borrowed' your work.

And then Worth saw, nestling between Geography's **what Mediterranean country is the only one in the world to display its map on its flag?**[13] and History's **what did cowpunchers use to protect their legs?**[14], the Entertainment question 'What's Columbo's first name?'

Very hard to answer, that one. Much easier to imagine Worth's response to seeing 'Philip' on the back of the card. 'I worked ten years for their glory and financial gain,' he said of the makers of Trivial Pursuit. He launched a multimillion-dollar lawsuit.

Worth kept the Columbo fact to himself when he announced the suit; meanwhile, Horn Abbot affected an insouciant air: 'It's kinda neat,' quipped the lawyer, Werner, who was also fending off claims from people who insisted that they had invented the game before Abbott and Haney, 'to hang around the bar telling people you're being sued for $300 million.' Worth mortgaged his house to pay his legal fees.

In total, Worth reckoned that 32 per cent of the questions in Trivial Pursuit had been lifted from his *Encyclopedia* and its sequel. Faced with the mutual misprints and errors – and 'just one more thing', as Columbo might have put it – Haney and Abbott could hardly challenge Worth's charges. Yes, well over a thousand of their questions had in fact been 'written' by lifting a fact from Worth and plonking a question mark at the end.

[14] Chaps.
[13] Cyprus; nowadays, Kosovo does, too.
[12] From left to right: blue, yellow, black, green, red.

All they could do was moot that that's what they thought encyclopaedias were *for*: to be a work of reference from which you can take what you like.

And that was enough.

The district court agreed, as did the appeals court; and the Supreme Court declined to hear the case. Game over. No doubt this seemed harsh to Worth, who was being simultaneously sued by his ex-wife for a share of the damages she thought might be due to him and was owed $50,000 by the now-bust publisher of his *Encyclopedia*. But writing down a fact about the world does not give you ownership of it, in law . . . or in fact.

To lock down facts, to make them the property of whoever wrote them down first, deemed the court, 'would stifle the very creativity which that law is designed to foster'. The ruling demonstrated an understandable wariness about assigning copyright protection in a fact to the first person who notes it down. Imagine the effect on quiz: every question, once asked, could never be asked again.

It's very hard to argue with the ruling that the 'discovery of a fact, regardless of the quantum of labor and expense, is simply not the work of an author' – but it's also a reminder that for every quiz answer, every reference-book entry, there's a schlepping schmo or harmless drudge who bothered to put it into words.

A year after Worth retired – he'd taken a job in local bureaucracy – he went for lunch with repeat *Jeopardy!* champion Ken Jennings. Jennings was interviewing Worth for a book about America's passion for trivia, but Worth insisted on buying the steak sandwiches and fries for the man whose quizzing had won him $2.5 million. He wanted to add to his stock of anecdotes one which conferred upon him some dignity.

*

Inevitably, Trivial Pursuit had, in turn, its own copycats: it was one of at least fifty general-knowledge board games vying for the money of the Christmas shoppers of America in 1984.

And before long, the official Trivial Pursuit family grew: the cinematic Silver Screen, the musical RPM and the frankly superfluous Baby Boomer edition. For the many who could not be persuaded to stray from the original Genus, there was merchandising, in that particularly 1980s form of aspirational tat: quartz-accurate watches, executive pencil caddies and a kit containing a brass box to hold the game and 'gold-electroplated' counters.

Horn Abbot also needed to jump fast to dominate the international market for general-knowledge board games – so fast that they ended up recruiting some bar buddies from Spain to set questions for the British edition. This version had questions from a pair described in a 1984 profile as 'penniless art historian Ray Loud and Steve Birch, a former kitchen designer', who had heard some of the prototype questions at a Nerja barbecue and concocted some less American-centric alternatives at speed in a Leighton Buzzard hotel. There still seemed to be a lot of baseball questions in the finished product.

This was all happening a long way from Montreal, and Horn Abbot knew still less about the non-English-language versions. 'It was selling so fast that licensees did whatever they wanted,' recalled Richard Gill, the man in charge of granting the licences. 'Companies launched it without getting the questions sanctioned.'

Across the world, Haney's vision had become a real thing, albeit one sometimes covered in dust: Trivial Pursuit was indeed something which everyone had stashed away in their closets. For most of them, though, that meant they didn't need to buy another set. The 22 million American sales in 1984 were followed by sales of 5.5 million in 1985. That was bad news for the ledgers at Selchow & Righter, whose worth fell from around $200 million to $75 million – which is what the makers of the Cabbage Patch Kids paid to absorb the company in 1986. When *that* craze faded, the parent company was itself absorbed by Hasbro – and the mainstream game industry finally accepted Trivial Pursuit.

Boom, then bust. But, like the nervous breakdowns and the various lawsuits, the fading of their fad couldn't stop Haney and Abbott, who had kept their moustaches and invested wisely, if louchely. Thoroughbred racehorses, a hockey team, a couple of golf courses: pretty much what you'd hope they'd buy. They were right to hope that other people around the world would enjoy what they had spent those evenings in the American Tavern doing.

People, if given the opportunity, tend to quiz. And the opportunities were multiplying. The year 1984 saw quiz appearing in new places (pubs, bars) and reappearing in old ones (a revived *Jeopardy!*). Today, it's hard to fathom that Trivial Pursuit could ever have been seen as anything other than a very promising investment.

And where do you come from?

2. Quite a quiz
Quiz's rise to ubiquity from nowhere

What colourful two-word phrase is believed to derive from the practice of dragging a malodorous *Clupea harengus* across a trail in order to put hunting dogs off the scent?[1]

The origins of the word 'quiz' are vague, but if you piece together fragments from the dusty memoirs of the worthies of late-eighteenth-century Dublin, a tale is told, and a legend is launched.

The launcher is Richard Daly, an incorrigible Galwayman, the subject of endless anecdotes, very good at challenging people to duels and very, very bad at duelling. Frequently caught by swords or bullets, he somehow never died, at least not in a duel. When he wasn't being dissolute he ran some theatres in Dublin; the rest of his time was spent on diversions like making 'wagers in reference to incidental matters, however unimportant'.

One such wager was made following the announcement that Her Grace the Duchess of Leinster had been safely delivered of a young Marquis of Kildare. The great and the good of Dublin toasted the happy news in the Eagle pub and, as a

[1] 'Red herring.'

magistrate recalled it: '[t]he evening had, as might be expected, a convivial termination'.

Among the celebrants was Daly, as convivial as a newt. A pleasant conversation about how words are coined was turned by Daly into first an argument and then a bet. Words were, he insisted, invented by such great men as himself, and he put twenty guineas to his claim that 'within forty-eight hours, there shall be a word in the mouths of the Dublin public, of all classes and sexes, young and old; and also that within a week, the same public shall attach a definite and generally adopted meaning to that word, without any suggestion or explanation from me.'

He boastfully added that the new word would not be derived from any existing word in any language, and demanded: 'Now, Alderman, what say you to taking my word or winning my money?'

The alderman in question, Mr Richard Moncrieffe, already regarded Daly as a nuisance: the more disreputable Dublin theatregoers were in the habit of throwing 'glass bottles and brick-bats' on to his stage and into his pit and, while Moncrieffe wished to prosecute them, Daly tended to let them get away and return the next day to buy another ticket. The alderman took the bet.

So Daly did what any theatre proprietor would do: he got his staff to work overtime. Issued with cards bearing Daly's coinage, they were instructed to go out into the city that night: 'In the course of this time the letters Q, u, i, z were chalked or pasted on all the walls of Dublin with an effect that won the wager.'

And, they say, since the unsuspecting folk who found their homes and businesses vandalized were furiously asking a question ('What in the name of all that is good and holy is "quiz"?'), the new word gained the meaning it has today: the world's first quiz question was 'What is quiz?'

In the discreetly appended words of one of the tellers of this tale, '[t]he parties to the wager . . . have all disappeared, but I have heard several of them narrate the particulars as I have stated them.'

In other words, there is just one problem with this widely told origin myth. It's balderdash: a herring as red, and probably redder, than that smelly *Clupea harengus*. Like the best etymological anecdotes (the acronym 'for unlawful carnal knowledge'; or marmalade being a headache cure favoured by Mary, Queen of Scots – *Marie est malade*), sadly, it doesn't stand up to inspection.

Far from being a word underived from anything in English or any other language, 'quiz' was already up and running before the apocryphal evening in the Eagle – even though the eighteenth century didn't have quizzes.

So what did 'quiz' really mean, and how did it come to mean a general-knowledge contest? The answer comes below, in the form of a short quiz based around the word 'quiz', a kind of ' "quiz" quiz'.

In the 1797 play *Heir at Law*, a pompous personal tutor uses 'a quiz' as slang for a weird-looking person. (**This character, Dr Pangloss, is named after the ever-optimistic Professor Pangloss in Voltaire's *Candide*, famous for insisting that 'All is for the best in . . .' what?**[2]) 'Quiz' moved from describing odd-looking people to describing puzzling and amusing objects. It was the name for a spring-action toy which was fashionable in the late eighteenth century and operated as a kind of

---

[2] '. . . the best of possible worlds.' (Accept, e.g. 'this best of all possible worlds', or any other reasonable translation of '*le meilleur des mondes possibles*.')

yoyo. (**What links the yoyo to the memory stick, the jacuzzi, the cashpoint, the autocue, the rawl plug, the portaloo and the hoover?**[3])

By the nineteenth century, 'quiz' had changed meaning again: it was used not only for amusing objects but also for amusing people: banterers, wits and practical jokers. ('**What a wicked girl you are!' cries Dickens's Mrs Todgers. 'You're quite a quiz, I do declare!' These lines are from** *Martin Chuzzlewit*; **can you name the seven other surnames which appear in the titles of finished Dickens novels?**[4]) And then, 'quiz' moved on once more: from being a noun describing someone who might mock, it became a verb meaning 'to regard mockingly', and then 'to interrogate with the eye', as in: '**Better quiz evils with too strained an eye / Than have them leap from disregarded lairs.' These lines appear in** *The Dynasts*, **a verse play by Thomas Hardy 'In Three Parts, Nineteen Acts, and One Hundred and Thirty Scenes', which is rarely performed, since it attempts to stage which conflicts of 1803 to 1815?**[5]

So 'quiz' moves from describing an odd person to describing a joker, then a critical observer; and then we have a final little leap from 'interrogate with the eye' to 'interrogate on matters factual for fun'. That leap needed some kind of push, and the process was sufficiently gradual that you couldn't confidently ask a quiz question about it. The *Oxford Dictionary* guesses that words such as 'inquisition' and 'inquisitive' may have helped along the meaning of 'quiz', but – pleasingly stubbornly – refuses to commit to anything stronger than a 'probably influenced'; Stephen Fry suggests that 'the first

3 They have all been proprietary names. (Accept any wording indicating commercial ownership.) The earlier in the question you got the answer, the better.
4 Pickwick, Twist, Nickleby, Rudge, Dombey, Copperfield, Dorrit.
5 The Napoleonic Wars; this question works best if you 'hear' it asked in the voice of Jeremy Paxman.

question in the old grammar-school Latin oral: "*Qui es?*" or, "Who are you?" ' might have done a similar job.

Perhaps no one will ever pinpoint the first use of 'quiz' as we now understand it. Also, quizzes have not always been called 'quizzes'. The first quizzes on BBC radio tended to be called 'bees'. In January 1938, the BBC broadcast a *Transatlantic Spelling Bee*, a co-production with the National Broadcasting Company of America, billed as a 'spelling match between members of Harvard and Radcliffe Colleges, and Oxford University'.

While this was more of a school-room exercise than a real quiz, it introduced listeners to such novelties as rounds and buzzers, and was successful enough that subsequent 'bees' pitted Age against Youth, Men against Women and the BBC against its Listeners. And once the format was in place, those Listeners were ready for the start of the British quizzing tradition: *General Knowledge Bee* was 'a contest across the Pennines' to establish whether the good people of Lancashire or those of Yorkshire knew more.

Tucked away on Regional Programme Northern, Britain first heard people buzzing to answer general-knowledge questions shortly after 8.30 p.m. on 19 April 1938 – **the same year as the invention of an early form of which pastime, in which 'quiz' should mean at least 22?**[6]

Two hundred thousand years of *Homo sapiens* – 'man who knows' – and, for the first time, Britain heard (inevitably) men competing to find out who was the most sapient.

As radio led, other media followed. Today, quiz provides filler for news websites which have forsworn journalism; in a previous technological epoch, it added value to CD-ROMS such as the *Encarta* encyclopaedia . . .

6 Scrabble (Alfred Mosher Butts considered calling the game 'It').

Name the conflict between thirteen British colonies on the eastern seaboard of North America and their parent country, Great Britain.[7]

. . . before that, its questions were posed by Bamber Boozle on Teletext; before *that*, they filled white space below the columns of coordinates in telephone directories.

And it's not just in the media. You might encounter quiz when you're trying to eat. Here's a question: **Which wind is shown as force 12 on the Beaufort wind scale?**[8] It's from the wrapper of a Quiz, a corn-syrup bar of the 1960s, and the answer could be found by unwrapping it.

A decade earlier, American diner tables boasted the Wise Owl Quizzette ('TURNS DEAD OVERHEAD NAPKIN EXPENSE INTO A PROFIT'), which dispensed trivia as well as paper napkins. Want to know the answer to Question 82: **What city is called the Hub of the Universe?**[9] Insert another cent for the answer, and for Question 83. 'TEST YOUR IQ' shouted the plaque next to the voracious slot.

The packaging, the accoutrements . . . but has anyone gone so far as to make the questions edible? Yes. Yes, they have. In 2004, Procter & Gamble began using food colouring to spray quiz onto individual Pringles ('It's a great way to add fun to the lunch'), from the vaguely high-brow (**What Shakespeare play is about the summer solstice?**[10]) to questions about other snacks (**What colour is the cool saxophone-playing M&M?**[11]).

---

11 Blue.

10 *A Midsummer Night's Dream.*

9 Boston, though since this title is geographically vague and about as official as 'World's #1 Dad', other places have claimed it: the town of Boswell, Indiana, even makes the boast on its water tower.

8 A hurricane.

7 War of the American Revolution (accept American War of Independence).

Quiz is in our conversations: it has given the language so many useful phrases that, if there's a situation which involves one of those essentials of most quiz programmes – truth, time and money (and that covers pretty much all of life) – one will fit. The phrases below are so well known, it's barely worth asking you **which programmes they come from:**

> **'Here's your starter for ten.'**[12]
> **'Is that your final answer?'**[13]
> **'I've started so I'll finish.'**[14]
> **'*That* is the sixty-four-thousand-dollar question.'**[15]

They're so well-known, in fact, that politicians feel confident using them when debating legislation. For example, **which Conservative party leader was the subject of the following political insult from prime minister Tony Blair in December 2000?** 'I know that the Leader of the Opposition is keen on summing up policy in six words. How about this: "You are the weakest link. Goodbye"?'[16]

Yes, the prime minister did an Anne Robinson impersonation as part of the debate on the Queen's Speech – and Chris Tarrant, too ('ask the audience').

More recently, Baroness Burridge did a better job when she told the Lords that 'the measure of progress for the Central African Republic will be when it is no longer a *Pointless* answer', deftly deploying a catchphrase at the same time as a quiz-show in-joke. (As *Pointless* established itself, so many people failed to name the Central African Republic when asked for, say, a

12 *University Challenge*.
13 *Who Wants to Be a Millionaire?*
14 *Mastermind*.
15 *The $64,000 Question* (though it entered common coinage as 'The Sixty-four-dollar Question' – see Chapter 12).
16 William Hague, who led the Conservatives from 1997 to 2001.

French-speaking country, or even for a country beginning with 'C', that new contestants were advised: 'If in doubt, say "Central African Republic".')

Back in 1954, Michael Foot evoked quiz host Wilfred Pickles in *Have a Go* when he summarized credulous governmental attitudes to military expenditure: 'Give 'em the money, Barney.'

In every instance, you know what they mean. Sometimes, politicians have to debate quiz itself: a vital part of the story of quiz is governments' decisions about what's fair and about how big prizes should be (see Chapter 12). And, before quiz began, it was thanks to a government report that people got into the habit of asking and answering factual questions in the first place.

3. Ask me another
The rise of the question

FA Cup finals quiz: Test your knowledge of last
fifteen years
BBC Sport, 28 May 2015

Back to the Future turns thirty! Take this quiz to
test your memory of the '80s movie
Today.com, 22 June 2015

Test your wits: tennis player or cheese?
Daily Telegraph, 26 June 2014

Imperial China knew how to test. Candidates for the civil service arrived at the examination compound with bedding, a
chamber pot and some ink and brushes, ready to spend three
days and two nights in an exam centre surrounded by a high
wall with, it was said, no opening big enough for even an ant to
intrude. If you died during the exam, the examiners wrapped
you in straw matting and tossed you over the wall.

The papers of those candidates who came out of the process
alive were transcribed by an official copyist, so that the person
marking couldn't exercise favouritism, should he recognize
someone's handwriting.

After about twelve hundred years of this meritocratic
recruitment, the West started to wonder whether there might
be something in it. The philosopher and jurist Jeremy Bentham

started banging on about it in the 1820s, and the British establishment, influenced by the Chinese model, soon began using tests to assess candidates. The 1854 Northcote–Trevelyan *Report on the Organisation of the Permanent Civil Service* found that 'Admission into the civil service is indeed generally sought after, but it is for the unambitious, and the indolent or incapable that it is chiefly desired.'

The indolent, the report noted, stuck around so long as they were moderately attentive and avoided 'any flagrant misconduct'. Who were these work-shy fops? 'The chief of the department . . . will probably bestow the office upon the son or dependant of someone having personal or political claims upon him, or perhaps upon the son of some meritorious public servant, without instituting any very minute inquiry into the merits of the young man himself.'

In less diplomatic language, the country's most important jobs were being assigned nepotistically to its biggest idiots. The examinations that followed the report were not conducted exactly as Bentham had dreamed: he had imagined that the questions in any particular examination were to be chosen on the spot by a very young child to prevent any jiggery-pokery, and that, of all the candidates who had passed, each job should go to the one who was prepared to accept the lowest salary: that's nineteenth-century utilitarian philosophers for you. Still, nepotism took a knock.

In America, the equivalent of the old-boys-and-their-sons network was known as the spoils system, and it was equally rotten. After an election, government posts would be doled out by the winners to their chums and to those who had helped them win. President James Garfield, however, had civil-service reform on his mind, and the issue became somewhat more pressing in 1881.

College drop-out and shyster lawyer Charles Guiteau thought that he was responsible for Garfield's electoral success on the basis of a public speech of support he had given a couple of times. This inspirational oratory, he fancied, had undoubtedly earned him a position in public life, preferably the Vienna ambassadorship, and when he was turned away from the State Department he decided to kill Garfield, which he then did, at the Baltimore and Potomac Railroad Station (**in which cities did the other three American presidential assassinations take place?**[1]).

Senators and the public realized that if a president could be shot in the back because of the expectations of entitlement encouraged by the spoils system, there was something amiss with America's patronage procedures. The spoils system joined Guiteau in the dock, and both were killed off. The Pendleton Law followed, and it insisted on civil-service exams.

Around the same time, the world of education was embracing and spreading the idea of assessing someone by giving them a timed test on what they knew – likewise a novelty. In the 1850s, the traditional Oxbridge exam was a curious ceremony in which candidates answered philosophical rather than factual questions, orally and on the spot.

'The academics in charge,' says historian Christopher Stray, 'would be sitting a little higher than the rest.' Local graduates gathered 'as a kind of audience' as some candidate was asked to advance, in Latin, a thesis such as 'God is good' or 'A triangle has three sides'. He would be argued against by another candidate, and by another participant: 'The jester had the role of making jokes, intervening to stir things in the disputation. He might make rude comments; in some cases, he would give a

[1] Lincoln: Ford's Theater, Washington, DC; McKinley: the Temple of Music, Buffalo, NY; Kennedy: Dealey Plaza, Dallas, TX.

witty or scurrilous speech, and sometimes this got so scurrilous that his speech, having been printed, was burned.'

Take away the Latin, and that could be a day-time game-show format – if it weren't for the fact that there wasn't such a thing as a 'correct' answer. The method of *elenchus* was preferred, **a disputational form of inquiry which is usually referred to using the name of which Greek philosopher?**[2] Change, however, was coming.

In education, as in the civil service, there was a feeling that the middle classes just couldn't get a look-in. For upper-class children, nepotism persisted in other areas of life. And even the poor had some chance, as religious societies and the state began enabling the young working classes to read and write at primary schools. Angry middle-class parents felt that their children were outflanked on both sides, especially if their school (grammar or private, but not top-tier) was coasting along.

Following the Northcote–Trevelyan report, Oxford and Cambridge extended this new notion of the 'test' to 'that large class of persons who cannot afford, or who do not require a University education for their children, by undertaking to examine boys, about the time of their leaving school'.

And so the written test, which had begun to accompany Oxbridge's (now jesterless) disputation, and which was to supersede it, spilled out into the wider world in 1858. Schools, it was felt, would up their game and provide children with more than 'bastard practical instruction', and the ablest boys (girls were not a consideration) would achieve the station in life they deserved, benefiting the nation as a whole.

Oxbridge's 'presiding examiners' began taking train journeys to far-flung schools, resplendent in academic finery and

2 Socrates (the Socratic method).

carrying locked boxes containing papers with questions such as these, from the University of Cambridge Local Examinations Syndicate:

> **Obtain the sum of forty-six times seven thousand and twenty, seventeen times one million and one, and thirty-three times thirty-three.**[3]
>
> **Name in order the Queens and the children of Henry VIII. On what grounds was he divorced from his first wife?**[4]
>
> **In what three ways was Our Lord tempted in the wilderness?**[5]

A practical advantage of the written paper over the disputation is its efficiency (accentuated by the railway and the penny post): you can in theory test everyone – and indeed, by 1870, more people (or, at least, more middle-class children) than ever before found themselves tested on what they knew (or, at least, what they could remember that they had at some stage known).

Within a generation, the whole idea of knowledge changed: it became something that could be chopped up into discrete parts – questions which you could be right or wrong about.

The American army chopped things up still further: recruiters regarded general knowledge as a good indicator of whether a potential soldier was smart enough not to give secrets away to the enemy, and testing vast numbers of young men became easier with the creation of the multiple-choice test.

Variants of the 'Army Alpha', which could be marked mechanically, were used for recruitment in civilian life. On p. 39

3 $322,920 + 17,000,017 + 1,089 = 17,324,026$.
4 Catherine of Aragon, Anne Boleyn, Jane Seymour, Anne of Cleves, Catherine Howard, Catherine Parr; excluding the illegitimate and those who died young: Mary, Elizabeth, Edward; he became the head of the Church (accept: she had married his brother).
5 Making bread from stones; jumping from a pinnacle and being caught by angels; worshipping the devil.

is **a 1921 example**[6] which shows how rooted in time and place an individual quiz can be.

The Army Alpha led in turn to the Scholastic Aptitude Test (SAT), which the president of Harvard in the 1930s hoped would bring him the ablest rather than the best-connected undergraduates. (**What does the modern-day SAT have in common with AT&T, CBS, KFC and BP?**[7])

The SAT went on to become a near-universal rite of passage for American senior students and, like England's Senior Local Examination, a source of intense anxiety. The Age of the Exam gave birth quickly to the Age of the Exam Nightmare, which Sigmund Freud thought had pervaded society and which he wrote about at length (though at less length than the Nudity Embarrassment Nightmare).

And yet we voluntarily tune in, turn up and sometimes pay to do pretty much that same thing the thought of which kept us awake at night when we were at school. Quiz has provided a kindly schoolmaster figure for contestants of every age: Bob Holness for

7 Their initials no longer officially stand for anything (accept orphaned initialisms, or similar).

6 1. Tobacco (the brand name became a nickname for Durham, North Carolina, and, in turn, the title of the baseball movie which springs more readily to mind today); 2. Sheep (also someone who emigrated to Australia through choice rather than because of a crime); 3. Red (another name for the pomegranate); 4. Author (Ade was a Twain votary); 5. Writer (although if Ade is an author, surely so, too, is Libby); 6. Hay (although also slilage); 7. Cambridge, Massachusetts (the Harvard Quiz Bowl team was stripped of National Academic Quiz Tournament titles in 2013); 8. Oysters ('pearl' originally referred to the pupil of an eye); 9. Bird (also a distinguished publisher); 10. Patent medicine (although, with 18 per cent alcohol, its use in the Prohibition era may on occasion have been non-medicinal); 11. Cannon (presumably weeding out military recruits who didn't know their arsenal from their elbow); 12. Color (unless you're French); 13. Fabric (pron. 'pun-JEE', from the cocoons of wild silkworms); 14. Lawyer (said to have remarked, 'You cannot live without lawyers, and certainly you cannot die without them'); 15. Six (their names are given in the Cambridge University question above); 16. The Merchant of Venice (unrelated to the Portia in Julius Caesar); 17. Law (Ambrose Bierce observed, 'There are four kinds of homicide: felonious, excusable, justifiable, and praiseworthy, but it makes no great difference to the person slain whether he fell by one kind or another – the classification is for advantage of the lawyers'); 18. Tennis (albeit via cricket); 19. Electricity (more precisely, electrical resistance); 20. Liver (it is the fluid formerly known as 'choler').

38

Notice the sample sentence:

People hear with the EYES **EARS** NOSE MOUTH

The correct word is EARS, because it makes the truest sentence. In each of the sentences below you have four choices for the last word. Only one of them is correct. In each sentence draw a line under the one of these four words which makes the truest sentence. If you cannot be sure, guess. The two samples are already marked as they should be.

SAMPLES { People hear with the EYES **EARS** NOSE MOUTH
{ France is in **EUROPE** ASIA AFRICA AUSTRALIA

1   Bull Durham is the name of a Chewing-Gum, Aluminum-Ware, Tobacco, Clothing 1

2   The merino is a kind of Horse, Sheep, Goat, Cow........ 2

3   Garnets are usually Yellow, Blue, Green, Red.............. 3

4   George Ade is famous as a Baseball-Player, Comic-Artist, Actor, Author 4

5   Laura Jean Libby is known as a Singer, Suffragist, Writer, Army Nurse 5

6   Alfalfa is a kind of Hay, Corn, Fruit, Rice.................. 6

7   Harvard University is in Annapolis, Cambridge, Ithaca, New Haven 7

8   Pearls are obtained from Mines, Elephants, Reefs, Oysters 8

9   The penguin is a Bird, Reptile, Insect...................... 9

10   Peruna is a Disinfectant, Food Product, Patent Medicine, Tooth Paste 10

11   The howitzer is a kind of Musket, Sword, Cannon, Pistol   11

12   Cerise is a Color, Drink, Fabric, Food 12

13   Pongee is a Food, Dance, Fabric, Drink...................... 13

14   Joseph Choate was a Merchant, Engineer, Lawyer, Scientist 14

15   Henry VIII's wives numbered 4   5   6   7   8   9   15

16   Portia is in Vanity Fair, Romola, A Christmas Carol, The Merchant of Venice 16

17   Homicide is a term used in Medicine, Law, Theology, Pedagogy 17

18   Lob is a term used in Football, Hockey, Golf, Tennis...... 18

19   The ohm is used in measuring Rainfall, Windpower, Electricity, Water Power...................................... 18

20   Bile is made in the Spleen, Kidneys, Stomach, Liver... 20

children (*Blockbusters*), Bamber Gascoigne for students (*University Challenge*) and Magnus Magnusson for grown-ups (*Mastermind*).

The terror of not knowing, after all, is balanced with the pleasure of knowing. There's a quiet history of trying to turn information into questions for the purposes of fun. It was not until radio, though, that any of them took hold.

Questions and answers for the sake of entertainment

In 1691, the enterprising London bookseller John Dunton found himself in some pain. A 'very flaming injury', he called it, 'loaded with aggravations'. One can only speculate on how he happened to come by this intimate inflammation, but we do know that it caused him enough embarrassment that he didn't want to approach anyone for advice. 'How to conceal myself and the ungrateful wretch,' he wrote, 'was the difficulty.'

> Whilst this perplexity remained upon me, I was one day walking over St George's Fields, and Mr. Larkin and Mr. Harris were along with me; and on a sudden I made a stop, and said, 'Well, Sirs, I have a thought I will not exchange for fifty guineas.' They smiled, and were very urgent with me to *discover* it; but they could not get it from me.

The idea, he presently revealed, was one of those new-fangled newspaper-type things, but with two twists: this one was to be read by women as well as by men, and it would answer questions sent in by its readers. It was called the *Athenian Gazette: or Casuistical Mercury, Resolving all the most Nice and Curious Questions proposed by the Ingenious of Either Sex* – at least until its second issue, when legal noises from the *London Gazette* prompted a name change to the *Athenian Mercury*.

Questions were answered by no less an authority than the Athenian Society, though readers were not to know that the Society comprised Dunton and two or three of his pals, who would gather in Smith's coffee-house and attempt to answer questions posed in the letters.

The questions have a delightfully wide range of subjects:

Q. What City is eſteemed the moſt populous in the World?

(London, replies the Society, whatever claims 'Foreigners' may make for Paris or Rome.)

Q. How came Monkeys firſt into the World?

(The Society insists that Monkeys came, 'As Man did, by the Power of God.')

Q. Whether Infinite Numbers are Equal?

(No, and furthermore, there is no such number as 'infinity', since any number can be doubled.)

One Querist was prompted to ask, 'Why do you trouble yourſelves and the world with anſwering ſo many silly queſtions?' ('Becauſe the World will trouble us, and never let us alone, unleſs we'll give 'em an Answer, which ſometimes we are forc'd to do, as to Beggars, meerly to get rid of them.')

Dunton was immensely proud of his 'question–answer project', and it was instantly popular, but in the words of Isaac D'Israeli, he was a man of a thousand projects, and financial ruin did for him and, thereby, for the *Mercury*. He had, though, created a use for the printed word that was not comment or reportage of the current, still less poetry or theatre, but entertainment in isolated pieces of information. He prepared the way for such antiquarian periodicals as *Notes and Queries*, which took its motto from Captain Cuttle, a character from a Dickens novel (**which one?**[8]), whose catchphrase was 'When found, make a note of.'

Throughout the eighteenth century, the literate early modern Englishman took to doing just that: compiling his own collections of interesting facts in what were known as commonplace books. A little branch of publishing grew from this tradition: miscellanies and almanacs intended more for entertainment than for instruction. As with the *Mercury*, the pleasure came from reading the information – but there's also pleasure in coming up with the answers *before* you read them.

The commonplace tradition inspired the 'journalist, educator and author' Albert Plympton Southwick of Charleston, Massachusetts (**not to be confused with his contemporary Alfred P. Southwick, who was credited with which invention after witnessing a drunk man killed by falling on to an electrical generator?**[9]) to make teaching aids based on discrete questions and answers.

Southwick's books, which included 1884's *Quizzism and Its Key: Quirks and Quibbles from Queer Quarters, a Melange of Questions in Literature, Science, History, Biography, Mythology, Philology, Geography, Etc., Etc., with Their Answers*, were intended to '[awaken] an intense interest in general study among the great body of teachers and students', but they can be reworked for the purposes of quiz with very little change. The answers below are as presented by Southwick, with my underlining added:

When and what was the first telegraphic message sent?[10]

How did the character '£' come into use to denote pounds, and what does it signify?[11]

What fugitive king concealed himself in an oak-tree?[12]

<hr/>

9 The electric chair.

10 In May, 1844, by Samuel Finley Breese Morse, LL.D. The message transmitted by him from Washington to Baltimore, at the suggestion of Miss Annie Ellsworth, was the expressive scripture 'What hath God wrought.'

11 It is from the old English black-letter £, the abbreviation for Libra – a pound weight; because, anciently, a pound in money was by law a pound weight of silver.

12 When Charles II fled from the Parliamentary army, he took refuge in Boscobel House, but when he deemed it no longer safe to remain there, he concealed himself in an oak.

Southwick was another pioneer of quiz – not least for that book title – but, like Dunton, he failed to make it into his fortune, and died in a hospital for the poor on New York's Welfare Island in 1929. Perhaps he should have had a gimmick – like the one deployed by Justin Spafford and Lucien Esty.

Spafford and Esty were graduates of Amherst College who, in 1926, had little to do with their time. They spent much of it smoking their pipes in Amherst's New York club and, like the inventors of Trivial Pursuit, took to asking each other factual questions. Q-and-A became a little hobby in their circle of chums and, being well-connected chaps, their hobby caught the attention of a far-sighted soul at Viking Press, on the lookout for something which might be as popular as the great crossword fad of 1925.

So they assembled some questions for a book, and their gimmick was great. They approached various among the great and good and put the questions to them before publication.

The actor and Algonquin Round Table wit Robert Benchley recalled being approached: he was 'a little impatient' when Esty asked for fifteen minutes 'in which to propound a set of questions'. 'I didn't quite understand,' he wrote, 'just what it was he wanted to do to me.' Less than a century ago, the very notion of quiz was enough to baffle, never mind its questions.

Spafford and Esty persisted, and printed the scores of the famous alongside the lists of questions they had had 'done to' them. Here are some of the questions from the round in which Dorothy Parker did rather well:

What two bodies of water does the Suez Canal connect?[13]
From what is linen made?[14]
What Stuart king of England was beheaded?[15]

[15] Charles I.
[14] Flax.
[13] The Mediterranean and the Red Sea.

Published as *Ask Me Another!* in 1927, this exam-as-fun sold 100,000 copies in its first month, but it failed to build into a tradition in the same way that crosswords did. Like flagpole-sitting, and indeed most of the fads of America's 1920s, it fizzled. (And if you're grimly wondering whether the apparent curse on the pioneers of quiz holds, Lucien Esty died of pneumonia two years later, aged thirty.)

Indeed, even while *Ask Me Another!* remained on the shelves, it was receiving hostile responses. Another Algonquin Tabler, Heywood Broun, protested that 'one might score a perfect tally and remain an oaf', and an editorial in the *New York World*, the newspaper which had created the crossword, reckoned that 'a man who treasures up a piece of information like the height of Brooklyn Bridge has a screw loose somewhere.'

A widely syndicated book review blamed Madison Avenue: 'Perhaps the vogue can be accounted for by those insidious advertisements which have been appearing, telling of the colossal knowledge of a certain anonymous gentleman who steals the interest of the evening by revealing his encyclopedic knowledge on this and that. Personally, such an individual would bore us to death.'

The same piece prefers a new collection by the poet Mark Van Doren, praising it for offering something quiet, elegant and memorable. Such words could also describe Van Doren himself, and his family: he was the brother of the literary critic Carl Van Doren, the husband of novelist Dorothy Van Doren and the father of a one-year-old boy named Charles, who went on to become an academic. Except that, once quiz had taken over the world, Charles would also collude in a piece of skulduggery which would make quiz a national disgrace (see Chapter 13).

Across the Atlantic, *Ask Me Another!* had its apparent imitators. Kathryn Johnson, who is frequently spotted answering the hardest questions in the country's hardest quizzes onscreen and off, is also responsible for a bibliography of British quizzes in print, and thanks to her I came across S. P. B. Mais's 1927 'question book', *Do You Know?*

Do You Know? combines Southwick's classroom philosophy ('a boy's ability', reckoned Mais, 'is better gauged by his answers to a General Paper than by any other form of examination') with the stardust of *Ask Me Another!*: the questions have this time been put to pairs of British eminences (Aldous Huxley and John Galsworthy; Sybil Thorndike and Noël Coward), so we discover that Sir Arthur Quiller-Couch outperforms H. G. Wells ninety to sixty-three in General Paper Number Six, on such questions as **who first illustrated *Alice in Wonderland*?**,[16] **What is a shag?**[17] and, unfairly, **What is Q's real name?**[18]

(And our last sorry end is that of Mais. His grandson recalled that, although Mais 'wrote more than 200 books and was a household name in his day', he never made enough to keep the bailiffs at bay: 'I'll never forget when my mother told me how she once had to hand over the contents of her piggy bank to his creditors.')

The printed page, it turned out, was not the natural home for quiz. After these false starts, it was broadcasting that made quiz into a real-time event with all the rules, gimmicks and personalities that radio and TV require. Quiz needs formats, and it's more fun when there's a person asking the questions. (This in itself can be half the fun of Trivial Pursuit.)

Getting the combination right, though, is not always easy . . .

[16] Sir John Tenniel, as alluded to in an earlier answer.
[17] A cormorant.
[18] Sir Arthur Quiller-Couch (from a modern-day Bond fan, perhaps accept Major Boothroyd).

The rules are
simple . . .

4. Starters for ten
A quiz *is* a format

Hornsey Town Hall, December 1966. Somewhere behind a whorling mist of cigarette and pipe fumes, David Vine can be made out introducing a new BBC programme, *Quiz Ball*. It follows a footballing metaphor, and the contestants – teams of three footballers plus a celebrity supporter – see their correct guesses represented by moves across a virtual pitch on a state-of-the-art electronic scoreboard.

Johnny Carey, Ian Ure, Ted Moult and the others have four tactics to choose from when 'in possession' of the ball, though the opposing team have, in certain circumstances, the option of a 'tackle'. The rules take an age to describe. Fully three and a half minutes of explanation pass before Vine recaps: 'Okay, then. Perhaps it all may sound a little complicated, I don't know. But we'll explain the rules as we go along.'

Once things do go along, they're discursive and fun, like when Vine says to Arsenal's Jimmy Young, 'Right then, Jimmy, **what do you associate – and you can't get around it by giving me some obscure answer – what does** *everybody else* **associate with the letters U, A and X?**'[1] After a long pause, Young repeats the U, as a question – 'U?' – which Vine confirms with another 'U', and then the same happens for A, and then again

1 British Board of Film Censors certificates.

for X, which prompts Young to suggest. 'I think you're going to lose this ball in a bit of a sticky circumstance,' and he's right in that Arsenal centre-back Terry Neill confidently 'tackles' by buzzing in, only to mentally grope his way to a guess of United Amalgamation of Ex-soccer-players.

'If there were such a thing as half a goal, Terry,' replies Vine, 'I'd give you it.'

Fond laughter follows, but the desolate feeling evoked in the viewer by that earlier moment, where Vine threatens to go over the rules *again*, is familiar to anyone who's struggled to make sense of a quiz which has so many mechanisms that it's impossible to tell what's happening, who's winning, or whether the next question is ever going to come.

The business of quiz, as mentioned earlier, needs some kind of structure. Very rare is the quiz which consists of nothing more than one question followed by another. When it is tried, it takes exceptional setting if it's not to seem dull and arbitrary. And so even the laziest pub-quiz host offers themed rounds and some kind of hand-out.

That said, the most enduring quizzes don't do a whole lot *more* than ask a bunch of questions: they may crank the tension with the dangle of prizes, or simply break the questions into 'starters' and 'bonuses', with the odd picture or music question to leaven the verbal dough. But the first quizzes had a very simple format indeed. They came from bees.

Noah Webster's spelling books gave nineteenth-century America the sense that there was only one acceptable spelling of a given word, and local communities devised impromptu contests to see whether their young people had been paying attention.

Spelling bees became, in the absence of other diversions, a popular place for teenagers to meet and do what teenagers do.

They might take place at mining camps as much as in schools, and became county-wide affairs; in *The Adventures of Tom Sawyer*, Mark Twain called one event a 'spelling fight'. In 1877, *The New York Times* reported on a bee gone wrong. Young Nellie Wilson misspelled a word; her friend Rosie McGrath retorted, 'I told you so' and: 'The expression aroused Nellie's wrath, and the match, which had been solely designed to settle the question of orthographical prowess, became a wrestling match, which ended with both contestants being taken to the station house after a desperate onslaught on each other's fair tresses.'

The repercussions might have been rowdy, but the format itself is staid and straightforward: contestants take it in turns to have words given to them by a host, give their best answers in front of an audience, and the one who gives the fewest wrong answers is the winner.

Over time, the media moved from reporting on bees to organizing them. In 1925 the *Louisville Courier-Journal* held the first national event. It became the Scripps National Bee and has run every spring to this day, except during the Second World War. In 1930, the winner (who ended their run by correctly spelling 'albumen') took home $1,000 in gold.

In 1933, the national bee became broadcast across America by CBS. An *international* bee seemed the next step . . . and one which brings us to an important broadcast of January 1938.

NBC and the BBC had a chance to test their cutting-edge radio telegraphy technology as Harvard took on Oxford in the *Transatlantic Spelling Bee*. Questions were asked over microphones, and British people heard, for the first time, teams competing with each other in mental sport. They liked what they heard.

It might have become an annual contest, but the outbreak of war in Europe put paid to that. The BBC, though, had discovered a format (questions, buzzers, audience, hosts, competition) and started to use it immediately. Listeners were quick to catch on – and, of course, to complain. The *Radio Times* of April 1938 announced:

> In view of the criticisms received from listeners after the last match there will be two small modifications of procedure tonight: –

> 1. The Spelling Master will exercise his discretion whether the mis-spelt word shall, or shall not be passed on to the corresponding member of the other side. That is to say, where the mis-spelling of a word makes the correct spelling obvious, another word will be given.
> 2. There will be a few seconds' pause before the competitors spell the word that has been given for the convenience of listeners who wish to write the words down.

No sooner had the quiz begun than audiences demanded that they be given a chance to take part themselves: such a key part of any broadcast quiz today that the commissioners have words for it: 'playalong', or 'playalongability'.

Auntie let them have their fun. A special kind of fun. Fun with a purpose. Here's the Regional Programme Western's *Agricultural Bee*:

> Tonight, on the principle of the Spelling Bee, teams of young farmers from Somerset and Dorset will compete in answering simple general knowledge questions on everyday agricultural topics. They will be the sort of questions to which most West Country listeners should be able at least to guess the answers, but which even a young farmer might just get wrong.

Just as *The Archers* was a collaboration with the Ministry of Agriculture, Fisheries and Foods which helped to disseminate the latest agronomic developments in the form of a 'farming

Dick Barton', so was the *Agricultural Bee* an improving exercise shaped like a quiz.

By 1939, the format was generally understood. The war brought its own variants, including an *Air Raid Wardens' Training Bee* 'from the Wardens' Post at the Odeon Theatre, Wealdstone' and the heart-breakingly titled *A Competition: Sons in France against Parents in England.* (The poignancy of this on-air family reunion was slightly undermined by the audible vomiting of one of the inebriated Sons and the BBC's concern that his equally jolly brothers-in-arms seemed constantly on the verge of giving away their location to the Germans.)

It was also the war that spawned two of the biggest, and best, quizzes which would appear once television arrived.

When the United Service Organisations (USO) entertainer Don Reid was tasked with devising a new form of entertainment for the troops fighting in the Second World War (or, in Jeremy Paxman's words, 'a way to keep servicemen from their more conventional styles of recreation'), he decided to test them on general knowledge, just as they had been during their recruitment – but this time he would put them on a stage.

Come peacetime, and Reid – who had been a basketball star at college – reflected on the colossal kudos granted to college sportsmen and wondered why those young people who attended American universities to actually study didn't have a forum offering the same recognition. 'There has to be some way,' he figured, 'to have fun with a sport of the mind,' and he adapted his wartime quiz for radio. His big idea was a sporting metaphor: basketball's jump balls and free throws – or, in quiz terms, starters and bonuses. And it's quite brilliant. In this format, some questions reward speed of mind and others a more reasoned approach.

Bunching them together allows knocking on for a hundred questions to be asked, without the half-hour ever threatening to drag.

In the popular radio series *College Bowl* (later renamed GE *College Bowl* and tag-lined 'At General Electric, progress is our most important product'), the horn-rimmed Alan Ludden asked questions from New York, hooked up to remote university teams who competed throughout the academic year for scholarship grants and glory. The TV version jumped around the networks, failing to find its place, and was cancelled in 1970: there was a dispute over the format's ownership, General Electric was feeling less warm towards students since many of them had begun protesting against its role in the Vietnam War, and – poignantly, given the show's ambitions to celebrate nerds over jocks – *College Bowl*'s cosy spot in the Sunday-afternoon schedule was given to American football.

There were 1,500 institutions on the waiting list for the cancelled 1970–71 series.

However, and as you may have guessed, the British spin-off proved more durable: the original *University Challenge*, with Bamber Gascoigne, ran for twenty-five years, and its revived form, with Jeremy Paxman, is merrily approaching the same age. It's fair to say that the source of the metaphor – sweaty basketball toss-ups – are not foremost in anyone's mind when the latter announces a starter for ten.

The other big beast of British TV quiz came out of a much less convivial part of the Second World War than the USO camp shows. Bill Wright had spent his war in the air as a wireless operator and later a flight-sergeant, until his Vickers Wellington was shot down en route to the Rhineland on Midsummer's Day, 1942. When he was captured by the Gestapo, they took him to be a spy because he was wearing civvies which he had procured from the Dutch underground movement.

Wright's captors repeatedly threatened to shoot him as they barked at him for his name, rank and serial number. They kept him in solitary confinement for three weeks and in prisoner-of-war camps for three years. After the war, he returned to his job at the BBC; by the late 1960s, he was in charge of the Outside Broadcast Quiz Unit and had to think up some new quiz programmes.

Quiz Ball was one of Wright's ideas. It was tremendously popular – so much so that its term 'route one' (risking a very hard question for potentially big rewards) soon became used in football itself, for the attacking tactic of a long kick upfield. Wright's next task was to devise a quiz to match the standards set by ITV's *University Challenge*, which was then drawing in 10 million viewers on Wednesday evenings, before *Coronation Street*. He tried shifting radio's *Brain of Britain* to TV, but it didn't really work.

All the while, he had been afflicted with nightmares in which a disembodied voice demanded his name, rank and number, sometimes intermingled with imagery from the Spanish Inquisition and the Geneva Convention. But one Saturday morning, he emerged from the darkness and told his wife, 'I've got it!' He replaced name, rank and number with name, occupation and specialized subject, but he kept the chair, the darkness, the interrogator and the sense of approaching menace.

The mechanics of his new show, *Mastermind*, could hardly have been simpler. Four contenders individually answer questions on their specialized subject, then do the same on general knowledge. The camera closes in on their torment. Save for the tie-break protocol, that's it.

Most quiz programmes are now born of the boardroom rather than the battlefield and, at any given moment, hundreds of people are experimenting with some new way of asking people questions. Some shows combine questions and answers with other games, sometimes before the question is asked (as in *Bullseye*, where darts determines the category), sometimes afterwards (as in *Wheel of Fortune*, where correct answers let you take a turn in Hangman).

And some are mutations of other quizzes: *Who Wants to be a Millionaire?* takes a similar increase-the-jackpot approach to (but is legally distinct from) *The $64,000 Question*. *Pointless* came out of a conversation about reversing the idea behind *Family Fortunes*, a programme in which contestants have to guess what answer has been given by most respondents in a survey. Turn that around, the producers figured, and you could reward obscure knowledge but still leave space for the more obvious answers. 'It felt,' recalls executive producer David Flynn, 'like you could start to create a quiz which could be sort of highbrow and populist simultaneously, which is quite a rare phenomenon.'

The show which engineered the biggest reverse of all came, its inventors relate, from a conversation on a 1963 plane trip. With the quiz-show scandals a recent memory, stalwart game-show host (and top-ten vocalist on the original 'I've Got a Lovely Bunch of Coconuts') Merv Griffin was grousing at his wife Julann about how the networks wouldn't allow shows based around questions and answers – in case the contestants had been given the questions. A fan of general knowledge, she was loth to accept that TV had abandoned quiz for gaudier stripes of gameshow, and wondered if the answer was to give the contestants the *answers* instead. She came up with an example. **If the answer is 5,280, the question is . . . ?**[2] Griffin got it (and many Americans, not having the decimal system, still would).

As they tell it, the format for *Jeopardy!* was in place by the time the plane taxied into La Guardia. (Their underwhelming working title was 'What's the Question?', while *Pointless* went for 'Obviously'. Both are probably worse than Trivial Pursuit's 'Six Thousand Questions', and both are certainly far, far better than *Have a Go*'s 'Quiz-Bang' and *Who Wants to be a Millionaire?*'s unspeakable working title, 'The Cash Mountain'.)

All these shows have relatively simple formats, and all became such scheduling staples that the public, even if they're not regular viewers, know them inside out.

Some quiz programmes become so familiar that they provide setting and plot for another show: one staple of a long-running sitcom is the episode where the main characters enter the quiz programme of the day.

> **In which violent slapstick sitcom do students from Scumbag College compete in *University Challenge* against Footlights College, Oxbridge?**[3]
>
> **In which Boston-set sitcom does Cliff Clavin appear on *Jeopardy!* to find that the categories are perfectly suited to him and include Stamps from around the World, Bar Trivia and Celibacy?**[4]
>
> **In which flat-share sitcom does Lee try to impress Lucy by appearing on *Pointless* with Daisy, cheating his way to a pointless answer in a tough category ('Shakespeare's History Plays including History Plays that were not in the First Folio of 1623') with *Pericles*?**[5]

---

[3] *The Young Ones* (not an authorized homage; see Chapter 15).

[4] *Cheers* – Cliff has a great lead in the final round, but wastes it by responding to Archibald Leach, Bernard Schwartz and Lucille LeSueur' with 'Who are three people who have never been in my kitchen?' (The correct response was, of course, 'What were the real names of Cary Grant, Tony Curtis and Joan Crawford?')

[5] *Not Going Out.*

One reason that quiz sticks around the schedules is that it's nice and cheap: one set, no actors, no scripts. But there's a danger in becoming part of broadcasting furniture: what if someone moves in and decides to redecorate? *Mastermind* got a decentish send-off in 1997, from Orkney's St Magnus Cathedral, and knowing it was over, the other Magnus took home the black chair. Ten years earlier, the future was less clear for *University Challenge*, which had been pinballed around the schedules following a loss of faith from LWT's John Birt and had suffered the further indignity of gimmicks, including actually placing one team above another and a round where the contestants passed around a baffling baton with lights indicating some scoring mechanism that neither they nor viewers had a hope of understanding.

On New Year's Eve 1987, Bamber Gascoigne signed off with the hauntingly vague 'It's goodbye now from our new champions Keble and from me until, may we hope, another series sometime in the future?' For a 'pro-celebrity' edition in 1992, he got to offer a proper farewell: 'Goodnight, so to speak, for ever.'

But it wasn't for ever. Like *Mastermind*, *University Challenge* was to return, albeit with a new and very different host.

Different host? That's some risky business, when so much of a quiz programme's personality is bound up with that of the person asking the questions . . .

5. Who wants to know?

Please welcome your hosts

While gameshows revealed folks' willingness to make fools of themselves, quiz shows redeemed the man in the street and revealed that the average guy wasn't as hapless as he behaved under the influence of [early gameshow legends] Art Linkletter, Bert Parks, or Ralph Edwards.
Gerald Nachman, *Raised on Radio*

The 'man-on-the-street' show was a staple of old-timey American radio: as cheap as it was cheerful, it made entertainment for the public out of members of the public themselves (sample show name: *People are Funny*) – the carnivalesque of the medicine show brought right into your home. 'Interactive', it would be called now. And in the 1930s, many Americans were in their homes, having neither a job to go to nor any money to spend. The radio stations, though, gave away money as fast as they could dream up new ways of doing so and find new celebrities to hand it over.

The man-on-the-street show was sometimes literally that: a microphone cable was strung out of an upper-storey window, connecting the people on the pavement directly to the studio above. Other man-on-the-street shows tried variants on the talent show: first asking members of the public for their opinions (Do you fancy the chances of Hoover or do you favour FDR?), then asking them trick questions, then silly, quasi-factual questions ('How many feathers are on the average hen?') and, eventually, general-knowledge questions, like those asked on the smash hit *Professor Quiz*, a series which started in 1936 by asking **what is the difference between a lama with one L and a llama with two Ls?**[1] (The contestant didn't know.)

The programme offered ten silver dollars to the contestant who correctly answered most questions (dropped audibly into his or her hand at the end of the show), and the identity of the professor was a closely guarded secret.

In 1937, the enterprising staff of *Radio Guide* magazine managed to identify the professor: he was in fact Dr Craig Earl. Or so they thought. 'Professor Quiz' was a pseudonym which the question-master used in his professional life; 'Dr Craig Earl' was another – the one he used in his personal life to avoid alimony and child-support payments. His disgruntled former wife had known him as Arthur E. Baird.

Baird claimed to be an orphan and a circus performer turned doctor (he was none of those things), and had previously jumped on to a fitness fad and, with phoney qualifications, presented an exercise programme in which listeners were encouraged to follow the instructions for some early-morning 'Setting-up Exercises'.

By the late 1930s, Baird was seen in promotional materials sporting a little moustache, some thin-rimmed specs and a

[1] A lama is a Buddhist (accept Tibetan) monk (accept priest); a llama is a South American pack animal (accept beast of burden).

selection of objectionable bow-ties, all, apparently, evidence of his erudition, and his fame made it inevitable that his family would eventually be reunited with him – at least in the court-room. In 1942, he paid $25,000 to his former wife, to make up for missed payments; highlights of his subsequent career include judging a competition by the Mother-in-law Association of Saks Thirty-fourth Street.

The figure of the quiz-show host was to become a short-hand for a smarmy, unreliable huckster, epitomized by the monstrous Prem Kumar in **Vikas Swarup's novel Q & A, which was adapted as which 2009 film?**[2] This might be unfair to the many legal, decent, honest and truthful hosts, but it faithfully represented their forebear, the odious Baird.

His immediate successors included the pompous and pre-posterous Dr IQ, but other models emerged. Baird was in not, in fact, the first choice to 'play' Professor Quiz: he swiped the job from a former vaudeville monologuist, Jim McWilliams, who had fallen ill. McWilliams rallied and returned to radio with *Uncle Jim's Question Bee* and *The Ask-it Basket* and, by presenting the host as friend rather than superior, exemplified a more approachable way of doing things.

Ah, but 'doing things' – what sort of things do hosts do? Even on television, much remains unseen, but they must arbi-trate on the fly, quite literally listen to voices in their head giving supplementary information through an earpiece while talking and keeping an eye on scores and timers, all the while not appearing to be mad. Mark Goodson, who was behind myriad TV quizzes, including *Winner Takes All* and *The Price is Right*, describes the ideal host as 'the kind of man who can conduct a

2 *Slumdog Millionaire* (as we shall see in chapter 17).

witty conversation with a complete stranger while at the same time driving a car with twelve gears backwards down a mountainside'.

There are different ways to drive that car. While American quiz hosts realized that they didn't have to pretend to have academic titles, in Britain, the role edged away from the classroom ambience of the bees and began to include far chummier presenters like Wilfred 'Give 'em the money' Pickles and the perma-mugging Hughie Green, who seemed so keen to slip a tenner to pensioners on *Double Your Money* that he'd be prepared to break the rules.

The British likeable everyman model (never done better than by Bradley Walsh on programmes such as *Wheel of Fortune*, *Spin Star* and *The Chase*) became one of many. In the early years of *Who Wants to be a Millionaire?*, for example, contestants were never sure whether Chris Tarrant was rooting for them or not. In America, there's less variety. Most quiz hosts there exhibit a duller strain, one not so much of likability as of stolid solidity.

There have been American exceptions, of course: the 1950s TV hit *You Bet Your Life* was introduced with an emcee intoning, 'Here he is: the one, the *only . . .*' and an audience hollering, 'Groucho!' before Groucho Marx appeared and proceeded to use the questions and answers as padding between which he would ad lib with the contestants. In his autobiography, *The Secret Word is Groucho*, he gives an example:

> 'Why do you have so many children?' I asked Mrs Story. 'That's a big responsibility and a big burden.'
>
> 'Well,' she replied, 'because I love children, and I think that's our purpose here on earth, and I love my husband.'
>
> 'I love my cigar too,' I shot back, 'but I take it out of my mouth once in a while.'

While it should be noted that Marxist scholars regard the book as ghost-written to the point of unreliability, and no tape of the episode is known to exist, Michael Barrymore would, in his *Strike It Lucky* heyday, take the idea of risqué banter to the borders of broadcastability. Also in the Groucho mould and also from the 1980s, *Bob's Full House* went further, by treating the questions themselves as set-ups for Bob Monkhouse's one-liners, with the scores a little-noticed side-effect: a question about **the inventor of snooker who shares his name with the prime minister who signed the 1938 Munich agreement**[3] is no sooner answered than Monkhouse remarks that Mrs Thatcher is going to privatize snooker with a plan to 'get rid of the reds and make the "queues" shorter'.

Of course, some quiz hosts seldom smile and are far from familiar. Here's Jeremy Paxman.

— Ten points for this. **'The liberties of England and the Protestant religion I will maintain.' Which royal figure made that claim when he landed at Brixham in Devon in 1688?**[4]
— UCL, Tyszczuk Smith.
— William I?
— No! William I!? I'm sorry, that's the *wrong* answer! You know it's *very* wrong!
— Sorry.
— It's only out by about six hundred years or so!
— I'm *sorry*.

And some have gone much further, though it's worth noting that the most abrasive host of recent times, *The Weakest*

[3] Neville Chamberlain.
[4] William III (accept William of Orange).

Link's Anne Robinson, drew attention in the UK and later in America as much for her gender as for her perceived cruelty to contestants.

For most of the life of the TV quiz, women have either stood next to the prizes in little more than their smalls or, if competing, stood as the questions are read to them, noticeably more slowly than they would be to a man, by 'the kind of man who can conduct a witty conversation with a complete stranger'. Nowadays, TV even allows them to read the odd question themselves. The industry still prefers men, though; as recently as 2006, a senior executive at one of the biggest producers of quiz told academic Su Holmes that the near-absence of women was down to *gravitas*: 'You always want to believe that the person giving you the answer knows the answer.'

Hm.

In 2001, on the Irish version of *Who Wants to be a Millionaire?*, Gay Byrne asked the contestant Shane O'Doherty his IR£125,000 question: 'Where in the human body is the lunula located – the heart, fingernail, eye, or ear?' O'Doherty phoned a friend, and the friend was a science teacher who immediately said 'heart'. Unfortunately, the human body has lots of crescent-shaped bits and bobs named 'lunulae', and so we can find them at the base of our nails (the answer entered into the show software), but also in our hearts. Someone had forgotten to check that all the 'wrong' answers were wrong.

When O'Doherty was sent home with IR£93,000 less than he'd been hoping for, the lunula became a topic of national debate. Heart surgeons were called away from their theatres to give their opinions and, eventually, O'Doherty was allowed to return, and faced a duly tricky £250,000 question about the **Dublin-born Olympic gold medallist who went on to**

become a Nationalist MP for South Kerry.[5] (Good luck with that.) He pondered for five minutes, muttered, 'My wife was quoted somewhere as saying she'd leave me if I got this wrong,' and took his IR£125,000 home to Knocklyon.

Of special interest was the role of Gay Byrne, who expressed regret but also his powerlessness to do more – a powerlessness accentuated by the producers' statement: 'It's nothing to do with him. Gay has absolutely nothing to do with the questions. He's just the presenter.'

I suspect that if it hadn't been issued in the middle of a febrile media hoo-hah, that statement might have been more thoughtfully phrased. I'm also not sure that most viewers believe that the person giving you the answer – whether he or she is of **the gender carrying XX chromosomes**[6] or **the one carrying XY**[7] – really knows the answer, but it spoils the fun when you're reminded outright that they're 'just the presenter'.

There are moments, of course, when you know that they do: Paxman is an example, as is his predecessor, with his gentler but no less firm rejoinders.

There is a small subset of hosts who would prefer, if time allowed, to understand every question they asked. (Michael Palin's reason for turning down the job of QI host was that 'I could just see that this was going to be something which you couldn't just *do*.'). Bamber Gascoigne says that he had nightmares about doing an episode of *University Challenge* unprepared. Early on, he bought every reference book that might be relevant, 'including a history of bicycling, in case a bicycling question came up.' Preparation involved taking delivery at his

[7] Male.
[6] Female.
[5] John Pius Boland (singles and doubles gold in tennis at the first modern Olympics, 1896).

65

home of questions typed on to blue cards (starters) and pink ones (bonuses), rephrasing them and ordering them into batches for each episode, then thinking around each:

> We had a question: Which English Romantic poet died young in 1821? And I wouldn't have had a clue whether the answer was Keats or Shelley, both of whom died young around then. So, the answer is Keats. When one looks up Shelley, to my absolute delight I remember, Shelley died a year later . . . So you put on your card '(Shelley 1822)'. And you secretly hope they will answer Shelley [so you can say], 'Oh bad luck, he died just a year later, in 1822. No, the answer is Keats.'

As is typical of the honest, Gascoigne presents this technique of informed research with *Britannica* as if it's an underhand trade secret which makes him appear better informed than he 'really' is. But for me, the mark of the informed host is not the correction of a wrong answer or the display of extra knowledge around the topic but some slip that indicates the topics he or she is *not* across.

With Gascoigne, it was the odd pronunciation of pop-cultural references such as 'Duran Duran'. Magnus Magnusson's Achilles heel came out in mispronunciations, too: his appalling French. On *Only Connect*, Victoria Coren Mitchell takes it a stage further by stating unambiguously the shakiness of her grasp on, say, even rudimentary astronomy, at one point reproducing onscreen the crude fruit model of the solar system with which I, as question editor, had, off screen, illustrated that a day on Mars lasts 24.62 Earth hours. These plausibly human moments remind the viewer that the host is a person – someone who knows some areas very well, but only some.

There are, though, also quizzes which are produced in great volume, sometimes broadcast daily, where the host's authority is granted by their reading of the questions, not by how well read they themselves may be. This is a different job, and a thoroughly decent one, but there's no room here for the host to suggest that they knew anything about what's on the cards before they were delivered to the dressing room. And it surely wouldn't work if the high-volume host tried to give the impression of omniscience: sometimes, the smartest thing is to read the words and keep a distance from what they mean.

If audience research is anything to go by, what viewers want most of all is to feel that the host is fair.

And fairness is just as crucial when it comes to the structure of the contest itself.

6. What are the chances of that?

The importance of luck

—We're not *losing*. The right questions aren't coming up.
—That's the whole point of a quiz, isn't it? It's
supposed to be random.
Chris Finch argues with Ricky Howard, *The Office*

In a 2006 edition of *Eggheads*, the odds appear irredeemably poor when the final round pits a complete set of the eponymous serial quiz champions against – playing solo – Jade Goody, the woman who had become infamous for statements such as 'Where's East Angular, though? I thought that was abroad.' This was not a celebrity edition: Goody was the sole survivor of the team representing her unpleasantly named salon Ugly's.

'Have a go – who knows?' counseled the host, Dermot Murnaghan, 'it could be done', before asking: **in which 1985 film does Harrison Ford play the role of Detective John Book?**[1] Goody considered the multi-choice alternatives, wrongly reasoning, '*Blade Runner*, I don't know, it doesn't sound . . . old', then offers the right answer. Her next question is **the yakuza is a criminal fraternity operating in which country?**[2] She rejects

1 *Witness.*
2 Japan.

Indonesia on the basis that the word 'yakuza' 'doesn't really sound Indian' and is again right. Even her conflation of India and Indonesia makes her – against the odds – luckier.

'If you get this right,' announces Murnaghan, 'and they get theirs wrong, you've done what's never been done on *Eggheads*, you've won £11,000. On your own.' Her final question is **Prince William graduated from St Andrews University in 2005 with a degree in which subject?**[3]

And *both* of these mismatched teams got their third question right, so the game went to sudden death (with no multiple choice). Murnaghan asked Goody, **in terms of one's speaking accent or accent, what do the initials RP stand for?**[4] She essayed, 'Something posh … "right pronunciation"?', so when the Eggheads are asked for **the fifth letter of the Greek alphabet,**[5] and give the correct answer, the natural order is restored. But the reason it's such a compelling moment of quiz is that chance has thrown up an improbably close-run contest. As Goody might have put it, the experience was 'random'.

But there's random and there's random.

We play in many ways. Some games are pure chance (Bingo, say, or Lotto, where everything is determined by the die); others reward nothing more than merit (the triple jump, say, or chess, where randomness is effectively eliminated). Where along the continuum does quiz come?

On the one hand, it's a game of merit: the contestant who knows the most should be the winner. And try setting a quiz where the questions veer – genuinely randomly – from **who wrote *As You Like It*?**[6] to **which character in *As You Like It* says**

---

6 William Shakespeare.
5 Epsilon.
4 Received pronunciation.
3 Geography.

'Let us sit and mock the good housewife Fortune from her wheel, that her gifts may henceforth be bestowed equally'?[7] and see how long you last.

On the other hand, quiz needs to appear random in some ways if it's to seem fair. Let's say one team is made up of old-timers and another of youngsters – it will seem that the deck has been stacked in favour of the former if a run of questions asks for **the only player so far to score a hat-trick in a World Cup final,**[8] then **the musical film which had the working title** *Eight Arms to Hold You*[9] and **the Secretary of State for war who misled the House of commons on 22 March 1963**[10]; in favour of the latter if the questions run along the lines of asking for **the messaging app with a logo known as Ghostface Chillah,**[11] then **the number of players on a quidditch team**[12] and **the leisure activity pursued by YouTube star Stampy Longnose.**[13] Mixing up the eras and the subject matter is just the start.

Randomness takes a lot of planning. The question pack for any decent quiz is the end result of agonizing over how to make sure that the information asked for comes across as consistent, whoever turns up and whatever way the dice fall. But you never know how it will play out.

Even if you tackled the luck-of-the-draw issue by giving two contestants *exactly the same questions* – well, luck could still creep in. One might be lucky enough to get the ones they find easier earlier, getting them into a zone of good guesses and right answers, while the other might find themselves trapped in a spiral of wrongness, with incorrect answers creating a panic

13 Minecraft.
12 Seven.
11 Snapchat.
10 John Profumo.
9 *Help!*, the eight arms being the Beatles'.
8 Geoff Hurst.
7 Celia.

that throws them off the scent of the later ones they really would have got if only they'd been lucky enough to get them early.

It's so much easier to make things *unfair*. Beware the quiz which makes a big deal of its apparently random question-selection. This tradition started with *The $64,000 Question*, which launched in 1955 when the vogue was for overwrought hoo-hah like bankers 'delivering' the questions onscreen, flanked by armed guards. The questions were provided by a modern, impressive and apparently impassive IBM sorting machine: luck, once thought to be the stuff of the gods, was now thought to be controlled and ostensibly eliminated by IT. 'Computer,' as they quaintly requested on *Who Wants to be a Millionaire?*, 'please take away two wrong answers.'

As viewers soon learned, the order of questions on shows like *The $64,000 Question* had already been decided by the human beings in charge, as well as which of the contestants was to get them right, depending on whether their 'likeability' gained the approval of the sponsors, Revlon.

Fifty years later, British TV took the lead in dishonest quizzing by going the other way: disguising rather than feigning luck. In 'call TV', viewers were persuaded to ring a premium-rate number on the promise of being connected to a studio during a live show and winning a cash prize. To compete, they just had to answer a question correctly.

But if a quiz's questions are very easy and if the contestants pay to play, it starts to look a lot like a game of mere chance – specifically, an unregulated lottery. As the regulators discovered, 'winning' was in fact all down to some telephonist watching the calls coming in, but being under instructions to ignore them; producers advised these underlings to read a book instead. For hours on end, all calls were diverted to a recorded message which took the callers' money – some were spending over a thousand pounds – and asked them to call again.

The racket originated with satellite and cable channels, but traditional broadcasters soon saw the opportunities offered by this gap in the light-touch regulation. (Nobody was sure whether this was the pigeon of the broadcasting regulator, the telephone standards committee or the Gambling Commission.)

They created spin-off channels, or used the same techniques in their biggest, most family-friendly shows – with pay-to-enter questions taking viewers in and out of the ads – until the syphoning was so loud that it became one of 2007's national disgraces and the TV industry had to find more respectable sources of revenue, like adult chat.

It's much more fun when the subversion of luck is effected by the contestants – like the young *Jeopardy!* victor from New York, Arthur Chu.

In *Jeopardy!* contestants tend to proceed predictably across the game board, taking turns to choose from six categories, attempting to answer the lower-value questions earlier and the higher ones later. But not Chu.

Chu's approach, during his 2014 reign, was to dart from topic to topic, diving in early at the higher values. Some of his many critics described this as 'random'. But it wasn't. When Chu was chosen as a contestant, he told himself, 'I'm not going to be able to learn all the things I don't know in terms of actual knowledge.' Instead of knowledge, he learned strategy.

Those higher-value questions are where the show's 'daily doubles' lurk: the device which allows players to answer questions in their stronger topics and top up their winnings if they're right. But Chu wasn't interested in being right; he wanted the daily doubles because the player who uncovers them

WHAT ARE THE CHANCES OF THAT?

retains control of the board, whether they've answered correctly or not.

Chu would breezily throw away chances to add to his jackpot and didn't even bother to guess at some questions (for example, **the sport for which Eddie Giacomin, Herb Brooks and Conn Smythe are known**[14]). This was, in fact, the elimination of random. Rather than subjecting himself to the luck of conventional *Jeopardy!* play, which is largely down to how you answer the questions, Chu was grabbing as much control of the luck as he could. And it paid off – over the course of twelve games, he amassed $298,200.

It wasn't his winnings that made Chu an item on news programmes throughout his run, but his style and the social-media opprobrium he prompted. They called him a 'mad genius' who used 'game theory': both misnomers which would probably not have been used if he weren't a bespectacled Asian-American.

In fact, Chu was not the first to use these strategies: the *Jeopardy!* strategy sites he 'trained' on attest that fans of the show have long scrutinized its workings. In 1994, ABC's *Good Morning America* ran a feature on quiz; among the interviewees was an aspiring contestant.

'I would like to play *Jeopardy!*,' announced Michael Larson. 'I think I've figured out some angles on that.' And Michael Larson knew a thing or two about angles.

In the evenings of the mid-1980s, millions of Americans were watching the expensive antics of the flush fictional people in programmes like *Dallas* and *Dynasty*. Not everyone, though: in south-western Ohio, the unemployed former ice-cream-truck driver Michael Larson was watching recordings of daytime quiz programmes.

14 Ice hockey.

Stacks of televisions were connected to video recorders which Larson had set to tape any show he came across which offered money as a prize. The long sessions of quiz-watching 'put a large strain on our relationship', recalled his common-law wife, Teresa Dinwitty. Daytime cash prizes were getting high – at one point, a contestant had won $40,000 – and the show which gave away the most cash, Larson concluded, was CBS's *Press Your Luck*.

Larson watched episode after episode, slowing down the tapes, until he knew the show inside out. In May 1985, he borrowed the airfare and flew to Los Angeles for the twice-daily auditions wearing a second-hand shirt he'd bought for 65 cents.

On *Press Your Luck*, contestants buzz in to answer general-knowledge questions. Correct answers and early buzzing are rewarded with spins on an electronic display board: lights flicker as it spins and it stops when the contestant presses their buzzer. This is the point when the contestant finds out whether the square they landed on has just flickered on to a cash sum, a consumer-goods prize – or a dreaded 'whammy'. The whammy would bring the appearance of a crude animation over their podium and reduce their winnings to zero, and the chances of getting a whammy were one in six.

One in six, that is, for contestants who hadn't watched myriad old episodes in slow motion.

In fact, the movement of the lights and the location of the whammies was not random, because not a lot really is. This is especially the case when it comes to computers, which are what's known as 'deterministic' devices: they follow instructions and are not given to arbitrary decisions. Computers can be programmed to come up with something that's not particularly predictable: you can ask them to give you a number (after all, it's all about numbers with them) from a seemingly muddled sequence, but that sequence needs to have been created from a set of instructions. (This is why some people roll dice to create their passwords: they're trying to add an element of genuine unpredictability.)

And, in 1985, television companies had access to a lot less processing power than we have today. There was a finite number of patterns for the movement of the lights across *Press Your Luck*'s prizes and whammies board. A finite number is inevitable, but a small finite number, which *Press Your Luck* had, might be a problem. (Bill Carruthers, co-creator of the show, recalled the conversations around the show's launch thus: 'I said, we can't go with six.') It might, in theory, be a problem which allowed a contestant to avoid whammies altogether.

What Larson had spotted was that two of the eighteen spaces never delivered a whammy – and one of them awarded extra spins along with its cash. This meant that all a contestant had to do was to answer a single question correctly and they could, in theory, add money to their jackpot indefinitely.

It *was* a problem.

And so, having answered some questions, including **in what season of the year does a dog normally shed his fur?**[15] and **the Polish call it their native dance, but it's really native to Czechoslovakia and it's one of Lawrence Welk's trademarks – what is this popular folk dance?**,[16] Larson takes control of the board.

His first spin gets him a whammy – it takes him a moment or two to establish what he'd been trying to gauge in auditions, the delay between pressing the buzzer and the light-pattern stopping. But when he does, he has the focus of a drone pilot. His eyes may flicker across the board, riotous as midges in a

[16] The polka.

[15] Spring (though some also shed in autumn).

Speyside summer; inside, he is coolly thinking as much like the studio software as he can.

Larson sees the board unlike any other contestant ever has: the prizes that the lights are illuminating are irrelevant. It's their position that counts: once you see that, say, spaces 2, 12, 1, 9 then 4 are winking on and off, you know when to press to make sure that you end up in a safe spot and are guaranteed more cash.

As Larson's fortune builds, the cheers of the audience are, naturally, deafening. Even on a normal day, *Press Your Luck* is not a ponderous quiz: contestants tend to howl, 'COME ON BIG BUCKS BIG BUCKS STOP!' when taking their spins, and the question-and-answer sections are punctuated by cultish phocine applause from all three contestants and a near-hysterical crowd as each and every answer is given. Money is mentioned constantly.

And everyone, producers and audience included, is expecting or hoping for an episode where a contestant hits a gripping streak, and Larson, it seems, is the one who got lucky. So when, in his first sequence of spins, he racks up $10,000, it's barely noticeable that he is in fact the only contestant who isn't loudly praying to the BIG BUCKS. He's concentrating too hard.

Larson's is a complex, compelling performance. In between his calculated presses, Larson has to feign surprise that luck is on his side and make it seem plausible that he's deciding to spin again rather than banking his winnings. He's helped in this by a couple of near-misses: he, like the audience, knows that a whammy could wipe him out at any moment.

But a whammy doesn't. He goes on and on and on. The presenter Peter Tomarken runs out of things to say to Larson; inside, he is thinking, pretty soon, I'll be working for him instead of for CBS. The clock-radio-like displays on the programme's podiums are designed to show a dollar sign followed by up to five digits. At one point, it reads '$99851'. Once Larson goes over $100,000, the $ is forced out. Still, he spins.

Fellow contestant Janie Dakan asks herself how long it can go on and, backstage, the people who will have to write the cheque are having similar thoughts. For Darlene Lieblich, an executive in the network's Program Practices Department, the first few spins raise the question: how is he doing that? A few more provoke the response: Oh my God, he's doing that. And then it gets very quiet.

'Program Practices' is a euphemistic title for a department tasked with matters like criminality and avoiding the skulduggery of 1950s quiz. Faking a power cut is not an option. All the TV people can do is watch Larson take their money.

In the end, it has to be Larson himself who decides the goose has laid enough golden eggs. It's exhaustion that does it. Another near-miss comes: it doesn't wipe him out, but it's a trip to the Bahamas rather than the cash he's after and, worse, it's in the same space where he accidentally got that first whammy. With a dollar-less '110237' on the podium display (five times the median national income), Tomarken announces, 'You have won more money than anyone's ever thought about winning on *Press Your Luck*!'

In the aftermath, the producers watch the tape back, pointlessly. Then they go through the release forms signed by the contestants. Among some executives, there's a feeling that Larson has cheated; but to cheat, there has to be some rule that you've broken or something that makes you ineligible to play. There's nothing, and Program Practices insists that Larson is paid the money he has won. They take some comfort in the network rule that contestants with winnings over $25,000 are not allowed to return for the next show.

In the 2003 Game Show Network documentary *Big Bucks*, the programme-makers are philosophical. 'You can like him or not like him,' muses Tomarken, 'but you can't help but admire what he did.'

And that should be the happy ending: a Goliath defeated by a David who knew when to quit. Sadly, Larson didn't. He had told Tomarken that he would invest his winnings in Ohio real estate, but he hit on another money-spinner. A radio station was offering $30,000 to any listener in possession of a dollar bill which matched a random serial number.

Larson hit on a way to dramatically increase the odds of winning: he withdrew tens of thousands of one-dollar bills and kept them in stacks around the house, waiting for some lucky number to come up. Later that year, he and Dinwitty returned from a Christmas party to find the cash had been stolen.

All that money – from shoppers' purses to the companies who advertised on CBS, via their advertising agencies to the broadcaster and then on to Larson – gone.

Understandably, Larson never was invited to be a *Jeopardy!* contestant.

Press Your Luck came off the air in 1986; when it was revived as *Whammy!* in 2002, the producers insisted that the prize board was 'much more random'.

7. Well done if you got that at home
When quiz gets hard

Most people don't know most of the answers. It is
nevertheless great fun to hear strange things that
you don't actually know about.
Bamber Gascoigne

When *College Bowl* was taken off the air in 1970, it wasn't just
the aspiring contestants who were bereft. 'We were basically a
TV company,' recalled the creator's son Richard Reid, 'and as
with everybody else in the universe, when you do something
you love, the notion that it has gone away dies hard.' Reid
Senior continued to receive some money from *University
Challenge* – Gascoigne ruefully recalled Reid's fee for each programme as being 'more than my pathetically feeble salary of
£40 a game' – but that was it.

However, Reid's company didn't close and, in 1975, he was
somehow still there, and asked his son to come and help out at
the office while he was ill. Helping with what? 'I didn't know
what helping him really meant,' said Richard Reid. Sitting in
the office of a TV company with no programmes, waiting for
the telephone to ring, is a bad and unhappy business, and
nobody did want to put *College Bowl* back on the TV. Another

phone call made a difference, though: it was from an assistant professor called Michael Decker who had figured out that the quiz-bowl format might work off-screen. (Those who love to quiz don't need broadcasters' blessings, as with the Master-mind Club, where former contestants compete for their own trophy in the form of a Toby-jug grotesque of Magnus Magnusson dubbed the Magnum, sport clothing bearing his reminder 'It's only a bloody game' and keep the spirit of the show alive during its absence.)

Reid Junior went to see a quiz tournament organized by Decker at Atlanta's Emory University and the pair hatched the notion of forgetting television and instead syndicating College Bowl on campuses. Without a sponsor like General Electric, it wasn't going to be TV money, but the format was back where it began: a real-world intellectual encounter, now with students instead of servicemen. By 1977, two hundred and fifty universities were playing; it kept growing, and the game has never gone away.

It reflects well on Britain that *University Challenge* has spent so long in primetime, but it's to America's credit that the same game is so well established there off-screen, its contestants merrily taking part without even the promise of their parents and two and half million other people watching them dressed up in order to get dressed down by Jeremy Paxman.

American 'bowl' quiz is also deeply hard. Its starters and bonuses resemble those of *University Challenge* in form, but the starters offer much, much more abstruse information before getting to anything that most people would find useful as a trigger to answer the question.

If you think you can bear it, here's an example, from the 2014 Chicago Open. It begins **Yang *et al.* proposed a link between a macroscopic form of this quantity and compressibility with** intuitions from the microscopic form of this quantity. It is pro-portional to the second derivative of energy with respect to the number of electrons in the atom when the molecular geometry is constant.** Not buzzed in yet? It continues for a further hundred words before finishing: **For ten points, name this quantity from an acid/base theory that is the counterpart of 'softness'.**[1]

Of course. The College Bowl Company Inc. offered, for a period, the only game on campus for those who fancied spending evenings in faculty basements celebrating and remembering the arcane. By the 1980s, schisms erupted, in part because of the fees which had replaced GE's sponsorship as College Bowl's revenue stream, and the practice is nowadays referred to as 'quiz bowl', with tournaments held by various sadistic bodies.

Who enters those basements? Quiz-bowl champions are people who have memorized lists, and possibly lists of lists. To perform well in quiz bowl, your knowledge needs to go deep. Not wide: unlike those in most other quizzes, bowl contestants disappear into their own rabbit holes of history, literature or science and often know surprisingly little about the rest. Jonathan Magin, who sets for the Academic Competition Federation, says that preparation 'can sometimes be a race to know harder and harder clues about something kind of peripheral' and likens it to what the Red Queen told Alice about Looking-glass Land: 'Now, *here*, you see, it takes all the running you can do, to keep in the same place.'

In 2014, I found myself asking questions at the Quiz League of London's annual bowl-like Buzzer Tournament. Apart from a half-hour lunch break, the contestants – who, despite the league's name, had travelled from far and wide to

[1] Hardness.

81

compete – answered questions from 10.15 a.m. until 7.15 p.m. There will never be a day in which I again say so many words.

The tournament is matier and, later, beerier than American quiz bowl, but no less fierce in its pugnacity. Some wander into league-quizzing when they fancy a stiffer challenge than pub quizzes; some begin as friends of other quizzers; others, following a tour de force on a show like *University Challenge*, are keeping that buzz going. And this day is like a fiercer *University Challenge* where the starters, as in America, give near-impossibly arcane information in their first few sentences.

Anyone who has read a bedtime story to a child will be familiar with the sensation of reading without being aware of *what* you're reading. At the Buzzer Tournament, I knew that I was saying the words correctly (thanks to little bracketed pieces of fuh-NETT-ick uh-SISS-tunce) and could often hear my voice somewhere, duly varying its pitch in a way that suited the length of the sentences, but that was about as close as I usually got to knowing what I was saying.

After five or six hours of these incantations, I emerged into a period of self-awareness in which I was conscious that my consciousness had become a Zennish trance. By now, the questions might as well be 'Colorless green ideas sleep furiously', a sentence devised by linguist Noam Chomsky which is easy to say but tricky to understand. The things I didn't understand included bonuses on 'Naval battles of the Ottoman Empire' (if you fancy it: **Named after the cape in southern Greece off which it took place, at which 1717 naval battle did the Ottoman fleet fight the fleet of an alliance of Venice, Portugal and the Papal States?**[2]) and on 'Hebrew linguistics' (if you haven't had enough: **Inflected forms of verbs and nouns in Semitic**

[2] Matapan.

languages are often constructed from stems or roots of this type. **This word denotes the presence of a certain especially common number of consonants.**[3]) I felt that I was now floating above a complete map of the universe, and everything human-kind has ever known about it.

And the miracle of it all is that the other people in the room – the contestants – *do* understand all these words, enough to buzz in and identify what they're about, and that they are gaining enormous pleasure by doing so.

Apart from good phrasing, one way that the setters of those long starter questions ensure that the contestant doesn't get utterly lost in words is the use of bold type, which, when stressed in speech, obligingly ensures that everyone knows what it really is that's being asked for: 'in **this conflict**, Syphax commanded Numidian troops'; '. . .the Adiri region of **this celestial body** is . . .'; and so on. Other quizzes achieve hardness precisely by eschewing this clarity.

'*Scire ubi aliquid invenire possis, ea demum maxima pars eruditionis est*,' as they say.

King William's College is a private school near Castletown on the Isle of Man which takes pupils from the age of three. It celebrates Christmas with a set of general-knowledge questions, originally designed, according to one report, 'in order that the boys shall have something to do other than breaking the house room windows or driving sheep into rival dormitories'.

The General Knowledge Paper (GKP) is structured more like a quiz than a traditional exam: they may not be called 'rounds', but the questions come in eighteen sets of ten. Pupils face the paper twice: once, unseen, at the end of term in

[3] Triliteral (or triconsonantal; accept roots with three consonants).

December (there are two points for every correct answer, and a typical overall score is two), then again in the new year, once they've had a chance to spend their vacation researching a new set of answers. Or, as a teacher put it in 1954, 'Their unhappy parents, their vicars, their lawyers, are pressed into service while the boy goes to the Cinema.' (Boys with lawyers? Plural? What on earth happened during Christmases on the Isle of Man in the 1950s?) In 1982, former chief setter Dick Boynes conceded that mileage may vary for international pupils: 'This admittedly may present difficulties if they happen to live in the Middle East or in a remote part of the African continent.'

The sets, at first blush, are baffling – but they might reveal a theme, so that some pieces of lower-hanging fruit . . .

> **What part is played by the third party at a lovers' tryst?**[4]
>
> **What is a hydraulic crane with a terminal railed platform?**[5]

. . . might help the hapless solver to discover the theme, and make sense of more cryptic queries: **What is Georgia?**[6]; and even have an inspired guess at the more specialist ones: **The eastward deviation of what was decreed by Teburoro Tito?**[7]

The GKP was first sat in 1905, with detention for the boys with the lowest scores and a half of bitter for those with the highest. At the beginning, its questions were more like those you would find in a traditional exam, but it started to express through its tone and themes the personalities of the teachers who set it. Denis Thompson – a familiar figure on the island, known for cycling up the windswept Hundred using his walking stick to stop his trilby from blowing off – was in charge from 1930 to 1958. He recalled: 'By 1915, [it] had enlarged its scope sufficiently to prompt a daily newspaper to publish an article entitled **"Why is the Red Sea red?**[8] What the little Manx boys learn".'

That this should be considered newsworthy is a little bewildering. What little Manx boy wouldn't want to know that? The same goes for other questions from the same set: **Why does a bad egg smell?**[9] And, indeed, **Where does the wind go to?**[10]

But this was before Britain started to quiz: after the first press reports of the existence of the GKP, reprints of the questions began appearing around the UK. And once the school became aware of the interest among folk on 'the adjacent island', 'one eye was undoubtedly kept on the larger public whom it might reach': it mutated into a new kind of leisure activity and not a bad bit of publicity for a fee-paying school.

Not everyone was convinced. A *Times* editorial in 1933 described the GKP as 'proof of the spread of a very dangerous form of mental disorder'; that mental disorder being recalling information for the fun of it. Until recently, the paper fondly remembered, those 'who would ask each other, even at breakfast, how many pints of blood there were in the human body' were, happily, 'few and shy of public notice'.

The floodgates keeping out enthusiasm for knowing things had been hurled open by 'the crossword craze' (*The Times* itself had only recently and reluctantly succumbed) and King William's was making matters much worse:

8 Tinge imparted by red seaweed.
9 Formation of sulphuretted hydrogen.
10 To an area of lower pressure.

This holidays it will be all over the place. Instead of dancing, or charades, or jolly, noisy round games, we shall have to sit still and be miserable under the exhibition of our own ignorance and the detestable conceit of some horrid little youth or girl, some pompous old man or sour old woman, who happens by luck (or through having got hold of the questions on the sly) to know the answers. It is a grievous prospect.

Another newspaper suggested that the GKP not be issued 'until Parliament had risen for Christmas, as the two could not be dealt with at once', and word reached the school that selections were being read out on American radio and distributed among delegates at the United Nations.

By this time, the questions had become much less on-the-nose than the Red Sea one and, to this day, among the regular features (the first set each time is on the year just passed, and the last on the events of a hundred years ago) are the sets which need some decoding before you know what you're being asked. These are often headed by a single word, such as the one which airily begins '**Locate**' before questions including **a a e e e b c b a**,[11] **e g c c b g c a a a g e**[12] and **g g g c c c a f c**.[13]

This variant of quiz – where you have to make lateral connections as well as recalling facts – is how various media make their challenges harder.

The BBC's *Round Britain Quiz*, a spin-off from *Transatlantic Quiz*, is the longest-running programme in the genre. Teams representing UK regions face gnomic challenges often submitted by listeners, with the host (currently Tom Sutcliffe) giving gentle hints that would probably be welcomed by GKP victims. At its 'softer' end are questions like **If a former Secretary**

11 'Scarborough Fair'. (The questions give the names the initial notes of the melody.)
12 'The White Cliffs of Dover'.
13 'America'. (*West Side Story*).

of State for International Development and the founder of the
English Folk Dance Society joined forces with Howard Stern,
why might the Mikado approve?[14]; at the tougher, **Where might
half an orang-utan and Leontes' daughter be spotted, along
with 99 others?**[15]

On television, lateral posers have been found since 2008 in
Only Connect's 'four apparently random clues'. The show set
out its unapologetic store early on, following viewer objections
to the Greek letters on the game board. Host Victoria Coren
explained all to viewers and to the teams, the Epicureans and
the Courtiers:

> It's a new series and something has changed. *Only Con-
> nect* is a much-loved show. There's only one thing that
> people have ever disliked, and it is the Greek letters. People
> have written in over the last few series and said that these
> are 'pretentious'. They're 'elitist' – 'snobbish', even. Some-
> body even said they were 'silly'.
>
> We listened. The Greek letters are gone. So, Courtiers –
> please choose your Egyptian hieroglyph.

Welcome, then, the Twisted Flax and the Horned Viper,
inspired by a cartoon which was making fun of the quiz's
abstruseness. Questions on *Only Connect* tend to get harder as
each tournament goes on, such that a series might start by asking for the connection between **Quintuple troth, Distress
signal, 1963 Lincoln Memorial speech and 1815 Belgian battle,**[16]
while a final might do the same for **Champion of 1981 Grand
National, It told of Pennywise the clown, Town where Battle**

---

14 Clare Short; Cecil Sharp: shock jock; the 'short, sharp shock' in *The Mikado*'s 'I am So
Proud'.
15 Latin name *Pongo borneo; Perdita* in *The Winter's Tale*; names of dogs in *One Hundred
and One Dalmatians.*
16 ABBA singles ('I Do, I Do, I Do, I Do, I Do', 'SOS', 'I Have a Dream', 'Waterloo').

Abbey lies and Had a 1974 hit with 'Killer Queen'[17] (which is easier than it seems if you look at the question for long enough).

Unlike these broadcast quizzes, GKP was compulsory for King William's College's boys (and, latterly, girls) – though no longer.

Pat Cullen sets the questions now; he first encountered them as a pupil in 1949, shortly before the *Guardian* made them a festive fixture, and 'solicit[ed] the help of a Commander Bliss at Scotland Yard and the head of transport at the National Coal Board' for his second shot.

'Participation is now voluntary,' he says, 'but competition no less intense.' The change came about in the late 1990s, because it was deemed inappropriate to oblige pupils to do something which might distract them from revision for national exams.

There's something sad about this and, perhaps counter-intuitively, less fun. The GKP did much to get Britain ready for quiz, and it did so by being a celebration of knowledge and a test in which you didn't know what was going to come up and everything was up for grabs. This gladdens the heart more than the teach-the-test, consider-your-CV thinking that character-izes today's approach to exams. If there's one thing you can say about life, it's that you really don't know what's going to come up. And, regarding the second time the pupils were obliged to take each paper: no one has ever suffered from developing a sense of where to look things up and who to trust.

The hardest quiz of all time, though, was surely the extra epi-sode of *Mastermind* in 1987 which Magnus Magnusson devoted to its contestants: the 'reservists who wait in the wings in case

17 The answer is in the clue (Bob Champion, Stephen King's *It*, Battle in East Sussex, the band Queen).

we have a last-minute cancellation'. Their specialized subjects were the Eighty Years' War, Australasian Fauna, the Life and Work of [physicist] Karl Gloping and the Life and Novels of C. P. Armitage.

These subjects were harder than any in the programme's history, mainly because they were entirely fictional, as were the contestants, their home towns – everything, in fact, except for Magnusson, gamely reading from a script written by Stephen Fry as part of a deadpan and consummately effected April Fool. It is remembered as no less entertaining a watch by those who took it to be straight quiz: proof that Bamber Gascoigne was right in the quotation above: it is indeed great fun to hear strange things that you don't actually know about.

Are you ready to play?

8. Everything you always wanted to know

How do you prepare for a quiz?

Who would be on your dream pub-quiz team? I'd save a space at the table for Sherlock Holmes's brother, Mycroft ('All other men are specialists, but his specialism is omniscience') – or, if we're restricting ourselves to real people, Thomas Young. Young was born in 1773 and worked as a doctor. Actually, perhaps that should read 'a writer'. Or 'a linguist'. . .

Put it this way: in 1816, the former child prodigy turned adult prodigy gave in to repeated requests to contribute to the *Encyclopædia Britannica*, then a recent arrival on the reference shelves of the curious. Reluctant to attempt definitive entries about anything he wasn't already deeply familiar with, he offered only the following:

Alphabet
Annuities
Attraction

Capillary Action
Cohesion
Colour
Dew
Egypt
Eye
Focus
Friction
Halo
Hieroglyphic
Hydraulics
Motion
Resistance
Ship
Sound
Strength
Tides
Waves

. . . sorry, and 'Anything of a medical nature'. And all this with no Wikipedia as a 'research tool': Young literally wrote the book on what was known of these subjects. In 2007, a biography of Young described him on the title page as *The Last Man Who Knew Everything*.

How was such omniscience possible?

It didn't hurt that Young was rich (see Chapter 15). This is not to say that he was idle: he was familiar with Annuities, say, through his salaried position as the Palladium Life Insurance Company's Inspector of Calculations, and, as Secretary of the Board of Longitude and Superintendent of the *Nautical Almanac*, he already knew a thing or two about Ships.

And then there's his day job, as a doctor, which is why he

wanted his *Britannica* contributions to be anonymous: if his patients knew of his various non-medical pursuits, he worried, they might think his mind wasn't on the day job and mistake him for one of the blood-letting quacks common among Georgian physicians. His scholarly peers included some who suspected that, if you knew about a lot of things, you probably didn't know much about any of them – you might call such people specialists, or perhaps spiteful.

The key to Young's extraordinary breadth of knowledge was that he couldn't go *too* deep – compared, that is, to today's sense of knowing a subject 'deeply'. In the exciting days of the early eighteenth century, you could still talk of science as 'natural philosophy'. In 1815, there was a lot that humankind had not yet noticed. As an illustration . . .

Give the decade in which knowledge was expanded in the following ways.

Following the abolition of publishing taxes and excise duty on paper, the British public starts reading magazines and periodicals in earnest – just in time for it to discover, through popular reviews, a new book by Charles Darwin: *On the Origin of Species*.[1]

Russian chemist Dmitri Mendeleev creates the periodic table, wisely leaving gaps for some elements which he thought would soon be discovered and which duly were?[2]

German physicist Wilhelm Röntgen detects a range of wavelength – X-rays – which will make visible the

1 The 1850s (1859).

2 The 1860s (1869): as Tom Lehrer rhymed, 'These are the only ones of which the news has come to Harvard / And there may be many others but they haven't been discovered.'

previously invisible, from inside the human body to the behaviour of the sun.[3]

Sigmund Freud turns his attention from exam-anxiety dreams to childhood development and publishes *Three Essays on the Theory of Sexuality*.[4]

Nuclear fission of heavy elements is discovered, which will *later* lead to some world-changing events at Hiroshima and Nagasaki.[5]

... and that only takes us up to 1938, the year when British quiz began, and leaves out many other figures who changed the way we think about knowledge and science: Wittgenstein, say, and Einstein, not to mention Frankenstein.

Not long after Young wrote his *Britannica* entries, humankind began to look at things that were previously so small or so far away (or so undiscovered or so subconscious) that no one knew they were even there.

It got worse for anyone who aspired to know everything. 'Natural science' split into disciplines, then sub-disciplines: from natural philosophy emerged chemistry, which presently split into organic chemistry and inorganic chemistry, then snapped, splintered and shattered into dozens of fields, from agrochemistry to zoochemistry, via chemistries including organometallic chemistry, supramolecular chemistry and, as if chemists were taking the mickey, solid-state chemistry.

So it is with everything else that even Thomas Young knew, to the point where a Wikipedia page on some topic is often so generous in detail, so nuanced and inclusive – put another way, so bloody *long* – that the non-specialist's eyes swim amid a longing for the clarity of the *Junior Pears Encyclopaedia*. Oh, to have a handle on something. On anything.

The epithet 'The Last Man Who Knew Everything' is compelling because it allows us to imagine a time when, if you just kept on learning, you might one day raise your hand and yell, 'Finished!'

But Homer Simpson speaks for humanity when he contemplates the thousand-odd cubic centimetres of storage in his head and complains that 'every time I learn something new, it pushes some old stuff out of my brain'. Worse, *remembering* can do the same thing – or, as a paper in *Nature* rephrased it, 'Retrieval Induces Adaptive Forgetting of Competing Memories via Cortical Pattern Suppression'.

Worse still for the quiz contestant, there's all that non-scholarly information that trickled then flooded in during the twentieth century: fact upon fact, each unmoored from its context, brought to us by more pervasive fact-bringing technologies. In the basketball movie *White Men Can't Jump*, the down-at-heel Gloria Clemente announces that her destiny is to pay off her debts by triumphing magnificently on *Jeopardy!* because her brain is overwhelmed with 'more useless goddamn information' than that of any other human being.

None of us can now aspire to omniscience, much less to Thomas Young's erudition – but, like Gloria and Thomas, outside the scholarly world we are all now generalists. Our knowledge is general. But what is the general knowledge that you need to know to win at quiz?

Put another way: what does a quiz setter expect a quiz contestant to know? The name of the game is guessing what a contestant might reasonably have come across since they started accumulating information so that they have a decent chance of guessing the answers. And the setter can reasonably assume that the contestant has been to school.

Except, of course, that your school career progresses from generalism to some kind of specialism, and the setter doesn't know which options you chose when you were fourteen. To be on the safe side, you need to strive for the knowledge you would have if you had taken all the GCSEs. (Those who sat their exams a while ago can have a moment to take on board that geography and history have been joined by textiles, statistics, citizenship, psychology and other topics which nobody taught in their day.)

You don't need to get a top grade in every subject, mind you: an A* in English literature might be useful in quiz, but for general science, a C will get you by (more on this in Chapter 10). Likewise, you might have daydreamed through much of your economics classes, but I hope you were paying attention during history. Older subjects over new; humanities over sciences.

And then there's the knowledge that's not taught in schools: all those questions about FA Cup finalists and Oscar nominees.

We're back in the world of John Dunton. We're back with newspapers. Those we met earlier, recruiting for the civil service and universities, expected their applicants to be regular devourers of (especially broadsheet) newspapers; the same pool of information makes up most of the rest of general knowledge. When a question setter is assessing how well-known or obscure some piece of popular culture is, their own memories of its appearances in newspapers (for which, now, read: news websites) is as good a bellwether as they're going to get. And, broadly, the more often that information appears, the less it will be worth in terms of points or cash.

(Incidentally, this vital setter skill could not be more different from the gift for retention needed by contestants. Those who set quizzes get used very quickly to the experience of attending a pub quiz, hearing a question that he or she has set in the past, recalling lots of interesting facts around the answer, and plenty of answers which are definitely wrong – everything, in fact, except the thing his or her team-mates are waiting for.)

And of all that mess of information, quiz especially values anything that can be quantified, tabulated, ordered or ranked: sporting and political contests, record-breakers and prize-winners, the tops of charts and of medal tables.

What sort of tables, charts and lists are we talking about?

After apparently reading a premature obituary of himself headlined 'The Merchant of Death is Dead', the inventor of dynamite changed his will to fund which annual awards?[6]

Those coming from Lausanne carry a CH, those from Karlsruhe have a D, and those from Zaragoza sport an E. What are these letters?[7]

Sculptures from *two* of them are in the British Museum, *one* remains intact at Giza and the remaining *four* are believed to be ancient history. What are they?[8]

The base-plates adorning what item are blank when presented, to keep secret the identities of their

[6] The Nobel prizes. (An ardent quizzer will also come to know who won what, when; also the periodic table, the set of SI units, the planets in order of distance from the Earth, their dimensions, etc., and their moons, etc.)

[7] International vehicle registration codes; accept IVR, stickers on cars, etc. (Quiz champs especially know those where the letter is not the initial of the English-language name of the country and will also get to grips with those 'CCTLDS' at the end of internet addresses, military ranks and their abbreviations, Morse code, etc.)

[8] The Seven Wonders of the ancient world. (Winners get to know the names of each and also bone up on the world's capitals, currencies, flags, etc.)

owners, but can be engraved immediately afterwards at the Governor's Ball?[9]

The Standing Fishes, the Rebecca's Camels and the Blasphemous Comma are notorious misprinted versions of which book, completed in 1611?[10]

The First Lord of the Treasury carries out duties that were previously held by the Lord High Treasurer, and the role is usually given to the person who has managed to secure what other job?[11]

. . . and of course, via the perennial pub-quiz pooch . . .

His voice was provided in a posthumous biopic by Harry Enfield, and he had a cameo as himself in the 1966 Eric Sykes spoof *The Spy with a Cold Nose*. What did Pickles the collie dog find wrapped in newspaper in a front garden in South Norwood earlier that year?[12]

That sort of thing. And Eurovision. Put them together, and you have quiz's periodic table. Or perhaps Rosetta Stone: as a coach of American college quiz teams told *Jeopardy!* champion Ken Jennings, 'The more facts you accumulate, the easier it becomes to learn new things, because you have a web of knowledge to fit those new facts into.'

Assemble a skeleton made of Kevin Bacon's filmography and his co-stars can cleave like flesh. Another day, master the

9 **Academy Awards** statuettes; accept Oscars. (Also, recipients of top categories, Booker winners, Poets Laureate, singles-chart number ones, etc.)

10 The **King James Bible**. (Also, names of books in both testaments, patron saints, Archbishops of Canterbury, cathedral cities, etc.)

11 **Prime minister** of the United Kingdom. (Also, all holders and their dates in office, monarchs and their houses, ditto popes and American presidents, etc.)

12 The **Jules Rimet trophy**; accept the World Cup. (Also, finalists, Olympic-gold-medal winners, athletics record-breakers, Wimbledon finalists, etc.)

rudiments of Dutch history and see how Spinoza and van Gogh click into place.

The prospect of getting those trellises of information into your head, though, may not seem irresistible; more like revision for an exam-on-everything than a leisurable activity.

So it's comforting to learn that when you ask quiz champions how they know so much, they're consistently keen to stress that it's not about memorizing lists. Most ardent quiz contestants, it turns out, read widely (non-fiction, largely) and for the pleasure of it.

Even within reference works, there are those which eschew dry cataloguing and offer something that's fun to browse through, hopping from topic to topic. I defy anyone to spend half an hour with *Brewer's Dictionary of Phrase and Fable*, Bamber Gascoigne's *Encyclopedia of Britain* or the Reader's Digest *Reverse Dictionary* without wanting to make it two hours – not to mention the appeal of all those points that will be gained in future quizzes as a result. But it's the news and 'normal' non-fiction that, quiz enthusiasts say, allow them to gather all those award-winners, monarchs and capitals without incurring migraines.

Here's part of a profile of *Eggheads*' Kevin Ashman: '[H]e learns best by simply reading – widely and very regularly. A book or an article or whatever it may be, even if some of the background context never comes up, or isn't likely to come up, might go towards answering a question,' he says. And this is *Mastermind* champion Gary Grant: 'I certainly never tried to learn "facts". That was something only geeks would do . . .' Finally, here's two-time International Quizzing Association world champion Olav Bjortomt: 'I would never advise anyone to learn lists. That's too boring. I practise learning through a much more organic way.'

Thank goodness for that. Oh hang on, though: there's more. Here's the next paragraph of the Kevin Ashman piece: 'Has he really achieved such eminence by just reading a lot? "I used to be able to learn lists if I had to . . . I tend to know the birth and death years of lots of people, and that helps. They're hooks to hang other information on." '

And we interrupted Gary Grant: 'That was something only geeks would do . . . or so I believed a few years ago.'

And there's a tiny caveat that follows the Olav Bjortomt quote: ' "The only exception," he says, is when he takes a week off to cram list after list of quiz questions until, as he puts, "I burn out." '

Yep, I'm afraid it's exactly as you feared.

These, though, are the champions. To be more precise, those who want to win the *hardest* quizzes do indeed learn lists. (Veteran quiz setter David Elias reckoned that a good question for auditions was 'What is Europe's highest mountain?': most contestants would guess at Mont Blanc or the Matterhorn; future champions 'would fire back "Mount Elbrus!" ')

Happily, the rest of us can indeed forget list-learning, relax and carry on reading one of those non-fiction books which convey a lot of diverse information as you keep turning the pages.

Besides, once the quiz starts, be it in TV studio or pub, it's no longer about what you happen to know. It's about how you fare in the format of the quiz.

9. Buzz before you think

How to answer a quiz question

The problem was that he had known the answers to
the questions the other players had been asked. He
had also known the answers to his own questions.
He just hadn't been able to get the words out to
answer them correctly.
Michael Scott's novella *The Quiz Master*

First, some basics.

You might have wondered why some TV quiz contestants give answers which sound odd, even unnatural. Here's a tough one: 'Name the film director whose experiences as a messenger boy on the show *Quiz Kid Challenge* influenced his 1999 Oscar-nominated movie *Magnolia*.'

The man in question is usually referred to as 'P. T. Anderson', sometimes as 'Paul Thomas Anderson', but – unlike Hitchcock, say, or Spielberg – rarely by his surname alone.

But 'Anderson' is all that contestants should write in a pub quiz, and certainly all they should say if it's a television quiz. Blistering in a windowless room under 4,000-lux lights, their minds primed to leap from topic to topic, the less their mouths do the better. The danger is that a brain, as brains do, might make a little link with Wodehouse, and the mouth might blurt 'P. G. Anderson', or the given name of some other directing Anderson: Wes, say, or Lindsay. 'Anderson' is enough to demonstrate that you know what the question is about, so the wily quizzer sticks safely with a surname.

Here's another. When they don't know the answer to one of those 'true or false' questions that pub-quiz setters are keen on, the smart contestants say 'True'. One study puts the percentage of 'true's at 56 per cent; I suspect it may be higher, since a question which asks contestants to consider that some interesting fact might be true, only to then add that it isn't, is, for setter, contestant and any witnesses, an outstandingly joyless exercise.

What about other kinds of multiple-choice question? Unless you suspect that the setter is hoping for a moment of surprise that the answer is more or less than common-sense suggests, follow the guidance doled out to those military candidates we met in Chapter 2: of A, B, C and D, consider the middle and, 'if in doubt, Charlie out'; in other words, choose C.

The most basic of the basics, though, is this: go easy on the booze. Long gone are the days when *University Challenge* contestants were routinely merry, at least on screen. 'When I said we had a drink,' recalls Malcolm Rifkind (University of Edinburgh team, 1967), who went on to become Foreign Secretary, 'that's probably an understatement. We were carefree and careless, and won the match.'

'I used to tell the teams,' says stalwart producer Peter Mullings, 'where the nearest pub was, and say: "An odd drink is not a bad idea. But a surfeit is a very bad thing."' He goes on, 'There was one occasion when one had had the surfeit, and shortly into the programme, his head fell – thump! – with an enormous thwack. Not to be raised. We had to stop the tape, go in, drag him out, put the reserve in, and start again.'

Today's debt-addled students are too responsible for day-time drinking, and health-and-safety regulations bar the tipsy from studios, but across all quiz programmes, there is not a producer without a sorry tale of a contestant or team which finished a day of repeated wins with a late-night celebration in whatever unfamiliar city the programme has brought them to. Time and again, the makers of a quiz hope that a team that shone yesterday will be the match of the questions today, only to see them knocked out in a hungover haze of ignominy in the morning's first recording.

The *last* night is the one for celebration or commiseration: for those shooting on a Sunday, no saturnalia on Saturday.

Presence of mind, you might call it.

A starter for ten from *University Challenge*:

The psychologist Raymond Cattell identified 'fluid' and 'crystallized' as factors of what human capacity, defined by one authority as the extent to which one deals 'flexibly and effectively with practical and theoretical problems'?[1]

And one from me:

In the Dean Martin song, can you remember what follows the lines about one girl and one boy, some grief and some joy?[2]

In 1974, a letter to *The Times* suggested that 'the fine word "mind"' was debased by *Mastermind*. 'Perhaps,' it went on, 'the BBC might be persuaded to call the game *Master Memory*, reserving "mind" for more elevated purposes.' A reply rapidly

[2] 'Memories are made of this'.
[1] Intelligence.

followed, insisting that the programme 'tests the acquisition, storage and retrieval of information: all processes of the mind', adding:

> It springs to mind that the game tests another human quality: presence of mind. During the quiz, we had also to keep our minds on the job, mind our p's and q's and not mind too much whether we won or lost.

Therefore, Sir, I remain with undiminished happiness,

PATRICIA OWEN, Mastermind of the United Kingdom

Owen was the show's second winner, and across the series her specialized subjects included Byzantine Art and Grand Opera, but it turns out she knew a thing or two about brains as well: her terminology is pretty much the same as that used by psychologists, who tend to break memory into 'encoding', 'storage' and 'retrieval'.

Encoding is the bit where, through reading widely and wisely, a contestant acquires information which might come up in a quiz. It doesn't necessarily involve codes, though it assuredly does no harm to know **what the following mnemonics represent**:

Richard Of York Gave Battle In Vain[3]
My Very Easy Method: Just Set Up Nine Planets[4]
No Plan Like Yours To Study History Wisely[5]

[3] The colours of the rainbow (accept spectrum): Red, Orange, Yellow, Green, Blue, Indigo, Violet.

[4] The planets in our solar system, outwards from the Sun: Mercury, Venus, Earth, Mars, Jupiter, Saturn, Uranus, Neptune and the beleaguered Pluto, which may or may not be a planet again as you read this.

[5] Royal houses since 1066: Norman, Plantagenet, Lancaster, York, Tudor, Stuart, Hanover, Windsor.

**Kindly Place Cover On Fresh Green Spring Vegetables[6]
Memorizing's Never Easy: Mnemonics Offer Nudges In
Capsules[7]**

As for storage: this is a physiological business about which
not a great deal is currently known, but it's enough to make you
question the wisdom of so many quizzes being held in pubs.

Then there's retrieval. The anti-quiz letter above claimed
that 'contestants are simply required to provide straight answers
to a string of (admittedly difficult) questions'. How simple is
that? Mind-magician Derren Brown was thinking of quiz in
much the same way in the 2008 TV show where he took a man
with a poor memory and subjected him to a speed-reading programme. After a week as a kind of human scanner, gazing
across pages of encyclopaedias, he professed himself astonished
to be able to give **the number of hummingbird types found in
the Amazonian rainforest**[8] (it's three digits) and **the currency
of Liechtenstein**[9] (it's someone else's) without remembering
having read this information.

He was then entered into a tough pub quiz in which, playing solo, he came a serviceably plausible second. Balderdash,
perhaps, but entertaining balderdash. Anyone who has ever reasoned their way to a moment of happy realization in a quiz,
though, will remember that *Rain Man*-style retention is not all
there is to 'retrieval'.

Part of it is what they call 'recall' (fishing out the answer
without apparent effort); the other part is 'recognition', where

---

[6] Taxonomic classifications: Kingdom, Phylum, Class, Order, Family, Genus, Species, Variety.
[7] The spelling of the tricky word 'mnemonic'.
[8] 319.
[9] The Swiss franc.

whatever is mentioned in the question – dates, places, and so on – form part of the reasoning which eliminates candidates and alchemizes the answer. As a way of getting a point, recognition can feel a lot more fun.

This is not to sniff at 'recall retrieval', which can also be described as 'crystallized intelligence' or 'knowing a bunch of stuff'. For one thing, it can be much quicker. For another, it's more valuable to some people than it is to others.

In a rare public encounter between the hosts of *Mastermind* and *University Challenge*, the issue of age came up. Jeremy Paxman teased John Humphrys: 'You must find this too, as you get to your very advanced stage of life: as you get older, you do find that knowledge sticks to you, like flies and fly-paper. You know more when you're fifty or sixty than you did when you were twenty or thirty, but the problem is the speed of retrieval.'

The psychological literature tends to agree here, again: it's the thinking on your feet and the making of connections that wanes as the raw stock of information waxes.

Still, however much information a contestant has acquired over however many years, they're never going to be able to pull out the answer to every question – hence the importance of 'recognition retrieval', which can also be described as 'fluid intelligence' or, in plain language, 'getting good at guessing'.

Good guess, good guess

It's not a bad idea to have some default answers knocking about. As mentioned above, 'Central African Republic' is the go-to answer on *Pointless*. A player at the 1984 Trivial Pursuit tournament in Chicago announced, 'When in doubt, I'm going to say Joan Crawford. This game has a lot of Joan Crawford questions.'

And in the sitcom *Two Pints of Lager and a Packet of Crisps*, Jonny coaches Janet for a pub quiz: 'If you don't know the answer, just say Shirley Williams or Uruguay. It's always one of the two.'

But the slow-witted Janet is doomed. When asked to say, *within a margin of three feet*, how high an alarmed springbok can jump, she guesses at 728 feet. This isn't just anatomically implausible: Janet has signally failed to use the margin of error to anchor her guess. (A few benchmark numbers, from **the length of an Olympic swimming pool**[10] right up to **the distance to the Sun**,[11] are handy points of reference.)

Sounder in reasoning is the narrator of the yuppie-satire novel *How Old was Lolita?*, who is asked the Trivial Pursuit question: 'Who was pope between June 4 and June 20 1963?'

> I am bad at popes. I am bad at geography, world wars, popes and rock 'n' roll hits of the fifties. But I'm good at deduction, and I conclude that such a short papal reign must mean an unorthodox answer. It may even be a trick question. I guess that the answer is no one, and I'm right. Not because I know popes but because I identify with the sense of humor of the Canadians who invented the game.

Or, from real life, there's *University Challenge* team captain Ralph Morley. In a quarter-final, Jeremy Paxman asks, **During the twentieth century, who held the position of Prime Minister of the United Kingdom for the ...** but gets no further before Morley buzzes in with the correct answer.

---

10 50 metres (164 feet).
11 Usually given as 93 million miles (150 million kilometres).

After a Paddington stare, Paxman asks:

— How did you know I was going to ask for **the longest period of time?**[12]
— Well, what else is it going to be?
— Okay, let's see if you get these bonuses right. They're on French land borders, you smart-arses!

When his team then guesses at 'Loire' as the answer to the question **Lying along the Belgian border and including the historical Dutch-speaking region of French Flanders, what is the most populous French *département*?**,[13] the host mock-reproaches them: 'Not all so easy, are they?'

Knowing the quiz can be as important as knowing the answers to its questions. This isn't about anticipating the questions themselves, though prospective contestants in the original *Fifteen to One* were known to watch videotapes of old episodes in the hope that some of them might be recycled by the time they were in the studio. And anyone who played the original Trivial Pursuit enough didn't just know that there were Joan Crawford questions, they knew the questions themselves, and the answer to them (Joan Crawford).

Even more importantly, it's about thinking like a setter of quiz questions.

Anyone who makes their living through words is effectively always on duty. If a crossword setter notices an ambiguity of language in his or her everyday life, it gets noted down – the same goes for comedy writers, along with any quirks of speech that might make for lively dialogue. With quiz setters, it's information.

13 Nord.
12 Margaret Thatcher.

Those who regard new information as setters do ('What kind of question might I make of this?') are tuned to the wavelength of contestants. Setting quizzes makes you better at answering them not because you necessarily acquire exactly the knowledge you need but because of how you look at all the stuff of the world. This is especially the case when it comes to information that's more interesting than the stuff of lists: not as quirky as the snappers, to use Trivial Pursuit argot, but the stuff that might be best described as mildly stimulating.

Here's a mildly stimulating fact: the word 'biscuit' reflects the fact that such snacks were once baked twice (*bis cuit* in French), the second time to dry them out. If you're thinking like a setter whenever you happen to come across that information, then you can bank that factoid and pounce like Ralph Morley, should you ever hear words along the lines of 'From the French meaning 'twice cooked', which . . . ?'

Getting to know the setter's brain is only half the battle, though.

Γνῶθι σεαυτον, as they also say

General-knowledge quizzes have long given psychologists a nifty way of gathering data to describe what people know, in particular, their sense that they're right or wrong about something.

Thanks to their toil, we know about something called the Over-confidence Effect. Knowing its name makes the findings less of a surprise, but the phenomenon is deserving of any quizzer's attention: with moderately difficult questions, we tend to pronounce ourselves 90 per cent confident when we've got about two thirds of them right, and our estimations approach 100 per cent when our score is around eight out of ten. So when you think you're on a roll, you probably aren't.

Another tendency, the Hard–Easy Effect, is towards over-confidence in harder questions and under-confidence in easy ones. Happily, no one loses extra points for a wrong answer just because they felt pretty sure of it. But getting to know what it feels like when you're right is as powerful a quizzing weapon as anyone can wield.

One skill is knowing when to change your mind. Candidates in multiple-choice exams are often advised to stick with their first answer. Likewise, the medical students who are told that good diagnosis begins with considering whatever seems the most obvious, known as Sutton's Law, in tribute to **'Slick' Willie Sutton, the prolific bank robber who legendarily answered the question 'Why do you rob banks?' with the six-word reply 'Because that's where ___ _____ ___.'**[14]

But wait. Don't these suggestions go against the spirit of the Over-confidence Effect? As the frenemy of **a sitcom character of the 2010s**[15] would say, 'Bear with, bear with,' for the next two paragraphs.

One study of multiple-choice tests in their educational context *first* asked teachers whether they thought that changing your initial answer was a fruitful strategy. It came out that 55.2 per cent thought it would damage your score. The researchers *then* assembled some numbers on the effect of changing your mind:

Wrong answer to right answer:	57.8%
Right answer to wrong answer:	20.2%
Wrong answer to another wrong answer:	22%

[14] the money is'. (Sutton claimed that the exchange was apocryphal, and that the real reason was 'Because I enjoyed it.')

[15] Miranda (the frenemy being Tilly).

So what should you do? The *first* answer – sticking with your hunch – perhaps feels intuitively right, but *then* that new option is starting to sound good, too . . .

In fact, the best bet is to fix a quick critical eye on each of the possible answers and work out why it might be *wrong* (including why the setter might have included it as a red herring). It's easy enough to fabricate some reason why a wrong answer might be *right* and to persuade yourself that it has about it a ring of famil-iarity. Contestants on *Who Wants to be a Millionaire?* were briefed to avoid making just this mistake, talking themselves so convinc-ingly into a wrong answer that when they then decided to ask the audience, the people in the studio had become persuaded, too, and 'confirmed' the money-losing, inaccurate option. (The audi-ence, incidentally, was apparently correct 91 per cent of the time when the contestant had not already expressed a preference, against 65 per cent of the Phone-a-Friends.)

It's also prudent to check that you're not in a bit of a flap. The first *Millionaire* contestant to see a million-pound ques-tion was Peter Lee. Having correctly named the **French Impressionist painter whose son became a successful film director**,[16] he was asked, for £500,000:

What does the Japanese word 'kamikaze' literally mean?[17]

A: sacred venture   B: divine wind
C: self-destruction   D: final attack

The quiz gods smiled. Lee had once led a study tour in Japan for dairy technologists and the group's guide had been a former (as in, surviving) kamikaze pilot. Lee had, as it hap-pened, asked him where the word 'kamikaze' came from.

[17] Divine wind.
[16] Pierre-Auguste Renoir, father of Jean.

He had been given the right answer then; he gave the same one to Chris Tarrant, then wrongly doubted himself when he became aware of 'a very audible intake of breath'. Hang on, he asked himself: 'had I blown it? Did the audience know something I didn't?'

In other words, he panicked.

Had this been his £8,000 question, it would have been worth a re-think but, of course, the real reason the audience made a noise was simple excitement at the amount of money being offered, so Lee was right to give the answer he was thinking of and take the cheque. It's sometimes good to change your mind, but it's always better to know when you're right and stick to it. (Peter Lee didn't fancy the £1 million question, which asked for **the county cricket side based at Chester-le-Street**,[18] despite his namesake town Peterlee being less than 12 miles from the ground.)

Panic can set in at any stage, of course. In 1989, a *Mastermind* contestant sat down and correctly remembered his name (Philip Wharmby) but froze on his occupation (clerical officer, gently provided by Magnus Magnusson). Happily, this was not the beginning of one of the programme's near-unwatchable 'pass spirals' (see Chapter 18).

As Patricia Owen said, a Mastermind needs presence of mind, and to avoid another kind of spiral: entering into needless Smiley-esque mind games. When a question suggests an obvious answer, like 'Which island was discovered on Christmas Day 1643?' the wrong approach is this:

- to consider whether it's a trick question (dismissing Christmas Island for some alternative, like Pitcairn) . . .
- then to worry that it might be a double-bluff (reverting to Christmas Island), before . . .

18 Durham CCC, at the Riverside Ground.

- twisting on to wondering if such things as triple-bluffs exist in quiz . . .
- and finally answering 'Manhattan' because it seems like that might be a thing you're expected to know.

The right approach is to answer 'Christmas Island', take the point and get a move on. (Assuming it was a quadruple-bluff would, admittedly, also get the point, but at the cost of your sanity.)

And so, even better than the setter, the person you have to know is yourself. This goes especially for those quizzes in which a buzzer is involved (and, in TV quizzes which use buzzers, any time you spend with the precise piece of kit you'll be using, get-ting to know its responsiveness and heft, is worth as much as any list of monarchs). Peter Richardson, one of the first quizz-ers who might be called a 'professional', pondered buzzer timing when studying for Norwich's 1970s flagship quiz *Sale of the Century*: 'It's no good waiting until you know the answer before pressing the buzzer. It's not even enough to buzz when you have heard the full question. You have to buzz just before the question becomes plain, banking on the fact that no question-master can stop talking instantly.'

Roger Tilling, who announces the name and institution after each bell- and buzzer-press on *University Challenge*, gives a further (if facetious) tip: 'I think it's strategic to have a long or difficult-to-pronounce surname on your team . . . it gives them at least an extra second to come up with the answer. If I was setting up a team, I'd have Drnovšek Zorko, Papaphilippopou-los, Warnakulasuriya and Bhattacharya. I think you'd win.'

Even if you're afflicted with a single-syllable surname, the right moment to buzz is not when you know the answer but when you know that you're *about to know it*.

And, for that, you have to have a keen sense of what you know and what you don't. **The American Secretary of Defense from 2001 to 2006**[19] may be judged by history as one of its greater monsters, but it's unfair to pillory him for his infamous 2002 distinction, apparently borrowed from NASA, between 'known knowns', 'known unknowns' and 'unknown unknowns'.

In quiz, knowing the difference between what you know you know and what you know you don't know is the most important knowledge of all. It's the difference between giving an answer and hanging back for a guess, and any decent team should cultivate at least a vague protocol for indicating to each other how confident they are in their guesses.

The only problem, in fact, with that Secretary of Defense's much-derided 'known unknowns' military briefing is that it leaves out the sweetest spot of all, the information you didn't know you knew: the unknown knowns.

On television, the moments when a contestant pulls an answer seemingly from nowhere are among viewers' (and thereby producers') favourites, but they're even more precious to the contestants themselves. The important thing is to ponder them – like you should with the terrible unknown unknowns, when you're surprised to be wrong – and to ponder them not in the moment, but later.

The difference between what it feels like to know something that you didn't know you knew and just thinking that you know it is something that you need to know, whether you know it or not.

And who knows? A greater self-knowledge might have little, unintended side-effects, like making you a better person outside of quiz.

19 Donald Rumsfeld.

All of the above, it should be added, assumes that you're facing good questions: ones which are largely consistent within the quiz itself and broadly so within quiz as a whole.

But there are also some very bad questions out there. Before we go into more detail, here's a good one: **I moved to the UK from South America in 1958, settling in Notting Hill. I had my own TV show in the 1970s, but did not appear on the big screen until 2014. Who am I?**[20]

20 Paddington Bear.

10. Good question!

Why is some
information more
enjoyable than other
information?

In the 1962 story 'Paddington Hits the Jackpot', our indefatigable ursine hero becomes a contestant on a TV quiz which is
unpopular with Mr Brown ('I wouldn't mind if he asked sensible questions. But to give all that money away for the sort of
thing he asks is ridiculous.')

Lucky for Some is hosted by Ronnie Playfair, a smarmster in
the model of Arthur E. Baird, as we see when he lamely wise-
cracks that Paddington will need to provide the 'bear facts'. In
other words, we are rooting for Paddington, who is offered a
choice of topics, and replies, 'I think I'd like to try my paw at
mathematics, please.'

Playfair reads the following question: **If you had a piece of
wood eight feet long and you cut it in half, and if you
cut the two pieces you then have into half, and if you then cut
all the pieces into half again, how many pieces would you
have?**[1]

1 Eight.

Paddington gets this right, and for the follow-up is asked how long each piece would be. 'Eight feet,' replies the bear. The answer on Playfair's card is 'one foot', but Paddington explains that he cut his down the middle, and had eight pieces, each eight feet long. Playfair splutters that 'it stands to reason' that anyone would cut the wood across the middle . . .

'Not if you're a bear,' replies Paddington, recalling his past adventures in carpentry.

Playfair becomes unprofessionally tetchy with Paddington; his frustration should, of course, be directed at whichever of *Lucky for Some*'s setters was responsible for the wording of the question, since it's flabby enough to allow more than one answer. In real-life quizzes where large sums of money can be lost, contestants often have to sign their agreement that the production company's decision on such matters will be binding.

Such awkward moments can, though, can be avoided by sticking to good questions.

Quiz questions are seldom written on the spot (though in the first *Mastermind* final, Magnus Magnusson managed to read all the questions on the specialized subject – the History of Music 1550–1900 – before the contestant's time was up and the recording was paused while some extras were hastily gleaned from *Pears Cyclopaedia*).

Most often, though, the questions are written in advance, far from the arena. Sometimes – and especially if a quiz nabob is involved, like William G. Stewart of the old *Fifteen to One*, or John Lloyd of *QI* – a TV quiz is created in an actual room which looks exactly as you would hope it might: well-lit, insulated with as many recherché reference books as will fit and redolent of curiosity and scepticism. There are companies which offer questions, such as the one set up by *Mastermind* semi-finalists Neville Cohen and Janet Barker, which went incognito for a while (they were working for *Who Wants to be a Millionaire?*, which affected the kind of grandiloquent security once associated with *The $64,000 Question* and *Twenty One*), and others which will offer stuff from a database to those who wish to assemble pub and television quizzes but who don't take any pleasure in actually setting questions. Most, though, are assembled using a disparate gang of setters.

Before questions began to exist as lines in word-processing documents or entries in spreadsheets, they were set by individuals researching, writing and rewriting in homes and libraries, and it remains the case that any question editor needs to create a network of the kind of people who actively enjoy wrenching facts into questions and answers (though they will probably never meet most of them in person).

And that distance from the arena of quiz has its costs: everyone involved in quiz has met examples of questions which worked well on paper but don't seem at all right once a contestant is actually trying to answer them.

For one thing, the questions have to fit unobtrusively into whichever quiz they've been written for. Different quizzes have different flavours. In the offices of *University Challenge*, the mark of a good question is referred to as 'inherent interest': 'even if you don't know the answer, when you hear it you think, Hmm, that's interesting, and not, So what?' On *Who Wants to be a Millionaire?*, it was 'shoutability': 'a chance for Dad to show off, for Mum to scream her disagreement and the kids to be amazed at how intelligent their parents actually are, or, just as often, how much brighter they are than their parents!'

Naturally, a question aimed at a team can be harder than

one aimed at an individual. Tie-breakers perform a different job, especially in pub quizzes, where they're written in a way that minimizes the risk of any two teams giving the same answer and of prolonging the tension beyond the point where it's fun (hence those demanding educated guesses along the lines of **What was the duration, in minutes, of the theatrical release of the 1994 film *Quiz Show?*[2]**)

For a normal question, though, the criterion, at its simplest, is that it has to make something happen.

Easy questions make nothing happen: they are a dreary call-and-response which the contestant barely notices until a feeling of irritation sets in. They're boring. Questions which are too *hard* for their contestants make nothing happen either: failure to answer is the ultimate non-event, unless you count a miserable feeling of degradation as an event. They're boring at best. Unfortunately, they're also the easiest kind of question to write.

Novice setters sometimes fancy that their job is to beat the contestant; it is not. Their job is to lose following a struggle. Failing to answer question after question is a joyless enterprise for the contestant; nor does anyone watching a quiz enjoy the harrowing moments of silence which characterize life in a points desert.

Even experienced setters sometimes underestimate the difficulty of a question: they think the answer is easier than it is because they've just typed it into some template and it becomes impossible for them to un-know – and so it becomes much more difficult to get into the mind of anyone who doesn't know it either. This holds even when the setters didn't know the answer themselves ten minutes ago.

2 132

Hard questions come in many forms. As anyone who has been to a bad quiz will recall, there are the dispiritingly obscure (**What colours are the star Regulus?**[3]). Then there are the arbitrary, the over-complicated, and those which ask for the wrong piece of information.

As an example, some raw material. A 1956 American programme which embraced the 'here-be riches' heart of American quiz was *Treasure Hunt*, with its accordion music, pirate girls and prizes in wooden chests. It also embraced the age's corruption: warm-up man Barney Martin picked contestants from the audience – so long as he got a cut of their winnings. The show was cancelled, and the dishonored Martin was banished from the broadcaster NBC – at least until the 1990s, when he returned in its most popular sitcom.

Is there a quiz question in this piece of trivia? It depends what the answer is. Barney Martin is not well-known enough to justify his being an answer, and anything which required a contestant to remember the forgotten *Treasure Hunt* would bring nothing to the quiz party.

But the name of the 1990s sitcom: *that* works as an answer (making the interesting back-story part of a gettable question, not a near-impossible answer). For example, **Barney Martin, who was implicated in the 1950s quiz-show scandals, went on to play a retired raincoat salesman called Morty, married to Helen, and father to comedian Jerry – in which 1990s comedy series?**[4]

This question works because – well, it asks people for an answer which they might very well know.

3 Blue and white (as asked on the Channel 4 reality show *Child Genius*).
4 *Seinfeld*.

Hey, what do you know?

Science is clearly regarded by quiz participants as **a tangent (hands up who knows what that is)**[5] to the mainstream of intellectual thought.

Bruce Durie, *New Scientist*, 1985

Working out what people are likely to know about landmark TV isn't the hard part. In pub quizzes and most TV shows, there's an unspoken assumption that a keen physicist will have come across Jane Austen, while a lover of literature might know the names of Einstein, say, or Newton, but not a lot about what they got up to, and may stand no chance whatsoever of identifying, say, **the physicist described as 'the most powerful scientist ever', who was Churchill's scientific adviser throughout the Second World War, and who said: 'It is more important to know the properties of chlorine than the improprieties of Claudius!'**[6] or even **the British physicist who shared a Nobel prize with Erwin Schrödinger and said: 'It is more important to have beauty in one's equations than to have them fit experiment',**[7] much less have a grasp on their work. (Double marks if you got those at home.)

There is indeed endless fascination in chlorine and beauty in equations, but the assumption remains fair. It is a truth universally acknowledged that a contestant needs only to have watched *Bridget Jones's Diary* or *Clueless* – or in fact the BBC on any given Sunday evening, or taken an interest in who's pegged to appear on the new £10 note – to be likely to have a chance of answering some Austen question or other. The cad

[7] Paul Dirac.

[6] Frederick Lindemann (accept Lord Cherwell or Viscount Cherwell).

[5] A line that touches a curve but does not intersect it. (Accept a plane that does the same for a surface, the trigonometric function, etc.)

Mr Fitzwilliam Darcy is known to far more quizzers than the eminent zoologist D'Arcy Thompson, he who inspired the work of Alan Turing and who remarked that, 'When I was young Science walked hand-in-hand with Art; now she walks arm-in-arm with Trade.'

This imbalance is sometimes called the Two Cultures Problem, after a 1959 lecture by novelist-cum-chemist C. P. Snow. Snow said when he heard apparently intelligent people snorting about scientists being literary ignoramuses, he liked to ask them to **describe the second law of thermodynamics**.[8] The artsy crowd tended then to go a bit quiet, he said, 'Yet I was asking something which is the scientific equivalent of: *Have you read a work of Shakespeare's?*'

Zing. In other words, Snow used impromptu quiz to shame the cultural snobs. This divide is in no way a healthy state of affairs, and quiz sometimes takes the flak. In the introduction to his *Encyclopedia of Britain*, Bamber Gascoigne reflects on a quarter-century of checking and then asking *University Challenge* questions, and divulges the most frequent complaint the programme received: the proportion of science questions: 'We tried to include more, and were usually rewarded with those looks of blank indignation unless there happened to be an appropriate scientist on the team (appropriate because a physicist would be flummoxed by any but an easy biology question, and vice versa).'

There's specialism again. The revived *University Challenge* asked those who had set its science questions to come to the studio to provide extra explanation to the host and producers. Despite the criticism, quiz doesn't have the civic duty to unravel

[8] Flanders and Swann summarize it in song as follows: 'That you can't pass heat from the cooler to the hotter / Try it if you like but you far better notter'. (Accept any reasonable summary of the law.)

the mess left by technocracy, nor can it. Its job is to come up with questions that contestants *as they are* have a fair chance of answering. Along with the odd play by Michael Frayn or Tom Stoppard, quiz is one of the few sources of entertainment where you might expect to meet a law of thermodynamics or two.

Here's another question: what subject matter is even more divisive than physical chemistry? Final answer?

Well done, you're absolutely right: it's sport. For some contestants, only a tough sport question provides a satisfying challenge, like this one from *Only Connect* . . .

What comes fourth in this sequence?[9]
100: Bannerman, Australia
200: Murdoch, Australia
300: Sandham, England

. . . while others struggle to identify **the shirt number shared by Pelé, Messi and Maradona.**[10]

The people in this second group do not read the back section of the newspaper, do not check results on their phones and do not pay attention to the sports sections of news programmes. They may not turn off, but what their brain stores is along the lines of '. . . after a disastrous first half, Some Team turned their fortunes, with a thrilling Technical Term from Some Player in the dying minutes bringing the final score to Some Number, Some Other Number.' These people are legion. They do not retain sporting data, they don't want to and they never will. And still they quiz.

There are subjects that most people feel they really ought to know about: history, science, and so on. There are popular-culture

9 400: Lara, West Indies (the first batsmen to reach these landmark scores in Test cricket).
10 10.

subjects which most people absorb a working knowledge of – music, say, or cinema – even if they don't really mean to. Light-years away, there is sport, with its devotees and its ignoramuses.

No one can keep both types of contestant happy at once for long: a sport round in a pub quiz tends to mean queues at the bar and loos made up of those who have glumly admitted that they have nothing to contribute. Yet sport offers so much to quiz: decades of largely unambiguous numerical results, tables and rankings begging to be turned into questions. A sport question is not a bad question, unless it is completely surrounded by other sport questions. The smart approach is to include enough sport to keep the first lot happy but to distribute it throughout the quiz so that the second lot don't spend too long feeling sad, bored and useless. (Unless, that is, you have a light-hearted format and access to sporting legends as your contestants, in which case you have the long-running TV staple *A Question of Sport* – but check, because you probably don't.)

Once a setter has mastered the trivial matter of understanding what everyone knows, he or she is ready to try to set questions in that Goldilocks zone (not too difficult, not too easy) and to try to get contestants to give the information that they didn't know they knew. This means writing, and rewriting.

Samuel Taylor Coleridge defined prose as 'words in their best order'. How did he define poetry?[11]
Which fictional character first spoke these words: 'How often have I said to you that when you have eliminated the impossible, whatever remains, *however improbable*, must be the truth?'[12]

11 'The best words in their best order.' (collected in *Table Talk*).
12 Sherlock Holmes (in *The Sign of (the) Four*).

Could you repeat the question, please?

Marcus Berkmann, pub-quiz doyen, spoke glowingly to Radio 4 about the phrasing of the questions on the original *Fifteen to One*: 'They're just beautifully constructed. They're very simple and they're well written, and some of them give you clues to where you're going to get the answer, so sometimes you end up answering the question correctly although you didn't know the answer'; while on a different programme, stalwart setter Thomas Eaton modestly reflected: 'It's not really a writing job – it's probably more of a craft. You're not coming up with anything extraordinarily imaginative, other than clever ways to use information, or re-use information.'

Whether quiz questions are things of beauty or the products of humble craft, there's more to writing them than copy-pasting facts from *Britannica* and whacking question marks at their ends. And since it's definitely possible to phrase a question badly, it must at least be possible to phrase it well. *Mastermind* creator Bill Wright tended to give this as an example of solid construction: **In which English city would you find the Dyson-Perrins museum?**[13]

The idea is that you don't need to be a devotee of ceramics collections to stand a chance: a contestant who has successfully found his or her zone might be prompted by the word 'city' to recall some notable cathedrals, and by the word 'Perrins' to recall a popular condiment, finding the overlap and feeling the answer surface in the time available.

Like many other questions, this one has its most useful

[13] Worcester (as in Lea & Perrins Worcestershire Sauce; now known as the Museum of Royal Worcester).

word ('Perrins') just before the end. It's often useful to phrase a question such that it allows multiple possibilities at the beginning and narrows things down as it goes, especially if the quiz is on the buzzer, since it rewards anyone who can get to the answer from the less revealing information.

Even if there's no buzzer, it's considerate to give the contestant as few mental bumps as possible. For example, see when the penny drops as you slowly read (or have someone slowly read to you) the following:

Which writer, born in St Petersburg in 1899, published eight novels in English in his lifetime, including *Pnin*, *Pale Fire* and one which is referenced in a song by The Police, *Lolita*?[14]

This phrasing, I hope, lets you refine the possibilities in a comforting journey of revelation not unlike the following. You begin by restricting your enquiries to writers (and, implicitly, writers whose names you think that I think you are likely to know). You narrow the field to Russian writers, then twentieth-century Russian writers. 'Novels' lets you eliminate any Russian known primarily as a poet or playwright and 'English' lets you put a question mark next to any Pasternaks and Solzhenitsyns on your list of candidates. Then the sample novels' titles begin, the more obscure first. Just before the end, you get a little extra non-literary clue which might have you singing in your head the couplet which rhymes 'starts to cough' with the answer, just as the kindest clue of all comes. Broad to narrow.

Here's a similar question, with a difference:

14 Vladimir Nabokov.

Which composer wrote the opera *Bastien und Bastienne*, which he reportedly first saw performed in a Viennese garden in October 1768 when he was twelve years old?[15]

Again, you start with composers, winnow out those who you don't think have written operas, concentrate on those who worked in Austria or thereabouts, finally getting the eighteenth century and the kicker that we're looking for a child prodigy. The difference here is that the words '*Bastien und Bastienne*' narrow the field *in principle* to one before we even get to Austria, but in practice do so only for irredeemable opera buffs – in fact, they are where they are to reward just those buffs who might get the answer very quickly, albeit at the expense of anyone hoping to play along.

'Which composer?', 'Which writer?', 'Which English city?' These are effectual ways to start a question, and not just to avoid giving away the goods too soon. Very often, the beginning of a question is not so much a clue as a way of telling the contestant the kind of thing they're being asked for. If a question has been worked on enough, its very first words can get the contestant thinking on the right lines. (And that word should probably be something like 'What?', 'Where?' or 'Which?'; if it's 'How?' or 'Why?', you're asking for trouble when you have to compare the contestant's answer to the one on the card, unless your quiz is modelled on the BBC's *The Brains Trust*, in which the 1950s panel answered viewers' questions such as 'What is happiness?' and 'Are thoughts things or about things?', neither of which I'll try giving answers to here.)

The importance of phrasing might sound obvious, but if you've ever found yourself wondering whether you're being

15 Wolfgang Amadeus Mozart (prompt on 'Mozart').

asked for the name of the singer or the song, you'll know that it's easy to omit these friendly directions.

It's no bad thing if your question could in theory be reduced to two words, like this one I wrote for a topical arts quiz in a Sunday supplement . . .

> **'In and Out', a poem by Frank Redpath, was recently misattributed to which poet by _The Times Literary Supplement_, following its discovery at the University of Hull?**[16]

. . . which could be brutally pared back to 'poet, Hull?'. The same goes for 'sitcom, Jerry?' and 'city, Perrins?' By the end of each sentence, there's something for everyone, but the whole thing, with the less revealing information, is more rewarding to answer – and to hear someone else try to answer – than a question like 'Which sitcom followed the life of a stand-up comedian named Jerry?' It's the appeal of the abstruse.

So is the other information mere adornment? No! The misattribution and the corruption, the pale fire and the ceramics museum, are part of the fun – in fact, sometimes, the lesser-known fact, even if it ends up incidental, is the thing that piques the setter's interest.

So what (apart from the etymology of 'biscuit') is interesting?

Very interesting . . .

In one sense, quiz privileges the interesting. First, take firsts. Every quizzer worth the name could tell you **the name of the first person on the moon**.[17] Many could tell you **the second**,[18]

---

16 Philip Larkin.

17 Neil Armstrong.

18 Edwin 'Buzz' Aldrin, who uttered the appallingly poignant line as himself on _The Simpsons_, 'Second comes right after first.'

but even by the time we get to **the third**,[19] we're only expecting an answer from the hardcore, never mind such relatively recent lunar lodgers as, say, *Apollo 17*'s geologist Harrison Schmitt.

Quiz favours the pioneers, the winners and the inventors – though the mark of distinction need not be enviable. **The only British prime minister to have been assassinated,[20] the only Spice Girl not to have a solo number-one single,[21] or the only part of the *Godfather* trilogy which failed to win the Best Picture Oscar, or a nomination for Al Pacino, or to be preserved in the American National Film Registry:[22]** these unfortunates are unusual, which makes them more memorable, in both the 'interesting' and the 'contestant-might-answer-it' sense.

On the topic of those Coppola–Pacino movies, here is one of the all-time best Trivial Pursuit questions, from the original Genus set: **What word was intentionally omitted from the screenplay of *The Godfather*?[23]**

Here we move to a more interesting sense of 'interesting': intriguing, revealing, beguiling. This question works so well not only because it satisfies that criterion of seeming fair, once the answer is given, even to those who failed to get it. It also offers a way into the tangled tale of how the movie and the mob came to an agreement about access to filming locations in Little Italy, and how the legitimate-sounding Italian-American Civil Rights League insisted that every instance of the word in question be excised from the original script (unbeknown to the League, it appeared only once, so that was an offer the producer was doubly loth to refuse).

19 Charles 'Pete' Conrad.
20 Spencer Perceval.
21 Victoria Beckham. (Accept either part of the name, or Victoria Adams, or Posh Spice.)
22 *The Godfather Part III*.
23 'Mafia'.

None of this backstory belongs in that terse and perfectly phrased question, but it need not go to waste. Hosts in some pubs and some programmes arrive armed with supplementary information which they can give to or elicit from the contestants, all adding to the fun of the quiz.

And there are facts which are interesting because they possess what you might fancifully call a kind of poetry. There are thousands of questions to be asked about the filmographies of Hollywood stars, but there's a little extra value in asking **who had a lead role in both *American Hustle* and *American Psycho***[24] or **who has appeared in Woody Allen's *Alice*, Aaron Sorkin's *Malice* and the Alzheimer's drama *Still Alice*.**[25]

A kind of anti-poetry is possessed by what you might call 'ironic facts': **How long, to the nearest five years, did the Hundred Years War last?**[26] **What animal caused the death of a Los Angeles pine tree planted in memory of George Harrison?**[27] **Which Californian valley, which contains the lowest point in North America, is carpeted by wild flowers and home to donkeys, sheep and dozens of species of birds?**[28]

Questions like the Beatle-y one above are assuredly fun, but they reward something different to most of quiz: the contestant gets there by wondering, why am I being asked this?, but isn't being asked to use anything more than the most rudimentary general knowledge. And some of the most interesting facts about the world are counter-intuitive, a characteristic which most quizzes avoid where possible. Most, but not all.

[28] Death Valley.
[27] Beetles.
[26] 116 years (1337 to 1453; accept answers in the range 111–21).
[25] Alec Baldwin (prompt on 'Baldwin').
[24] Christian Bale.

QI, by the cunning of being a quiz which rewards interest-ing rather than correct answers, is perfectly able to ask about things that would be far too difficult for most quizzes. The programme's begetter, John Lloyd, talks of how, on learning that he was to become a father, he tried to read the 'nine yards' of the *Encyclopædia Britannica*, which led him to the three interesting facts which formed the basis of the *QI* philosophy. Reworded as quiz questions, they are:

> **Which organ normally occurs once in human beings, but three times in kangaroos?**[29]
>
> **What alteration to the basketball kit was introduced twenty-one years after the game was invented, doing away with the need for a step-ladder?**[30]
>
> **Which eight-legged, millimetre-long micro-animal can survive out of water for ten years in a suspended-animation-like state, then come back to life when rehydrated?**[31]

The cunning plan that makes *QI* such an inspired format is in taking the kind of information which in a normal quiz could be used sparingly at best and making it the meat-and-potatoes of the programme.

And that leads us to a deflating but liberating observation: the truly interesting fact is not the meat-and-potatoes of quiz.

It is, of course, generally better to include something inter-esting in a question than not to, and it makes the setter's day-job more rewarding if he or she manages to include something that feels fresh. More often, though, 'interesting' means 'not gener-ally known', which means that any interesting fact needs to be

---

[29] The vagina.
[30] A hole in the bottom of the net (the official Olympic history gives the innovation as hav-ing happened 15 years later).
[31] Tardigrades (accept water bears).

coupled with some less interesting ones, if anyone is to have a chance of answering – or it means 'surprising' or 'counter-intuitive', which means that it risks misdirecting the poor contestant.

Worse is the precedent set by the interesting question. Too many of these, and the 'landfill' facts which inevitably make up much of any quiz start to seem more mundane than they really are.

As pub-quiz attendances and TV viewing figures attest, there is real appeal in a quiz which derives its content *solely* from those Eurovision and Cup Final lists mentioned above. In fact, another mistake often made by the novice setter of, say, a work-place quiz is to show off with a series of baroque mind-benders, leaving the contestants literally crying out for questions demanding **the capital of Somalia**[32] or **the chemical symbol for sodium**.[33] Viva landfill!

As you will know if you've ever volunteered to provide a quiz for work, school or family, there's still plenty of work involved in assembling those meat-and-potatoes questions: maintaining consistency in terms of difficulty and diversity in terms of subject matter; giving enough clues to avoid the possibility of saying, 'Ha, um, well, I guess you know it or you don't' to a sea of blank or hostile faces.

Mentioning these pitfalls is in no sense to denigrate the honest setter or host of quiz who does it for pleasure rather than money. Especially since, when there's no money involved, there's no budget to pay someone else to check the answers. And *that* opens the door to legions of gremlins . . .

[32] Mogadishu (accept Xamar).
[33] Na.

11. We're just checking that for you

Who decides whether a 'fact' is correct?

Question setters tend to be barely visible. The more respectable pub-quiz hosts take the time to write their own questions, and later defend them in person against beery challenges, but in radio and TV, the setters appear only in a stack of credits, unnoticed by most viewers and by all industry awards.

Peer even further into that murky list of names which is routinely squeezed into a corner of the screen and talked over by an unrelenting continuity announcer, decipher the job titles, and you might get a dim sense that the questions have been not merely created but also checked.

Question verifiers – and there are very few of them – prefer it this way. There are practical reasons for this – big money can be riding on the answers – but it's also a matter of temperament. Verifiers are monumentally cautious by nature.

For a swathe of British quiz programmes, especially the more serious ones, the questions are sent to a small team led by a woman in the rural south-west of England who prefers to remain anonymous and who spends her non-quizzing time doing precisely what you would expect the wife of a clergyman to do.

Questions arrive in batches – until recently entirely on hard copy, but increasingly attached to emails – and are assigned to individual verifiers. Some of them were brought together by the church, but what really unites them is a collection of and a devotion to reliable reference works. Shelves of *Wisden Cricketers' Almanack* for some; volumes and supplements of the *Dictionary of National Biography* for others. If you're picturing a largely pre-digital environment of ink printed mindfully on to paper, you've got it right.

If the question can't be checked in a book, they proceed by whatever means necessary: I have known them to zoom in on a clapperboard prop in a DVD of *Singin' in the Rain* to ascertain the precise title of the film-within-a-film, *The Dueling Cavalier* (not *Duelling* or *Duelin'* or even *Duellin'*) – and, to check a question about **the shortest verse in the King James Bible**,[1] one verifier wrote a computer programme and fed the testaments into it, effectively creating a new concordance. All for quiz.

Sending a question to them is, as I know, an act enveloped with foreboding. However careful setters have been, *their* aim, at the end of the day job, is to create new quiz questions. Verifiers seek to destroy.

That isn't to say that the destruction isn't done with charm, with regret, or with helpful suggestions as to how a question that you thought was perfect might be salvaged from the rubble. You need not despair that your question 'How many English kings have been called Edward?' has led you into

[1] 'Jesus wept.' (John 11:35).

the sticky meta-question of whether to acknowledge such pre-Norman Edwards as the Elder, the Martyr and the Confessor, since the verifiers will have suggested a wording which restricts things to the ones you were thinking of – you know, with the Roman numerals after their names: **Since the Norman Conquest, how many kings of England have been called Edward?**[2] Still, you feel a little foolish and resolve to copper-bottom all future questions. In vain, of course.

You do, though, quickly develop a sense of which areas of knowledge are more liable to throw up inconvenient truths. Only a chump would stray into such evidently subjective areas as 'Who is the greatest footballer of all time?', but only a novice would approach an area like, say, geography, expecting it to provide nice, clean facts.

Take coastlines. They have lengths, which can be measured, and so while they're not especially guessable, they might offer up a nice multiple-choice question, right?

What is the length of the coastline of the United Kingdom?
(a) 7,723 miles
(b) 11,073 miles
(c) 19,491 miles

Wrong. Or rather, they're all right, depending on which geographers you ask, which islands you're including, how high the tide is when you're measuring, and so on. And should you manage to resolve those issues, you then run smack into what cartographers call the Coastline Paradox.

Imagine you're looking at a map of Wales. You could measure the length of the line that separates sea from land, from the

2 Eight.

137

Dee Estuary round to the Severn. But now imagine you'd chosen a more detailed map.

You're now confronted with more bits jutting in and out, and so, if you start tracing the same line, you run the risk of travelling the distance suggested by the first map before you even reach Llandudno. Zoom in further still and, again, you face the prospect of measuring *around the edges of* rocks – maybe even pebbles – that you would previously have gone straight *through* . . . and the coastline approaches infinity. It's bonkers, of course, which is why it's called a paradox, but it's a reminder that the fairest answer to the question 'What is the coastline of the United Kingdom?' has to be:

(d) it depends.

Small wonder, then, that verifiers suck their teeth when a question begins 'What is the longest river in . . . ?' Dear old Mount Everest isn't even the highest mountain if you're including those which start underwater.

Human geography is, if anything, more perilous for quiz than physical. Sometimes, you've got no further than the words 'Which country?' before you're asking for trouble, especially if the answer is considered a country by some people but very much not one by others:

> **What W. S. is a disputed territory which shares borders with Mauritania, Morocco and Algeria?**[3]
> **What S. O. is a disputed territory which hosted a brief war between Russia and Georgia in 2008?**[4]
> **What N.-K. is a territory which is disputed by Azerbaijan and Armenia?**[5]

[5] Nagorno-Karabakh.
[4] South Ossetia.
[3] Western Sahara.

If you've ever wondered why *Pointless*'s Richard Osman spends so much of his life intoning 'As always, by country we mean a sovereign state that's a member of the UN in its own right,' that's to avoid such gnarly geopolitical conundrums. The status of the United Nations non-member permanent observers and non-member signatories of declarations may (or may not) be determined by the arbitrarily blowing winds of politics, but a quiz needs a definitive list and UN membership is as good as it gets. Arguably.

And if you've ever wondered why there are so few questions about Israel and Palestine, that's partly because a good verifier will tell you that, even with as many qualifiers as you can squeeze into the question without its starting to resemble a dissertation, your question is still going to get complaints from viewers, and everyone involved in making quiz would rather spend their time editing one series and preparing for the next one than writing carefully worded responses to viewer complaints about the previous. (And while letters about the Middle East can get heated, the ones about dog breeds and computer operating systems are far more fervid.)

Verifiers also remember that what was once not a country may become a country, and that what was a border may become nothing at all. Yes, the world can change between the moment a question is written and the day it is asked. The anonymous verification boss above told me that 'future-proofing' is an especially elusive part of the job when it comes to 'longest's and 'smallest's: 'There's always a new bridge being built somewhere or a tiny hamster being found in Outer Mongolia.'

Likewise, if you ask for the name of a celebrity's spouse, you're flirting with quiz disaster, as some of them get through another *Hello!* nuptials shoot by the time the question is asked in studio, and two more before the relevant episode is broadcast. Or repeated: the existence of TV channels such as Challenge, which broadcast old quizzes, is a splendid thing, but it does have the dreary side-effect of encouraging questions to be cumbersomely reworded so that the questions make some semblance of sense not merely when they're first broadcast but also years later.

Anyone who has recently played the original Trivial Pursuit has experienced this tendency to obsolescence. **The woman who has won the most Wimbledon singles titles**[6] is no longer Billie Jean King. **The three countries which share land borders with Finland**[7] no longer include the Soviet Union. And craps is no longer **the biggest money-maker in Las Vegas casinos**.[8] (All the answers below are accurate, and all the countries exist, at the time I am typing these words.)

Once in a blue moon, a quiz question itself changes the thing it's asking about. Not so long ago, a 'blue moon' was the third full moon in those rare seasons which had four: rare enough to make excellent sense of the phrase 'once in a blue moon'. Nowadays, it's usually taken to denote the second full moon in any given calendar month (making the literal sense of the phrase a deal weaker), and that change in meaning, the *Oxford English Dictionary* believes, is down to a misunderstanding found in the Genus II edition of Trivial Pursuit, asked and answered so many times that it actually became correct.

Verifiers know this kind of thing – and they also know what people think they know about this kind of thing. A question might be copper-bottomed, backed up with incontrovertible evidence from infallible sources, but still sound wrong to some contestants and viewers. It's not enough merely to avoid answers

[8] Slot machines (accept slots).
[7] Norway, Sweden and Russia.
[6] Martina Navratilova (nine to King's six).

which are based on fallacies which are popularly believed; you have to stop those fallacies making right answers look wrong.

For example, if a viewer heard a contestant give the right answer to **The French folk song 'Ah! vous dirai-je, maman' provided the melody for which well-known English-language astronomical lullaby?**,[9] he or she might lose faith in the quiz because they had understood that the song in question had been composed by Mozart. Worse, the contestant might decide to not give the right answer, thinking that, since Mozart hasn't been mentioned, it must be something else.

A verifier, then, will remind you of the popular misconception so that you can rephrase the question along the lines: 'The French folk song "*Ah! vous dirai-je, maman*" was adapted in twelve variations by the young Wolfgang Amadeus Mozart and later provided the melody for which well-known English-language astronomical lullaby?'

Anticipating likely wrong answers also helps a host. If you ask **What natural features are the subject of the national anthem of Austria?**,[10] it's useful to know that there's a chance a contestant might offer edelweiss flowers, since the host then has a chance to explain that while 'Edelweiss' was written for *The Sound of Music*, it is widely mistaken for Austria's national tune, and that its singer Theodore Bikel recalled elderly Austrians thanking him for reviving a traditional song they thought they remembered from their childhoods.

From qualifying phrases to complete rewrites, rare is the question which returns from the verifiers without some kind of suggested change. These are people who actively take pleasure in teasing out ambiguities, infelicities and potential

---

10 Mountains and river ('*Land der Berge, Land am Strome*').

9 'Twinkle, Twinkle, Little Star.'

legal nightmares. Many of them, in fact, no longer enjoy quizzes: they can't trust those they haven't verified and they can't bear to watch those they have, in case they spot some kink too late.

It is, though, never too late to rephrase a question, or to entirely rewrite it, even when an unambiguously duff question has been used in public. I'm thinking especially here of the very first question asked on *Mastermind*, back in 1972. The specialized subject was 'The Visual Arts' (contestants took much less specialist specialisms in the early days), and Magnus Magnusson asked this toughie: **Picasso's *Guernica* was a protest about the bombing by Spanish planes of a village. What was the year when the event took place which inspired the painting?**[11]

The answer was fine, but the bombers were German.

A quarter of a century later came the final *Mastermind* final to be chaired by Magnus Magnusson (and, as far as anyone knew at the time, the final final of all). The team decided that, so long as the outcome would not be affected by how the contestant answered, the last question to be asked would also concern *Guernica*: 'Sixty years ago, during the Spanish Civil War, which town in the Basque country was destroyed by German bombers, an event which was commemorated in a painting by Picasso?'

The contestant got the answer right but, more importantly, a twenty-five-year-old wrong had been righted. After that early question, *Mastermind* soon learned the value of having people pick through every word of the question as well as the answer and check each against sources. *Reliable* sources.

In the sitcom *After You've Gone*, Celia Imrie's cut-glass mother-in-law Diana enters a pub quiz which comes down to a

11 1937.

tie-break question: **What is the capital of the Republic of Congo?**[12] She sticks up her hand and announces 'Kinshasa!' The host's book says otherwise and, after loudly delivering a potted history of Kinshasa, Diana declares the book to be 'shabbily put together, without any consideration for the truth'.

'Hold on,' insists another contestant, 'you can't challenge the quiz book!' But you *can* – regardless of the awkward fact, revealed later in the episode, that Kinshasa is in fact the capital of **another African country, one which is easily confused with the Republic of Congo, but which isn't the Republic of Congo.**[13]

It's ironic that many quiz books, which stand or fall on their accuracy, are indeed shabbily put together and risk challenges or worse. Books in general, though, have long been the natural resources of quiz. When quiz started to get serious, paper was the thing. David Elias, who set for the original *University Challenge*, recalls that if questions were not backed up by the thirty or so 'approved books' (*Britannica*, *Whitaker's Almanack*, *Halliwell's Film Guide*, *Kobbe's Opera Book*, and the like), they still needed to be rendered in paper form, by photo-copying the source: 'Once I sent in a question based on the masthead of the English edition of *Pravda*, which I'd seen when browsing in W. H. Smith's, and was told sharply that I ought to have bought the paper and sent in either the original or a copy, but we eventually agreed that some items (like the opening credits of *Star Wars*) couldn't easily be found in printed form.'

Indeed. But even within those approved books, errors are possible (sometimes ones which have been carried over from the sources they themselves used: William Smellie, who wrote much of the first edition of *Britannica*, confessed that many entries were assembled with the aid of his best friend, 'a pair of scissars [*sic*]', 'clipping out from various books a *quantum sufficit* of matter for the printer', a practice which propagates fallacies like Columbo having a Christian name).

Verifiers get to know where the goofs linger in even the apparently trustworthy sources (the *Encyclopædia Britannica* briefly and inaccurately listed **the number of jumps in the Grand National**[14] as thirty-one) and if – like me – you're interested, they can discreetly tell you which newspapers' obituaries are less reliable when it comes to sportspeople but good enough for the details of the lives of, say, minor aristocrats. This is deep, deep scepticism, a kind of meta-knowledge about the corpus of apparent information, all put to the service of quiz.

Still, if you trust the printed word more than the pixel, you're taking the same approach as most verifiers. Many questions may begin at a Wikipedia page, and any setter who claims not to use that resource is spreading some inaccurate information of their own. But then there's the checking. Some prefer paper when reading fiction; in the quiz world, the same goes for non-fiction, and the happy coincidences and byways that physical books can bring. 'All my Team,' my anonymous verifying friend tells me, 'would still rather be using book sources', and, without wishing to divulge trade secrets, what sources they be: David Pringle's *Imaginary People: A Who's Who of Modern Fictional Characters*, William Rose Benét's *Reader's Encyclopedia*, Debrett's *Kings and Queens of Britain*, the House of Commons librarians' *Facts about the British Prime Ministers: A Compilation of Biographical and Historical Information*. Who needs fiction?

14 Thirty.

When I'm setting questions, the sources I think of as reliable are those who take it seriously (more seriously than a tiny correction on page 23 of a newspaper) when they get something wrong (as always happens), and for that, it helps if I've been in their offices and seen them at work. So I'm confident with what I'm told by the BBC (especially when it comes to the facts and figures of news), the *Oxford English Dictionary* (never happy to support a conveniently appealing origin of a piece of language), the *QI* multi-media imperium (you can imagine) and, both especially and naturally, Penguin Books and its imprints (those written by other people, anyway). The credibility of these operations lives or dies on the basis of their trustworthiness, and while print is less important to some than it is to others, the ethos of print is in them all.

Here's what you've been playing for

12. What do points make?

The slow-slow-quick embrace of prizes in quiz

When *Who Wants to be a Millionaire?* arrived in America in 1999, there was shock in some quarters of the TV industry that it became so popular so fast. A few months in, executive producer Michael Davies mused: 'Everybody said beforehand, "Oh, a prime-time *quiz* show? Are you crazy? What do you *mean*, a quiz show in *prime time*?" But people forget that this is a foundation of American television.'

He was right. Still, it had taken a long time to get to the point where *any* quiz was giving a million of *anything* as a prize.

When Professor Quiz began handing out those ten-dollar prizes in 1936, the use of ten silver dollars, rather than one of the combinations of $1s, $2s and $5s which would have made up the same sum (**how many are there?**[1]) was to make the money itself audible: to make it one of the show's stars.

Some listeners and critics would have preferred the prizes to have been less prominent, or absent altogether, since they were

1 Four (ten $1 bills; five $1 and one $5; two $5; one $10 – though if you've somehow managed to find a $2 bill in circulation, the combinations number ten).

149

yet more evidence of what they thought of as the insidious 'something-for-nothing' culture. Letters to the radio regulator, the Federal Communications Commission, worried that 'numerous addicts are neglecting family duties endeavoring to win something'; as well as gambling, angry listeners associated prizes with the twin threats of 'inflation' and 'Communism'.

Money, it was argued, should be earned through toil and trade, not doled out by the radio for simply knowing some things. Quiz was, for some, an affront to the American Dream.

A similar charge has been made in Britain since radio quizzes here first offered prizes, though the most outspoken critics have long since appeared to have at best a shaky grasp on how easily a certain kind of prizes might be won. Here's how the cultural critic Richard Hoggart (**Whose son presented which radio show with 'quiz' in its title?**[2]) spoke for the great and the good to a government-appointed committee in 1960: 'We don't like the quiz shows. They pander to the need for quick money, having people up to produce the astounding fact that Cleopatra's Needle is on the Embankment and being told they are terribly clever, and here's a refrigerator.'

And here's the Liberal Lord Airedale addressing the Lords in 1984: 'One gets someone being asked, "Who is the prime minister?", but they look quite blank and are told, "We will give you a clue: it is someone whose name begins with T". The contestant says, "Of course!" and finds he has won a grand piano. Anything that gets rid of programmes of that degree of absurdity must be good.'

Absurdity indeed. Another objection to any programme offering prizes was that it enticed listeners without necessarily being excellent in itself (the expression often used on both sides

[2] Simon Hoggart presented Radio 4's *News Quiz*.

of the Atlantic was 'buying the audience'). It was not merely the prize-winners who were demeaned, but audiences, too. A BBC memo put it curtly: prizes 'inevitably introduce an element of bribery rather than adequate reward as a means of stimulating interest'.

And that memo pre-dated quiz: it was prompted by a mere proposal to include a competition on a children's radio show. (One of the qualmless pirate stations, Radio Luxembourg, experimented in pioneering fashion with *The Symington's Soups Film Star Competition Programme*, where listeners could win a packet soup.) In 1930, all heads of BBC 'programme branches' received a memo informing them that any suggestions for competitions on shows outside of *Children's Hour* should be referred to the Director-General, and that the Board of Governors was in any case 'in principle not in favour of competitions in our programmes'. At the very least, the director of programmes thought, prizes should be seen to be in a programme which 'stimulates thought and creates intelligent interest'. It seems so long ago, but the effect of this caution was that many programmes underplayed their prizes for a long time.

The 'educational' dressing of American radio shows *Professor Quiz* and *Dr IQ* gave a sense, however shaky, of respectability, and the child-prodigy showcase *Quiz Kids* purported to celebrate the classroom (and had among its champions **a boy who went on to share a Nobel prize with his colleague Francis Crick for the discovery of DNA[3]**).

Another show tried to raise quiz's moral bar. Radio producer Dan Golenpaul found *Professor Quiz*'s 'professor' infuriating 'when he made such a great fuss over the fact that a contestant didn't know an answer. A bit sadistic, I thought.' His reaction

3 James Watson.

gave him an idea for a new programme: 'I wish I had these quizmasters and so-called experts in front of me. I'd like to ask them some questions. They're probably not that much brighter than the average listener.'

And so in 1938 he created NBC's *Information, Please*, in which a panel of clever-clogs tried to answer questions posted in their tens of thousands each week by the audience; those listeners who confounded the experts received prizes, but appropriate ones – a multi-volume set of the *Encyclopædia Britannica* with your $10. This was an age when a quiz programme might, as *Information, Please* did, launch its own almanac.

At the same time, the BBC had a similar show: *Confound the Experts!*, which was, if anything, even higher-minded in its prize-giving protocol:

> The BBC is so confident in the ability of its experts to keep the flag of knowledge flying that it has backed them to the extent of five shillings per question. That is to say, should no member of the team be able to answer a question accurately the sum of five shillings will be paid into the fund for the Week's Good Cause.

Five shillings is not the kind of sum that should be handed out willy-nilly. Likewise, in 1949, Wilfred Pickles claimed that, following his insistence that his producer 'Give 'em the money, Barney!', the various prizes of two shillings and sixpence here and a guinea there would often be 'returned at the end of the programme to help some good cause'. And so was created the austere spirit of today's celebrity editions of popular quiz programmes, where well-known folk soberly announce the charity they're hoping to raise money for.

In 2014, Radio 4's *John Finnemore's Souvenir Programme* spoofed the apparent magnanimity of quiz's celebrity specials.

The prizes are much bigger in the sketch's *Celebrity If You Say So* than they were in *Confound the Experts!*: we hear a charity raising funds for fresh water in Africa discover that it will receive £6,000 rather than the £25,000 jackpot because the contestant 'Richard Bacon thought Sooty was a dog'. The representative of the charity suggests that since the £25,000 was in the programme's budget, it would be possible to pretend that Richard Bacon had got it right:

> — Yeah, I'm sorry – I just don't think that would be ethical.
> — You don't think *that* would be ethical?
> — Yeah, I'm sorry – we just have to be really careful with ethics on TV, you know, in this climate?
> — But you're fine with withholding £19,000-worth of life-saving water sources because Richard Bacon didn't know Sooty was a dog?

(What *should* Richard Bacon – and the (equally wrong) charity representative – have said Sooty was?[4])

And the leap from Pickles's shillings to *Celebrity If You Say So*'s thousands came in the mid-1950s, when two things happened to change quiz: in Britain, a new channel and, in America, a Supreme Court ruling.

You've never had it so good

Parliament has long been split on the issue of fun. One urge is to keep the lower orders in check and protect them from their baser urges. Another is to get out of the way when the lower orders want to have fun (and to let other people make a lot of

---

[4] A bear of indeterminate species.

money while they do so). And so the debate around the Television Bill of 1954, which proposed bringing advertiser-funded TV to the UK, included a proposed amendment to 'preclude the possibility of prizes' on programmes.

The Conservative Lord Balfour of Inchrye worried that such a ban would have to apply to the BBC and would 'have the effect of washing out those very harmless but enjoyable little gifts that Mister Pickles gives'. The Labour peer Earl Jowitt, who favoured the amendment, was unmoved, announcing, 'I do not know anything about Mister Pickles's programme.' The sparring continued:

> Lord Balfour of Inchrye: He gives away a few shillings.
> Earl Jowitt: I have not competed in that particular programme or won a prize, but I think it is best to have no prizes at all.
> Lord Balfour of Inchrye: You would spoil a lot of people's fun.

The bill did become law, but without the amendment, and some at the BBC were fretful. If the new ITV was not going to play by the old rules, and if it was going to lure viewers with less responsible practices, how should the BBC adapt? Controller of Television Programmes Cecil McGivern hoped that prize-giving programmes could 'be fairly intelligent!' and tentatively offered, in one of the more BBC-ish memos ever issued: 'It could be argued that the sensible way is to admit a human weakness (the desire to win a prize and get something for nothing) and, while catering to it, at the same time try to control it and try to keep it decent.'

So far, the BBC had managed a compromise between the edification of the nation and the exhilaration of offering them prizes – and McGivern and his colleagues believed that they still could. They may have been naively optimistic about that; they were right at least to expect big changes.

In 1955, the launch week of ITV's London region borrowed a programme from Radio Luxembourg for its first quiz: Associated-Rediffusion's all-conquering *Double Your Money*, in which Hughie Green, introduced as 'the man with the greenest hue' by hostesses including a young Maggie Smith, offered a cash prize of a gargantuan £1,000, with the draw of the cash right there in the title. Broadcasting historian Louis Barfe describes the launch episode as a piece of TV 'in which dolly-bird hostesses, pimply, recently demobbed National Servicemen, and people who would have remembered the Jack the Ripper murders as local news all co-existed. It was bright, brash fun for all the family and the viewing figures reflected as much.'

Other regional services (quizzes were a smart way for ITV to meet its required hours of 'local' programming) were launched with similar big-money shows, like Wales's *£1,000 Word*, that evening's top-rated show across the two then-existing channels.

The shift towards big prizes was neither tentative nor slow. As early as January 1957, a typical week of ITV had ten 'give-away' programmes. As part of *Sunday Night at the London Palladium*, Tommy Trinder invited audience members to *Beat the Clock*, while Mondays saw *Two for the Money*, shortly after David Jacobs's *Make Up Your Mind*. Midweek had only one prize show each night: Bob Monkhouse's *Do You Trust Your Wife?*, the general-knowledge *Double Your Money* ('WITH THE £1,000 TREASURE TRAIL') and *Spot the Tune*. Friday evenings began with Michael Miles's *Take Your Pick* (the *Deal or No Deal* of its day) and finished with *Lucky Spot Quiz*, while Saturdays offered *State Your Case* and the quiz proper of *64,000 Question*, where Jerry Desmond offered 64,000 shillings.

Now, Wilfred Pickles didn't seem quite so generous with his 38 shillings and sixpence. The independent-television regulator politely and unobtrusively wondered whether there was 'on the whole rather more giving away of money and prizes in programmes than is good for the reputation of the programme companies'. ATV's Richard Meyer candidly acknowledged the concern but insisted that 'We must use every possible endeavour to obtain maximum audiences in the initial stages of the development of the medium so that we can be certain of getting worthwhile sales of advertising space'.

In other words, the public liked (or at least could not resist) watching other members of the public having their lives transformed by the arrival of money. And by 1955, as Roland Gillette (controller of Associated-Rediffusion and adviser to the Conservative party on matters televisual) put it, the BBC's idea of trying to control human weakness was already broadcasting history: 'Let's face it once and for all. The public likes girls, wrestling, bright musicals, quiz shows and real-life dramas. We gave them the Hallé orchestra, Foreign Press Club, floodlit football and visits to the local fire station. Well, we've learned. From now on, what the public wants, it's going to get.'

And what the advertisers wanted would, similarly, be provided.

Had ITV been given its licence a year earlier, Jerry Desmond's Saturday-night show would have had a markedly different title. It was borrowed from an American show but, in the America of 1954, there was no *$64,000 Question*: the programme's title – and the original version of the adage – was *The $64 Question*.

It took the Supreme Court to add the zeros.

In the week approaching Independence Day 1941, the Federal Communications Commission found its remit getting much bigger. Television arrived, and it arrived with quiz. NBC announced itself by putting into vision two of its radio stalwarts: *Uncle Jim's Question Bee* and *Truth or Consequences*, a quiz so popular that it later offered to broadcast an episode from whichever American town was the first to supplicate by renaming itself to advertise the show – and so it was that, in 1950, Hot Springs, New Mexico, became Truth or Consequences, New Mexico. CBS also launched with a quiz: no recordings exist, but it had both the distinction of being unrelated to any radio show and the indistinction of its title: CBS *Television Quiz*, which can hardly be criticized for mystique.

Just as theologians are characterized as debating the number of angels that can dance on the head of a pin, so did the FCC, the priesthood of American broadcasting, concern itself for many years with the question of what constituted a lottery in order to divine whether quiz-show prizes were morally meritocratic or unlawfully and awfully aleatory.

This being America, the whole thing had to be decided by the courts. Broadcast lawyers debated FCC restrictions on prizes and challenged the commission's 1949 ban on granting new licences to stations which planned to 'award prizes to induce persons to listen to the particular program'.

The issue rose through the district courts and, in April 1954, the American right to quiz was considered in the highest court of the land. The Supreme Court's justices ruled 8–0 (with one absence) that quiz was not gambling, and that the attempts to curb prizes violated **the constitutional amendment which prohibits the impedance of freedom of speech**.[5] Chief Justice Earl Warren (**whose 1963 Warren Commission would investigate which historical event?**[6]) wrote that 'it would be stretching

the [lottery] statute to the breaking point to give it an inter-
pretation that would make such programs a crime'.

Tellingly, the judgment added, 'Regardless of the doubts
held by the Commission and others as to the social value of the
programs here under consideration, such administrative expan-
sion of §1304 does not provide the remedy.'

One FCC lawyer had frankly confessed that his real aim
was to improve the quality of programmes, using the lottery
issue as a way to enhance general standards in broadcasting.

Quiz producers had their hands untied, and Louis G.
Cowan wasted no time. He had acquired the rights to *Take It
or Leave It*, which had evolved into *The $64 Question*, and he
worked out how to make it sing on TV.

And so, in 1955, the proverbial question added $63,936 to its
value as the Revlon-sponsored, IBM-showcasing quiz was
launched on television. It was said that the crime rate fell while
The $64,000 Question was on, and that President Eisenhower had
asked not to be disturbed on Tuesday nights so that he could
watch.

There followed some very good years to be in quiz – or
rather, to sponsor it – but only a few. By the time the sixties
found their swing, two more things had happened. In Britain,
it was a government report. In America?

We'll be right back after a word from our sponsors.

Commercial break

13. Say it ain't so, Charles

The 1950s scandals

On 5 December 1956, in the most exciting episode yet of the NBC quiz *Twenty One*, two contestants who had become nationally renowned met each other for the final time. The stakes were reaching preposterous levels; the champion defending his position was a former General Issue soldier and his challenger was a university teacher. Here's how it was introduced that evening:

— Good evening, I'm Jack Barry. Tonight here on *Twenty One* Herbert Stempel, our 29-year-old GI college student, can win $111,500 – the highest amount of money ever to be won on television. But to do this he's risking much of the money he has won thus far. So right now let's meet [our] players, as Geritol, America's number-one tonic, presents *Twenty One*.

In fact, Geritol, an iron supplement said to 'revive tired blood', was the real star of *Twenty One*. Geritol was the real winner, too: sales went from $10.4 million to nigh-on $14 million when the company became the quiz's sponsor.

It was the same on other American quiz programmes of the big-prize era: when Revlon began to promote *The $64,000 Question*, profits went from $1 million to $11 million; at one point, the corporation simply ran out of lipstick. Advertising agencies bankrolled – and typically owned – quiz, and the business had become very big, very fast.

— Herb, you've got your $69,500 riding here at stake. How do you feel? . . . We're going to be playing for $2,000 a point. Were you aware that this would, would happen, could happen?
— Sure I was, Mr Barry. I knew it all along . . .

Herb Stempel knew all right. The producers of the show had explained what the host would announce, and how falteringly Stempel would respond. They had also chosen his clothes: an ill-fitting suit with frayed shirt would be better than his own clothes at presenting the picture of a penniless ex-GI.

Stempel wasn't penniless, but if a shabby Jewish guy from the Bronx could get stinking rich on TV from his smarts, then *Twenty One* had a fair claim to embodying the American dream. And this, they hoped, might help assuage Geritol's anger about their initial unsatisfactory ratings. So, none of Jack Barry's banter was a surprise to 'Herb'.

They'd also told him the answers to the questions.

— I'm certainly risking an awful lot of money, but by the same token I could win a lot of money, too . . .
— Yes, indeed you can. You can win or lose a lot. All I wanted to make clear was that you knew certainly that this could possibly happen.
— That is right, Mr Barry.

The other big quiz programmes were doing the same. 'You'd think I was Marlon Brando,' recalled a contestant on *Dotto*, one of the most tightly scripted quizzes. 'I was told how to bite my lips, clench my fists and look agonized as I supposedly struggled to find the answers. They even told me how, at the last moment, to make my face light up as if the answer had suddenly come to me.'

The coaching and casting was intended to make the contestants into everyman and everywoman, even when they already were. 'We want personable, although not necessarily good-looking people,' remarked *The $64,000 Question*'s executive producer. 'People who look like your neighbors.'

Many 'contestants' found it easier to answer the questions in rehearsals – before they had been supplied with the answers – than to get their onscreen performances right. 'Everything had to be done exactly,' Stempel later recalled. 'Woe betide you if you did not do it as it had been planned.'

And on this night, Stempel knew that he was to lose to his challenger, Columbia University teacher Charles Van Doren.

— Now, Mr Van Doren, I guess you know pretty well from last week how to play this game . . . The first category is the Civil War. How much do you know about it – you tell us, from one to eleven?
— That's an awful big subject. Uh, I'll try for eight points.
— For eight points: because of a disagreement with his commanding general, Ulysses Grant was virtually placed under arrest for a brief time early in 1862. **Who was the commanding general of the Union Army at that time?**[1]

[1] Van Doren replied, correctly: 'Oh, yes, uh – I know his name. Halleck, General H. W. Halleck.'

Charles Van Doren had a friend in common with one of the producers of *Twenty One*, who decided that he should topple Stempel. A stammering, sweaty GI getting rich was one version of the American dream, but Van Doren offered quite another.

The Van Dorens were a literary dynasty: Charles's uncle and father both had won Pulitzer prizes; he himself mixed literature with maths (his master's thesis was on inversive geometry) and music (his clarinet was essentially concert standard). He was also really very handsome. A clever, attractive teacher getting rich – now there was an American dream which might even compete with *I Love Lucy*. Indeed, when *Twenty One* was rescheduled to compete with that immense CBS sitcom, it held its own. Geritol were delighted.

Van Doren was also a natural actor. When he performed in an amateur performance of *The Male Animal*, the play's author, James Thurber, beseeched him to take up theatre professionally.

— Mr Van Doren, you have no points at the present. The category is Movies and Movie Stars. How many points do you want, from one to eleven?
— I think I should take about seven, but I just can't risk it – uh, I'll try for ten points.
— For ten points, one of the tough questions. In 1954, the Oscars for the best supporting actress, best director, and best story-and-screenplay writer all went to people who had worked in the film *On the Waterfront*. **Name these people.**[2]

[2] Elia Kazan, Budd Schulberg ' . . . and she's the only [actress] I can remember – let's see – she was that lovely, frail girl – Eva Saint – uh, Eva Marie Saint.'

Van Doren was initially taken aback when he was told that 'the sponsors want ["this fellow Stempel"] to be beaten . . . they want somebody more sympathetic' – but once he internalized the idea that a successful educator might make education attractive, he put his acting skills to far more lucrative use than they would have found on a stage. (Among the interpreters at the United Nations, the practice of reading out a prepared statement as if you're translating it in real time is to this day known as 'doing a Van Doren'.)

— Herb Stempel, you have sixteen points . . . All right. What motion picture won the Academy Award for 1955? Do you need some extra time to think about it?
— Ah . . . I sure do.
— I'll tell you when your time is up.
— I don't remember . . . I don't remember . . . *On the Waterfront*?
— No, I'm sorry, the answer is *Marty*. *Marty* – you lose five points, which puts you back down to eleven. Better luck on the next round.

Stempel was a decent performer, too. But he was less bid-dable than Van Doren – and he felt the power of the 'story' of Van Doren's quashing him as keenly as the producers hoped the audience would. If it were a fair fight, he figured, he would remain the winner, and he offered to reduce his winnings if he could play an unfixed match. Unbeknown to him, Van Doren wanted the same thing.

But their wish was not granted. Stempel had to go: he con-sidered himself betrayed, and especially resented the indignity of feigning ignorance regarding *Marty*, a cinch of a question about a favourite film of his (and one which happened to portray a schlub from the Bronx).

When he overheard a comment while leaving the studio floor for the last time – as he recalls it, 'Now we have a clean-cut intellectual as champion instead of a freak with a sponge memory' – it was inevitable that he would turn from quiz's greatest champion to quiz's greatest whistle-blower.

After he left the competition, Stempel took his story to the newspapers. They were reluctant to run with the testimony of a possibly unreliable witness. Even when the truth about quizzes like *Dotto* started to emerge, there was a sense that *Twenty One* was different: more honourable.

In an April 1957 piece which began 'Are the quiz shows rigged?', *Time* magazine described apparently tackier shows before noting, 'On *Twenty One*, candidates cannot qualify [without] taking a four-hour, 363-question test that ranges across the spectrum of subjects used on the show.' It approvingly went on to note that the test papers were burned to maintain the quiz's integrity and that Van Doren (still, then, the reigning champion) 'feels certain that no questions were being form-fitted – to his phenomenal mind'.

— Mr Van Doren, you have eight points. The category is kings, K-I-N-G-S. How many points do you want?
— I'll try for ten points.
— For ten points: it's well known that some of Henry VIII's six wives fared better than others. He divorced his first wife, Catherine of Aragon, married his sixth, Catherine Parr, just a few years before he died. Name the second, third, fourth and fifth wives of Henry VIII and describe their fates.

— Oh, my goodness. You want me to **name the second, third, fourth and fifth wives and what happened to all of them?**[3]

— That's right.

Van Doren went to the press, too, but with more rarefied misgivings. By September, he was a former contestant but a regular fixture on NBC educational programming; for *Life* magazine, he wrote of the differences between being well educated and doing well in quiz: 'The world of the educated man is full of mysteries. It is foggy and dark; with lots of unlighted passages going off to who knows where.' In quiz, by contrast, 'Only those questions are asked which have answers, and then only if the answers are available, on a card held in the MC's hand.' It reads as if it's constantly on the verge of a confession.

In fact, Van Doren was given many more chances to be more direct about the difference between academia and the American quiz of the 1950s. In April 1957, another contestant was instructed to take a dive about one of his cultural favourites, when asked for **the poet who wrote 'Hope is the thing with feathers/That perches in the soul'.**[4] It was as if the producers enjoyed abasing the smarter players. He not only gave the right answer on air but sent the questions to himself by registered post, dated before the show was recorded. So there was the proof of the fix.

3 'Now the second one was, uh – Anne Boleyn . . . Uh – and of course the poor woman was beheaded. Uh, now the third – the third was Jane Seymour . . . And I believe she died a natural death – she died in childbirth, uh, after the birth of the future Edward vi. Now the fourth now – uh, let's see – two Annes – Anne of Cleves, and I don't think he beheaded her – no, uh, did he divorce her? He – he divorced her. The fifth – one more – uh, uh, one more. Oh! I think that Henry viii married three, three Catherines. Now . . . Catherine of Aragon, Catherine Parr – Catherine Howard. Yes, what happened to her? Considering Henry viii, he probably divorced her . . . uh . . . he – he divorced his – did he behead Catherine Howard?'

4 Emily Dickinson.

And as the great quiz scandal began, so did the lies. The lawyer for *Twenty One*'s producers advised them to commit perjury if questioned and to flee to the Cocos Islands (on the mistaken basis that they had no extradition agreement with America) if things got serious.

They did. Van Doren lied to his lawyer and then to the district attorney, who told him, 'You can lie to me, but I'm not going to let you lie to the grand jury.' Then he lied to the grand jury. But the scandal would not go away.

— Congratulations, Mr Van Doren. Herb, in the few brief moments we have, what are you going to do with your dough?

— . . . I would like to make a small contribution to the City College fund to repay the people of the city of New York for the free education which they have given me . . . and I would also like to thank you and the members of your staff for all the kindness and the courtesy which you've extended to me . . .

— Charles Van Doren, come back next week . . . Goodnight to Charles Van Doren, ladies and gentlemen. Friends, we don't have much time. Remember Geritol and Geritol Junior.

When the deception reached the hearings of the House Committee on Interstate and Foreign Commerce, Van Doren offered to give evidence, hoping he wouldn't have to. The committee called his bluff and subpoenaed him.

Van Doren finally pleaded guilty (to the sin of cheating and to the actual crime of second-degree perjury): 'I was involved, deeply involved in a deception . . . I have a long way to go. I have deceived my friends, and I had millions of them.' Quiz was on trial, and his was the most important testimony: if the professor was rotten, everything was rotten.

Stempel, who had cheated but not committed perjury, went on to become a teacher. Van Doren could not continue as the same, as became clear when he returned to Columbia and a student yelled from a dorm window, 'Charlie's going to be in the quad tomorrow to give out the answers to the Comparative Lit. exam!'

He worked quietly instead for the *Encyclopædia Britannica* and later wrote a rather good book with a rather good title: *A History of Knowledge*. In the 1990s, he was offered $100,000 to act as a consultant to *Quiz Show*, Robert Redford's film version of the scandals. His wife told him, 'Please don't be a fool.' While he was considering the offer, he heard a song in his truck with the refrain 'I don't need money/All I need is you' and decided she was right.

The producers were less contrite. Sure, they, argued, the perjury was wrong, but the original deception was no different from rigging wrestling. John Steinbeck, for one, disagreed; he thought the fraud symptomatic of an American sickness and wrote this response to his friend, the former presidential candidate Adlai Stevenson:

> We can't expect to raise our children to be good and honorable men when the city, the state, the government, the corporations all offer higher rewards for chicanery and deceit than probity and truth. On all levels it is rigged, Adlai. Maybe nothing can be done about it, but I am stupid enough and naively hopeful enough to want to try. How about you?

Congress agreed. This was the end of outright sponsor control of programmes, and Geritol would presently have to buy space between programmes rather than owning the programmes themselves. Others went further and called for television free of commercial influence altogether, which led to America's public-broadcasting service.

As for quiz, Congress criminalized 'deceptive practices in contests of intellectual knowledge'. Quiz-show ratings had plummeted, in any event, during the scandals and effectively disappeared from American screens for decades, replaced by gameshows and other formats where it's safer to control the outcome.

For a long time, it was up to Britain to keep quiz alive.

Welcome back

14. Here's what you could have won

From rotary irons to a million pounds

The American scandals did not pass unnoticed in the UK. *The Times* called them *l'affaire Van Doren*; other papers preferred 'the great Quiz Swizz'. And they all began to wonder about home-grown quiz.

ITV had its own version of *Twenty One*; in 1959 the *Daily Express* reported that one of its contestants – a waiter called Stanley Armstrong – had been given 'definite leads' which helped him to win all of £30, and there followed a briefer British hullabaloo. The production company, Granada, appointed no less a figure than the former attorney-general Sir Lionel Heald QC to investigate its own programme.

The producers had, it turned out, given contestants a kind of reading list; Sir Lionel found this 'highly imprudent' and 'Pharos' in the *Spectator* described the tip-offs as 'a common, perhaps universal, practice in this type of quiz where the money is big', adding that the programmes' appeal relied on the offensive lie 'that these supermen (or women) have wonderful encyclopaedic minds'.

Sir Lionel agreed that the issue was one of trust: 'It would perhaps be going too far to compare a television producer to Caesar's wife, but in my opinion it is only natural, if programmes of this kind are to be presented, that the public should expect some positive guarantee from the Network itself that the competition is genuine and the chances even for all.' (Sir Lionel's allusion is to the proverb 'Caesar's wife must be above suspicion', Julius Caesar's ungallant reason for divorcing his second wife after Publius Clodius tried to seduce her. **What was her name?**[1])

The independent-television regulator insisted that quiz programmes produce a little booklet clearly stating not only their rules and rewards but also how contestants were to be advised. Granada promised that its questions would be verified properly, and that only contestants who had performed well in auditions would appear.

So the British quiz bubble didn't burst – but it was prevented from getting too big. And the perceived nasty niff around quiz was lingering still when, in July 1960, Harold Macmillan appointed the Pilkington Committee.

Under the chairmanship of glass baron Harry Pilkington, the committee was to consider the future of broadcasting. Quiz came under particular scrutiny, and this submission, from the National Union of Teachers, was typical:

> Children may also see a succession of 'quiz' shows, especially on the commercial channel, in many of which not only are valuable prizes awarded for futile performances, but the whole atmosphere is calculated (or seems to be) to encourage greed and acquisitiveness. In the schools we attempt to teach, by precept and example, the value of service and work, and it is difficult to escape the conclusion

[1] Pompeia.

that this attitude and that of the 'give-away' shows are not entirely compatible.

The Pilkington Report was published in 1962, and quiz in particular was excoriated. Quiz programmes, it said, 'do not stand on their merits', relying instead 'upon the appeal to greed and fear'. They were letting the country down; they were letting broadcasting down; worst of all, they were letting themselves down: 'These programmes abandon the objective – light entertainment which amuses because it is good – for light entertainment which is poor in invention and needs the support of extraneous appeals.'

'Accordingly,' it concluded, 'we recommend that the maximum value of prizes should be greatly reduced.'

This was not, the report insisted, because 'an intellectual minority finds the programmes trivial.' *The Sunday Times* disagreed, and commissioned a survey. It found that 75 per cent of respondents said that they watched quiz programmes, but only 20 per cent agreed with the statement that they 'appeal to greed and fear'. (The proportion sympathetic to Pilkington was higher among men, the middle classes, Liberals and Conservatives, and those who had been educated beyond the age of eighteen.)

ITV, in particular, came in for criticism (Associated-Rediffusion soon lost its franchise; *Double Your Money* went with it) and the steady-as-she-goes BBC was rewarded for its general restraint and good behaviour with a new TV channel. Three months after the report was published, ITV pulled its socks up and gave the nation *University Challenge* (thus begetting *Mastermind*). It was, said Bamber Gascoigne, 'an incredibly bold step' by the young company Granada to launch 'a quiz that the public wouldn't know the answers to', but it was also a canny one, given the bad smell around the genre. And even for the shows with big prizes, the prizes didn't get too big. TV quiz entered a three-decade holding pattern.

Until the end of the eighties, no British quiz was allowed to give away more than £6,000 (one benchmark was the value of a small family car, but the UK version of *The $64,000 Question* stretched it to £6,400 in 1994), and most offered far less. This led to strange situations, like when Jimmy Tarbuck explained to a contestant, 'You've got twelve-hundred pound on the board, but the rules are you can only win a thousand pound . . .', then turned to the audience (and the regulators?) with a peevish: 'That's the rules of television, we're only allowed to give a thousand pound away on this show.' Such announcements inevitably undermined the programme's title, *Winner Takes All*.

Many quizzes offered household goods instead, often announced in tones somewhere between post-rationing glamour and chic urbanity. In the early days of the darts quiz *Bullseye*, the things to be won on Bully's Prize Board were intoned with little ceremony before we returned to the important business of staying out of the black and in the red. (It's important to remember that you in fact got nothing in this game for two in a bed.)

But something was missing. Darts commentator Tony Green recalled the change of policy: 'They said, "Can we get something with a little bit more oomph into it?" and that's when it all came out. I said, "Right-oh. I'll give you it." '

For one lucky generation, nothing evokes Sunday-afternoon treats more than Green's voice intoning, 'Iiii-in one!' before listing the prizes. This is a collection of my favourites:

In 1: The food will go further, and stay hotter – in this hostess trolley

In 2: A touch of class, in glass – a crystal rose bowl

In 3: Mum can sit there and have a good doze, and wake up and find she's got sparkling clothes – with this automatic washing machine

In 4: If you take home this cuddly pink hippo, they'll be shouting 'hippo-ray'

In 5: Aye aye, Skipper, put it there – in this pine captain's trunk. Ah-arr, Jim, lad

In 6: Put yourself in the picture – this compact camera has got a self-timer

In 7: You'll score elevenses out of tenses if you take home with you – this coffee-maker

In 8: For the woman in your life, or the wife – a complete beauty set

And Bully's Special Prize this week – a VHS video recorder

'Worth a lot of money,' remarked host Jim Bowen after the last. 'There you are.' Not as much as the speedboats that appeared on *Bullseye* more regularly than you might expect a speedboat to appear, but he was right. In the 1980s, before the era of 'buy one, get one free and throw the free one away', TV still talked about making food go further and equated cut-glass with class.

But being a prize on *Bullseye* and its ilk rendered cut-glass less classy and VHS video recorders plummeted in price, so there came a point where enough households already owned these items (or, in the case of hostess trolleys, had put them into a car-boot sale) that they no longer brought the same sparkle to a quiz. Gone were the days when, in the words of one concerned critic, television routinely broadcast 'the extraordinary event of an entire studio audience applauding a rotary ironer'. Keith Chegwin tells me that when he hosted the revived *Sale of the Century*, contestants would ask the producers for the value of the prizes they'd just won and offer to take a smaller sum in cash.

By the 1990s, in fact, pretty much everything we've discussed above had gone, too. Lotteries as an evil? Broadcast Saturday nights, prime-time, by the BBC's flagship channel, with *its* prizes approaching £100,000. 'Buying' viewers seen as cheap? Ratings ruled. And unearned wealth was, through the coming credit boom, what would propel the economy.

And as to 'stimulating thought', a populist editorial in Rupert Murdoch's *Times* expressed best the spirit of the age: 'The family with the single parent and the single television set pays the same as the opera-loving tycoon with a television in every room; and the tycoon's favourite television Shakespeare is subsidized by the very quiz shows that so successfully keep the children quiet.'

Hm. Do tycoons really turn over from *Telly Addicts* to catch an act or two of *Timon of Athens*? Reality was beside the point. Quiz was, again, a political football. Big business wanted big prizes, and the regulation of TV was to be portrayed in the press as snobbery. It was time for another official report. A successor to Pilkington, Margaret Thatcher's Peacock Committee, was less interested in what intellectuals and teachers had to say: it was so pro-business that the licence fee only just survived it.

And so, just as 1955 had heralded the £1,000 prize, 1998 went seven-figure.

In 1956, Frank Sinatra and Celeste Holm sang the Cole Porter song 'Who Wants to be a Millionaire?' (**in which musical?**[2]). The refrain was a defiant 'I don't' ("Cause all I want is you'), but the question was not to remain rhetorical.

[2] *High Society.*

In 1995, the former Capital Radio executive David Briggs was pondering his years as the station's head of competitions and executive producer of Chris Tarrant's breakfast show. On some radio shows, the quiz is left for an intern to cobble together. Not at Capital in the 1980s, where 'Competitions' were, literally, a big deal. Listeners called to enter, and the station had an arrangement with telephone companies to share the revenue.

Briggs approached two chaps called Steve Knight and Mike Whitehill who had also worked with Tarrant at Capital before going on to write jokes for Jasper Carrott. Come 1995, they were working in development at Carrott's small production company, Celador (named after **a two-word phrase which is fancied by some to be the most pleasing combination of sounds the English language can produce**[3]). In particular, their job involved concocting quiz ideas in the wine bars of Covent Garden.

Briggs showed them what he persisted in naming *Cash Mountain*. There were other differences to the programme it became: a booth called a 'sweat box', for example, and prizes which started at £10 and reached a frankly unnecessary £5,242,880. But the basics were there: the unprecedented prizes, multiple-choice questions and, vitally:

> The prizes would be funded by the revenue to be derived from the use of the premium line.

Just as the first wave of TV quiz came from radio, so would its revival.

The three of them thrashed out what worked and didn't work with Celador boss Paul Smith, an indefatigable TV exec who was famous for taking the oft-repeated clip of an animal

[3]. 'Cellar door'.

(**what kind of animal?**[4]) named Lulu voiding her bowels live on to the *Blue Peter* studio floor and turning its appeal into a whole new show: the internationally lucrative *It'll Be Alright on the Night*.

They were certain Tarrant was the right host. They considered various devices, such as offering the advice of a panel of *Confound the Experts!*-style boffins: Carol Vorderman, say, and Patrick Moore – perhaps Stephen Hawking? And they eventually realized that a million pounds was probably enough. Following the Peacock Report, ITV had a new regulator which had effectively done away with limits on prizes – but no one had successfully exploited the opportunity. In Yorkshire Television's *Raise the Roof*, Bob Holness had offered an actual house as a prize, but audiences had preferred BBC1's *Casualty* of a Saturday evening and *Raise the Roof* lasted only one series. (Holness would later lament that the ethos of television quiz was 'turning much more to avarice – the want of . . . money, money, money. The general interest and the learning side of it is probably fading.')

And when Smith took Celador's revamped version of *Cash Mountain* to the channels, there was similarly scant interest. ITV's director of programmes was convinced that there was no appetite among members of the public for seeing other members of the public winning indecent amounts of cash. But he did commission some market research. The respondents said, broadly, that they would probably give the show a try, but that its title was wretched. 'Million' was felt to be the word which best conveyed what the programme was about; a suggested new title was *To be a Millionaire*. (The punters also

4 An elephant.

thought that the show didn't need its proposed interludes from a live band.)

Still, ITV was sure that the future for evening television was in scripted programmes: soaps, sitcoms and the odd classy drama with a posh bird in it. Certainly not quiz. The category known in the industry as Entertainment had by common consensus breathed its prime-time last.

Smith, though, was nothing but tenacious. When a new director of programmes took over at ITV, he returned to the channel. But having been round every *other* channel, he was weary of pitching a sheaf of paper. As he turned up for his appointment on the Gray's Inn Road on 8 April 1998, he came instead with a flip chart and four envelopes stuffed with increasing amounts of his own cash.

He had decided to make the new boss play the game.

The new boss was David Liddiment. He'd been given the gist, but thought that it was madness to show the contestants the next question before they decided whether to continue, and that using multiple-choice questions would risk losing a million pounds every night by quite literally giving contestants every answer.

Smith opened by asking the man he barely knew to empty his wallet, hoping it might contain £250. Liddiment had two hundred-odd pounds but tentatively added an IOU. Smith offered him the envelope containing £500 if he could answer this question:

What would an aborigine do with his wurley?[5]

    A: eat it   B: hunt with it
    C: play it   D: live in it

5 Live in it: a hut, from the Adelaide tribe's *wodli* or *worli*.

Liddiment used two lifelines at once: he phoned an actual friend and went fifty-fifty before getting it right. Smith then proffered the envelope containing the £500 – but he didn't want to give him that. He wanted Liddiment to give *him* much more. He next offered a tricky, £1,000 question: **What was the length in feet of the *Titanic*?**[6]

History does not record the multiple-choice options (you can have fifty feet either way), but Liddiment wanted to phone a friend again (the rules were not as readily understood as they are now), then asked the audience (some nearby secretaries) before deciding to keep the £500 he'd won. Smith considered the loss worth it.

Finally, the show was going to happen.

Still, Liddiment had very reasonable concerns. If not enough viewers called the number to enter, who would end up bankrolling the prizes? It would not be ITV. Plan A was that the show would fund itself; in a moment of reckless courage, Smith nominated himself – or rather his shares, his savings and his family's home – as Plan B. Celador's investors were notified and scenarios tabulated. As gameshow nabob Peter Bazalgette describes it, the planning 'was beginning to sound more like financial risk management than television production'.

Liddiment wondered whether the show could be ITV's rival to the BBC's 1998 World Cup coverage, but Smith wanted to get everything right first and produce an impeccable pilot later that year. Everyone eventually agreed: you can't get a series right if you haven't absolutely nailed the pilot.

The pilot was awful.

What really strikes you – in the sense of aurally assaulting you – is the music. Smith had earlier approached Simon Cowell;

his plan was to have the theme tune released as a single and in the top ten before the show began, to whip up anticipation. Next to the resulting 'Cloud Nine', *Going for Gold*'s notoriously perky theme sounded like a funereal dirge: 'You take me over the rainbow / And up to cloud nine / I'm flying *high* . . .'

It wasn't just the music that was too jaunty. The lighting was too bright. It presented itself as just another tiresome gameshow. Worst of all, the graphic design gave almost all of the screen to the multiple-choice, squishing the contestant's face into a tiny box. Smith's reaction was 'Someone's deliberating whether they're going for half a million pounds! You want to see the sweat on their brow. You want to see their nostrils dilating. You want to see all the signs of panic.' Someone had noticed what had made the recently cancelled *Mastermind* work.

Celador had a matter of days in which to redesign everything, ready to record episode one on Thursday, 3 December, for transmission the following evening (with another to be broadcast on Saturday, and on Sunday . . . ITV had cleared the schedules).

And so Friday at 8 p.m. saw a dark-suited Tarrant against a black background. His stately address began, 'Tonight and for the next ten nights, you'll be watching British quiz-show history.' He ended with the more important: 'To find out how *you* can take part . . . join us for *Who Wants to be a Millionaire?*'

After the titles, the revamped set was revealed: it looked like the invasion-planning deck of an imperial spaceship. The colour of money, and tension, it transpired, was blue. And 'Cloud Nine' had been replaced with relentless hum and ominous fanfare. The imperial spaceship's invasion began. The first night's viewers played along in a new way: you could choose your answer but also consider whether you'd be confident enough about that answer to risk losing £32,000. They did not see the making of a millionaire and, in fact, Tarrant was beaten to the punch a year later by another DJ: Chris Evans, who gave a million on his Virgin Radio show to Clare Barwick when she correctly identified **which of George Eliot and T. S. Eliot was a woman.**[7]

But giving money *away* wasn't the most important thing – not yet. Would viewers be tempted to risk their own cash to enter? It helped that Rupert Murdoch's *Sun* newspaper was the show's marketing partner and, on the first evening, the show received 200,000 calls. Even if many were individuals multiple-dialling, the show was away.

And after the weekend came more calls, not to premium numbers, but even more lucrative: TV folk from around the world had heard about this big show from this little company and wanted to license their own versions.

In which countries has *Who Wants to be a Millionaire?* been known by the following titles?

Qui Veut Gagner des Millions?[8]

¿Quién Quiere Ser Millonario?[9]

Alles ist Möglich — Die 10-Millionen Show[10]

Legyen Ön is Milliomos![11]

Hvem Vil Være Millionær?[12]

Кто хочет стать миллионером?[13]

[13] Russia (1 million roubles).
[12] Denmark (1 million kroner).
[11] Hungary (25 million forints).
[10] Austria (10 million schillings).
[9] Spain (50 million pesetas).
[8] France (originally 3 million francs; as the answers indicate, some countries had to use their equivalent of pennies rather than pounds).
[7] George Eliot (aka Marian Evans).

184

'Never mind taking coals to Newcastle,' remarked David Briggs when *Who Wants to be a Millionaire?* hit America in 1999, 'we have sold light entertainment to the Americans. We ought to get the Queen's Award for Export.' (Where quiz led, talent shows – *American Idol*; *Dancing with the Stars* – followed.)

The show arrived to find a different America. There was an attractive stock-market bubble based on the new technologies of the internet (even though there was plenty of smart money to be made from the century-old telephone). If you missed out on that, there was another way to get rich with little effort. Here's how media professor Robert Thompson put it at the time: 'In the case of *Who Wants to be a Millionaire?*, we've bypassed the entire length it takes to achieve the American Dream and compressed it into twenty minutes.'

Trivial Pursuit may have given a quick kiss of life to American TV quiz in the 1980s, but this was a resurrection for a bloodless genre: the few gameshows that had shambled on towards the millennium had barely any true quizzes among them. But the lessons of *Twenty One* had been learned: when the fourth episode of *Who Wants to be a Millionaire?* offered a sackful of duff questions (ambiguous phrasing, two right answers, computer malfunctions), the show fessed up, invited contestants back and generally showed that quiz had grown up.

America also offered the first million-winner in any country's version of the show: taxman John Carpenter, who had all his lifelines intact at his final question . . .

Which of these US presidents appeared on the television series *Laugh-In*?[14]

A: Lyndon Johnson   B: Richard Nixon
C: Jimmy Carter   D: Gerald Ford

[14] Richard Nixon.

. . . and used his phone-a-friend to say, 'Hi, Dad. I don't really need your help; I just wanted to let you know that I'm going to win a million dollars.' Where do you go from there? The American copycat *Greed* presently offered $2.2 million, but what's a million or so between shows? It lasted one season.

That leap to a million seems to be as high as quiz has been able to go so far. And, in fact, prizes have since come down. As *Who Wants to be a Millionaire?* entered its second decade, the late-nineties boom had gone bust. Fewer and fewer people wanted to be a Millionaire. 'People were saying: "I've got ten grand, I'm not going to risk that,"' recalled Tarrant in 2013. Where he had once given away an average of £100,000 per episode, he said, it was now taking three or four shows to get to that amount.

And, he added, he no longer felt comfortable encouraging contestants to risk a six-figure sum that they would be happier to bank. Here's the same thought, in different words, from explainer-of-economics John Lanchester, who described the programme as 'a welcome casualty of the Great Recession: as times got harder, contestants realized it made much more sense to cash out their very useful £50,000 or £75,000 rather than risking the money just to make better entertainment for the audience at home on their sofas.'

In February 2014, on a celebrity edition, Chris Tarrant asked his penultimate question:

Which of these royal couples were born in the same year and reputedly had the same midwife in attendance at their births?[15]

A: Victoria and Albert   B: Charles and Camilla
C: Elizabeth and Philip   D: Edward and Mrs Simpson

[15] Victoria and Albert.

Countdown's Rachel Riley and Hairy Biker Dave Myers hoped to win £20,000 with their guess of Charles and Camilla; Tarrant put them in an unnecessary double headlock and told them that the money they'd amassed for a hospice and a children's charity had just 'plunged back to £1,000'. His last question was addressed to the audience at home:

> That means that the viewers' grand total stands at £48,500. To be in with a chance of winning *all* that cash *and* that holiday to the Maldives, *here's what you need to do.* If someone appears extremely attractive, they're said to look like a million . . . what? A: euros. B: dollars. C: pesos. D: rupees. Call 0904 16 19 333. Calls cost no more than £1.54 from BT landlines; other networks may be higher and mobiles considerably more.

'Knowledge Its Own End'

In quizzes at the trickier end, the kind of questions which came as a contestant's fifteenth on *Who Wants to be a Millionaire?* might crop up five or six times in an episode. But those shows don't give away five or six million pounds.

Take *University Challenge*, which in the Gascoigne era included, as well as reference books, some end-of-series prizes which would not have been out of place among *Bullseye*'s lesser offerings (a glass swan; a rose bush; a VHS recorder) and some which would (a copy of *The Rake's Progress*; a punt christened *Bamber 1*). Luckier teams also received special crystal goblets from Asprey's; one year, each was engraved with the legend 'University Challenge'.

For the show's revival, the Mancunian sculptor Adrian Moakes created a stainless-steel trophy in the shape of a book. Trinity College, Cambridge, was the first to take the prize home, though not to keep it. The production company Granada presently asked for its return so that it could be passed on to the next champions; Trinity claimed not to have it, but Granada proved that a college porter had signed for it, and it was eventually duly handed to Imperial College London.

Mastermind outdid the rose bush and glass swan by combining them in the form of its handsome rose bowl, designed and engraved using a copper-wheel lathe by Denis Mann of Wick's Caithness Glass, with variations on the theme of **the nine Greek goddesses Calliope, Clio, Euterpe, Thalia, Melpomene, Terpsichore, Erato, Polyhymnia and Urania, who are better known as what?**[16] But it's still not money, and no Mastermind's bowl is known to have been sold on. (Dave Clark, who won the 2008 final with the specialized subject, the History of London Bridge, took his to the *Antiques Roadshow* and had it valued at around £500, but insisted, 'It will never be sold because it would have to be prised out of my cold, dead fingers first.')

An earlier Mastermind, Philip Jenkins (1979, History of Wales 400–1100), subsequently became a professor at Pennsylvania State University and found that not only did his victory mean nothing there but also that, in Magnus Magnusson's words, his colleagues 'were amazed to hear about a TV quiz which didn't give thousands of dollars in prize money'. Even *Jeopardy!* sends its top contestants home with plenty of bucks.

Both those shows, though, are positively brash compared to *Only Connect*'s closing ceremony, in which a trophy costing less than £300 is handed to a tournament's eventual winners in semi-darkness *as the credits have already begun* and the theme tune obliterates their mumbled words of triumph.

16 The Muses.

And tough radio quizzes often don't have any spoils at all: unless you're banging those silver dollars against the microphone, there's not much point in booty that no one can see.

But, of course, it's not about the trophy. Olav Bjortomt, who at the time of writing wins pretty much every quiz going, wrote in 2002, 'A fellow *University Challenge* alumnus, David Stainer, told me he would trade the £64,000 he won on *Millionaire* in a nanosecond for the UC trophy he missed out on when he was beaten by the infamous Open University team, accused of being professional quizzers.'

More on that in the next chapter; in the meantime, another Mastermind, Fred Housego (1980, Tower of London), recently spoke to *The Chase*'s Bradley Walsh about whether he wished he'd been a champion in the era of big-money quiz. He said, 'It would have been nice but you've got to think of the culture at the time. Because the expectation of winning vast sums of money wasn't there, to me that was fine. It was genuinely wonderful.'

Kudos, then, to those who quiz without expecting material reward. And the cabbie Housego also appears in the next chapter. Because, to have enough cultural capital to compete as a gentleman quizzer, perhaps it helps also to have some *actual* capital . . .

15. Knowledge is power, and vice versa

Quizzes for the rich, quizzes for the poor

The words 'pub quiz' summon to mind many things: ale, waggish team names, intense rivalry – and most of all, blokes. But the people who shaped the form were women.

In the 1940s, impromptu quiz events, inspired by the new radio shows, were advertised in local papers. With a Women's Institute or a Mothers' Union often overseeing matters, these were typically wholesome affairs with specialist rounds on road safety, farming techniques or local matters.

Presently, quiz leagues – regular rather than one-off events – were sharing space with whist drives in the youth clubs and town halls; by the 1970s, they had taken things to the pub, some setting the questions themselves, others forming teams for competitions like the *Sunday People* Great Pub Sports Quiz. But what if you had a pub and fancied the regular custom of quiz devotees, but no locals had taken it upon themselves to form leagues or teams?

In the mid-1980s, the sometime landlady Sharon Burns

cashed in on publicans' aversion to quiet evenings by selling a 'quiz night' package to loads of them. Burns, too, recognized the importance of format and accoutrements, and handled tournament structures and publicity as well as supplying the questions. Thatcher-era press profiles wrote glowingly of 'the woman behind all those pub competitions', of the 150,000 matches a year organized by her enterprising initiative and of the million pounds Burns had accumulated.

By the time she sold up and bought a hotel and a Manchester drive-in hamburger restaurant, the habit of quizzing in pubs had been taken up by more than the hardcore. You might find anyone playing. Well, not quite anyone.

In Alan Bennett's novella *The Uncommon Reader* a mobile library visits Buckingham Palace. The queen does something she hasn't done before – reading for pleasure – and her courtiers are horrified ('While not exactly elitist, it sends the wrong message'). But the kitchen porter Norman is supportive, and they pursue a mutual love of the written word. One afternoon, a thought strikes her about the 'area in which one would truly excel':

> 'The pub quiz. One has been everywhere, seen everything and though one might have difficulty with pop music and some sport, when it comes to the capital of Zimbabwe, say, or the principal exports of New South Wales, I have all that at my fingertips.'
>
> 'And I could do the pop,' said Norman.
>
> 'Yes,' said the Queen. 'We would make a good team. Ah well. **The road not travelled. Who's that?**'[1]
>
> 'Who, ma'am?'
>
> 'The road not travelled. Look it up.'

[1] Norman looked it up in the *Dictionary of Quotations* to find that it was Robert Frost', and, the reader notes, tactfully does not give the poem's title ('The Road Not *Taken*').

The queen at a pub quiz? It's so seductively *wrong*: pub quizzes are for money: they're part of one strand of British quiz – with cash up for grabs, open to all. And for a very long time, this was kept well apart from the other strand: the one that retained a whiff of the classroom and to which only certain classes needed apply.

The genteel tone of the early BBC bees persisted with the Light Programme's *Top of the Form*. Special post-office lines connected two schools to London, and children competed to answer questions politely and win 'the coveted Owl of Wisdom trophy'. The hosts, who included a brace of Dimblebies, asked questions largely based on school syllabuses:

Who in history was supposed to have burned the cakes?[2]
What was the name of the ship in R. L. Stevenson's *Treasure Island*?[3]
What bird did Noah send out of the ark first?[4]

The children often addressed the hosts as 'Sir', and didn't tend to get much wrong. In fact, they often appeared staggeringly well informed . . .

— What is a relativistic velocity? Ann Gilchrist?
— It's velocity considered in, um, Einstein's type of space – relative to space–time curvature.
— Very good.

. . . though they *had* all completed a nine-page questionnaire which asked them for the set texts they had studied and

[2] Alfred the Great.
[3] The *Hispaniola*.
[4] A raven.

their extra-curricular interests. Their responses influenced the questions: not as a fix, but to avoid humiliating the nervous young contestants, much like *Mastermind*'s habit of starting the specialized subject with a question the contestant can comfortably answer while overcoming the terror of the Chair.

These children were well turned-out and well spoken (especially, representing Latymer Upper School, **a boy who would go on to star in *The Englishman Who Went up a Hill but Came down a Mountain*,**[5] who said that he was only chosen because the master in charge of selection 'had always, well, frankly, had a crush on me'). They came across as the product solely of the classroom and of their unstintingly wholesome hobbies. Not surprisingly, since they were typically chosen as those who would reflect best on their schools, right up to the squeaky final toast: 'Three cheers to the boys of Kingston Grammar School. Hip hip . . .'

Top of the Form moved to BBC1 in 1962 but was expelled from the TV schedules in 1975. (It reappeared in parodic form in the wonderful 1995 comedy *Natural Born Quizzers*, where Steve Coogan and Patrick Marber play homicidal brothers who have never got over failing to **name the Banana Splits**[6] twenty years earlier.) Chris Woodhead, former Her Majesty's Chief Inspector of Schools, thought that because it made children compete on the basis of how much they knew, the programme became 'increasingly out of step with the dominant movements within education'. It lived on until 1986 on Radio 4, though its orderly theme tune, 'Marching Strings', was pointedly replaced by producer Paul Mayhew-Archer with 'Fanfare for the Common Man'.

---

[5] Hugh Grant.
[6] Bingo, Fleegle, Snorky and Drooper; Guy Crump said 'Drayfer', though the real *Top of the Form* would hardly have asked about a brash American variety show.

The show's title certainly had the smack of elitism, but its content? Comprehensive schools had featured on *Top of the Form* since the late 1960s and their performance demonstrated that there was nothing elitist about its questions and answers; *Top of the Form*'s problem was one of presentation: as alternatives to the old-school came along, it started to come across as uppish.

Likewise, its elder brother.

In 1975, the letter asking Manchester's student union if it would like to submit a *University Challenge* team was misdirected and landed in the hands of a communist undergraduate who then hatched a plan with his flatmates. They replied to the letter, putting themselves forward as the Manchester side and arrived at Granada Studios with some forged tickets for their mates and a plan to sabotage the show.

One of them was David Aaronovitch, now a columnist for *The Times*, then a critic of the establishment. He recalled standing alongside Bamber Gascoigne in the Gents before the recording, mulling that he was 'a legendary figure, for all that he was the class enemy . . . and yet we were going to have to destroy his programme, his baby'.

Manchester's objection was that *University Challenge* did not accept teams from polytechnics or colleges of further education, yet for Oxford and Cambridge, 'even the smallest theological college had its own owlish and cloistered team'. This was a legacy of the early days of the show, when Britain had only thirty universities: allowing each Oxbridge college (and those of the Universities of London and Wales) to field its own side increased the pool of entries.

As time moved on, other reasons for maintaining the tradition were offered: the Oxbridge colleges were separate teaching institutions, and the statistics suggested that any series with one team apiece from Oxford, Cambridge and London would give each city a free pass to the semi-finals.

For Manchester, this was counter-revolutionary nonsense. A more nuanced critique of elitism might have been directed at schools and universities, but an invitation to a TV show was what Manchester had, so quiz became the arena for their protest. And it was an arena with a big audience: as Clive James, who captained Pembroke in the same year, put it, 'The whole country watched *University Challenge*. They watched it in working men's clubs. The Queen Mother watched it, knuckles white, running to the telephone to place bets.'

Emboldened by booze, the team from Manchester entered the studio and, whatever the question, buzzed in and gave the name of a different revolutionary icon: 'Trotsky', 'Che Guevara', 'Karl Marx', and so on. After a while, they ran out and started recycling them, in particular Trotsky. After another while and a few recording breaks, they were told that if they didn't start playing properly the programme would be scrapped.

They then began to quiz more conventionally, finishing the match with forty points. After the recording, Gascoigne recalled, the Manchester team joined him in the pub 'and they turned out to be very endearing. By the end of the evening, we were very fond of them.'

ITV changed its ticketing system to prevent future gate-crashers in the audience, but was left with the dilemma of whether to broadcast the sabotaged contest. Nowadays, any programme would ditch the episode and re-record with a new team, so it's cheering to reflect on the fact that this bizarre encounter was put out like any other edition of the programme. It's such a shame that the recording appears to be lost: alongside the 1972 parliamentary special, featuring Enoch Powell and David Steele, it's the one I'd most like to watch. Perhaps it will resurface; in the meantime, we have to make do with the episode which opened the second series of student sitcom *The Young Ones*.

In 'Bambi', Vyvyan, Rick, Mike and their captain, Neil, represent Scumbag College; their opponents are Mr Kendal Mintcake, Miss Money-Sterling, Lord Monty and their captain, Lord Snot, playing for Footlights College, Oxbridge, in a real-life Oxbridge invasion of alternative comedy by Stephen Fry, Hugh Laurie and Emma Thompson which prompted co-writer Alexei Sayle to bark on set, 'I thought these people were the enemy!'

The Scumbag boys have amassed precious little general knowledge in their lives so far and their only material for preparation is *The Daily Mirror Book of Facts: Did You Know?*

Worse, the quiz is biased against them. As Footlights chant, 'Rah rah rah! We're going to smash the oiks!' the host ('Bambi') remarks, 'Yes, that's the spirit,' and after Miss Money-Sterling answers a question about chemistry by giggling 'My father's got a Porsche', he gives Footlights the points: 'Yes, well, that's not exactly what I've got written on the card, but I knew your father.'

Hm. Alternative comedy skewered many sacred cows, but when you impugn the impeccable integrity of Bamber Gascoigne, you go too far. The real-life Gascoigne, recalling the episode with a chuckle, told me, 'We were as eager as anyone to see a university that wasn't from Oxbridge win, which quite often happened. We were thrilled.'

Stephen Fry (who had been on the Merton side which lost the real-life 1980 semi-final on a tie-break, having successfully interrupted on questions like **The man who partnered George Burns in the film version of** *The Sunshine Boys* ...[7]) recalls

[7] Walter Matthau.

Gascoigne uber-sesquipedally: 'A wise and kindly man, he seemed aware that other teams knew that he was a Cambridge graduate himself and therefore went out of his way to be scrupulously fair, without ever toppling over into self-conscious countercantabrigianism.'

And *The Young Ones* can perhaps be forgiven, since it was his fond memories of the spoof that helped convince a BBC Manchester controller to bring the programme back: 'An extreme or comedic view can,' reckoned John Whiston, 'fix in your mind what was special about the format in the first place.'

More importantly, if there is any bias in a quiz which asks the kind of questions featured on *University Challenge*, it doesn't need to be the result of favouritism. Cerebral pursuits have tended to require money (and for you not to be exhausted from a day's toil), and the kind of cultural capital that the smart end of quiz demands has been greater in some families than in others.

I'm thinking of the kind of families that you saw on *Ask the Family*.

> Just reached an edition of *Ask the Family* in which one of the families live in Scotland. But they still have a daughter called Camilla.
>
> cultural critic Robin Carmody

Once its incongruous raga theme tune had ended, *Ask the Family* was surely the squarest quiz ever conducted. It was also unremittingly fun, and not just for the sight of four hands of varying sizes piled on to each of the buzzers, or 'interesting buttons', as the host termed them. Robert Robinson gave introductions like 'two more families put themselves at the vaulting horses of abstraction, stripped to the intellectual buff' before posing questions such as this . . .

At a bloodstock sale, a racehorse is sold for 750 guineas. (It probably only had three legs at that price.) **How much was this in decimal currency?**[8] Ah! Straightforward but, ah, nasty to do on your fingers.

. . . to two families of four, when that set-up was considered the national norm. Its middle-class contestants were spoofed on *Not the Nine o'Clock News*, with its 'Robert Robinson', like 'Bambi' above, played by Griff Rhys Jones (who would later host BBC4's genuinely recherché *Quizeum*): 'Taking part tonight are the Brainie family from Croydon. Mr Giles Brainie is a quantity surveyor. His wife Serena Brainie is a quantity surveyor, and their children are Julian, 16, and Nigel, 15, who are quantity surveyors.'

Where, the parody asks, did they find these people? It wasn't easy.

'I'd spend half the year choosing families,' recalled producer Cecil Corker. 'I'd been to their homes and spoken to them all. That's what you had to do. It doesn't happen by itself.' He also acknowledged that only a certain type of contestant tended to appear: 'My one regret is that I could never convince families other than white middle-class viewers to take part. How different it would be now.' And this was despite the worry among many members of the professional classes that they would be embarrassed by getting the wrong questions. Lord Quinton, former president of Trinity College, Oxford, recalled the Quinton family's appearance in 1970:

> I remember being very concerned about being made to look as if I didn't know anything. We lost out in the semi-finals to a family much worse than us because I had a sheer

8 £787.50: Robinson said of the father who got it right, 'By God, you're a computer, Sir!'

mental aberration and forgot the answer to a very easy question . . . All the family were displeased with me and said: 'Oh, father!' But at least they had the prize money of about £30, which Joanna spent on clothes and Edward spent on LPs.

(For those who might be interested, the other Quintons dispute Lord Quinton's account. Joanna insists that 'he deliberately pretended to be slow on the buzzer because he just didn't want us to be known as TV family of the year. It would have been all too embarrassing.' Quinton *père* went on to chair *Round Britain Quiz* in the safer space afforded by Radio 4 on Sunday evenings.)

Ask the Family continued looking for intact families that could bear the indignity of winning a few bob on telly – until it was canned in 1984, three years before *University Challenge* took its sabbatical. Robinson's quiz likewise reappeared without its original host. But few revamps have been iller advised.

The 2005 *Ask the Family* was fronted by **the raucous presenters of *In Da Bungalow***[9] and innovations included requiring the families to eat a colossal wedge of cream cake before answering. It was a shock to the show's creator, Patricia Owtram. 'I was disgusted,' she wrote to the *Telegraph*, that 'a boy who gave the wrong answer was forced to wear a donkey mask and be hooted'. The new hosts presently disowned the make-over, describing it as 'absolutely shoddy', adding that it 'shouldn't have been called *Ask the Family* – it was just an awful programme,' and the BBC cravenly replied that it 'wasn't a good programme and whose fault that was is neither here nor there'.

The revival set a new and surely unbeatable benchmark for

9 Dick and Dom (accept Richard McCourt and Dominic Wood).

dumbing down. Here's Robinson in 1978, airily introducing one of the distinctive graphics created by Eric Ilett:

The names of five musical compositions you now see before you. If you place the initial letter of the composer's name of each, you get the name of another composer. It's only a matter of speed.[10]

Clock Symphony
Tales of Hoffman
I Pagliacci
The Mikado
Swan Lake

And here's a current-affairs question from 2005:

Is the name of the US Secretary of State Bondagoozza Noodle or Condoleezza Rice?[11]

Most quizzes, especially the serious-looking ones, are accused of dumbing down at some stage. The charge is usually along the lines of this 2004 lament from the shadow culture secretary Julie Kirkbride: 'It used to be about Jane Austen novels and Beethoven symphonies. Now there's just too much popular culture. *Mastermind* was meant to be about intellectual purity. I'm not persuaded that subjects like *The Simpsons* and *Only Fools and Horses* have a place on such a programme.'

As the Bondagoozza Noodle question shows, though, you can dumb down a question about serious subjects. Kirkbride was working from a set of assumptions built over decades in which quizzes which featured middle-class contestants tended

10 Holst (via Haydn, Offenbach, Leoncavallo, Sullivan and Tchaikovsky).
11 Condoleezza Rice.

to ask questions on literature, the fine arts, history and the like – the canon of culture perceived to be high-brow.

Quiz champions, by contrast, tend to look at it all as information which you either remember or you don't. 'For my *Doctor Who* round I had to know about 158 broadcast shows,' replied the 1993 champion Gavin Fuller, who also took the Mediaeval Castle in the British Isles and the Crusades. 'You could argue that that's much harder than being quizzed on Jane Austen, who wrote only six novels.'

And regarding the dominance of middle-class contestants, it doesn't always hold, not even on *Ask the Family*, nor on the radio (the pub pianist Irene Thomas, in her words, disturbed 'the monastic calm of *Round Britain Quiz* with the presence of an ex-chorus girl') and, most notably, not on 1980's *Mastermind* final. Of the 18 million people who watched Fred Housego take the title, some were perplexed and others delighted that a cabbie had beaten two civil servants and a postgraduate researcher.

The specialized subjects taken by the contestant who became known as Fred (but was referred to by *The Times* as 'Mr Frederick Housego, aged thirty-five, a London taxi driver, who left school with one O-level pass') were King Henry II, Westminster Abbey and, for the final, the Tower of London. The sanguine victor, like the fictional queen above, attributed his knowledge to his day job:

> You can't study general knowledge, but being a tour guide and a cabbie is the closest thing to it. I had studied all aspects of London's history. There are all sorts of fascinating people who've passed through the city down the years: Lenin, Marx, scientists and architects. So, all the time I was reading history, I was unconsciously training in general knowledge. By the time I came to *Mastermind*, I knew an awful lot.

Or rather 'day jobs': he wasn't just a cabbie. The information Housego possessed was down more to his other post as a Blue Badge Guide, but his ability to retain it was, it seems, linked to his given occupation of 'Licensed Taxi Driver'. It later transpired that cabbies in general may be better built for remembering. A paper by Eleanor Maguire, 'Navigation-related Structural Change in the Hippocampi of Taxi Drivers' announced that the hippocampuses of cabbies are significantly bigger in the parts related to memory, and that they get bigger still as the driver exercises more of the Knowledge.

Housego recalled the moment of winning. 'In any other show,' he said, 'I would've jumped up like I'd scored a goal in the World Cup . . . I was elated, but because *Mastermind* was an "upper-class" quiz show . . . I just raised both hands in a gentle fist. And I thought, you twerp.'

But Housego was no twerp. Viewers were used to seeing the Fred Housegos of the world on a completely different kind of quiz.

In Stan Barstow's 1960 kitchen-sink novel *A Kind of Loving*, a housing shortage and an unintended pregnancy force Vic Brown to move in with the family of his girlfriend, Ingrid. 'I always used to like television,' he remembers, 'but now I hate the sight of it.'

'We shan't ever be able to talk about books we've both read,' he sighs, because the most serious issue in Ingrid's home is 'whether she liked *Criss Cross Quiz* better than *Double Your Money*, or *Take Your Pick* better than both'.

For Vic, quiz is symptomatic of ignorance. For one thing, it's not British. 'It's all Yankeeland these days . . . if it goes big in America it takes here.' And it's not about knowledge; quiz is something that gets in the way of knowledge. To some extent, he's right. The other strand of British TV quiz – from *Double*

Your Money through *Sale of the Century* to *Wheel of Fortune* – is about much more than the questions.

Quiz was the first type of programme to include 'members of the public' – much of the appeal of *Have a Go* was the novelty of hearing working-class people bantering with Wilfred Pickles – and in Ingrid's favourite programmes, the contestants' personalities are played up. Name and occupation are just the start of it: we hear anecdotes and backstories long before the first question is asked, and personal tales like Housego's (the exception around *Mastermind*) are the rule.

Even so, Vic is a little harsh. Brasher quizzes are still tests of general knowledge: ones which are more likely to ask about phrases and sayings than about allusions and quotations, with more of the parts of general knowledge that contestants can pick up from TV and newspapers and less of those they get from books and journals. (**In the Scottish proverb, what does many a mickle make?**[12] **Which country has a lottery prize known as El Gordo – 'the fat one'?**[13])

We can only imagine what Vic would have made of the show produced by William G. Stewart before *Fifteen to One*: *The Price is Right*, where general knowledge was restricted to the recommended retail price of consumer durables, putting money into the questions as well as the prizes. Ingrid would have been glued to the screen. Stewart said that people who watch *The Price is Right* 'instinctively think, "That could be me" because other ordinary people are appearing in them. And with quiz they can join in.'

It's the money which really separates the two strands of British TV quiz and accounts for why it was difficult to recruit for *Ask the Family*: for most families, the idea of subjecting

[12] A muckle (though 'mickle' itself originally meant a great deal).
[13] Spain.

themselves to questions 'for father and elder child only', only to win some pocket money for the daughter's LP collection, is pre-posterous, when they could expend the same effort to appear on a money show and be part of a story where some 'ordinary people' take home something useful, like serious cash or a car.

And while people like Fred Housego appeared only rarely on cashless quiz programmes, middle-class appearances on money quizzes were even rarer. For the typical *Ask the Family* family, it simply wouldn't do to be seen making a quick buck.

Until the 1990s, that is.

The second-ever contestant on *Who Wants to be a Millionaire?* fulfils the programme's life-changing promise, while winning nothing near a million. Chris Tarrant asks the nervy twenty-year-old Rachel Mendez da Costa what she'll do if she wins the jackpot. 'Clear my debts, clear my fiancé's debts, sort out our business,' she splutters, 'and get married.' The wedding is planned for May 2000, two years away.

The audience coos, the cameras pick out the fiancé, and Tarrant tells him, 'It might be May 2000 – but it might be tomorrow!'

And so when the audience helps her to name **the café-owner in *Casablanca***[14] and get to £4,000, they are as loud as they will later be for million-pound wins, and da Costa spills her water. 'You can't be sick in front of your fiancé,' Tarrant advises her.

Two questions later, she's asked, for £16,000:

Which English county has a border with only one other?[15]

    A: Devon   B: Norfolk
    C: Cornwall   D: Kent

footnotes[15] Cornwall.
[14] Rick Blaine.

She phones her father Jack in his hotel room, who says, 'I'm sorry, Rachel, I can't help you on geography.' As the seconds click away, she yelps, 'Dad, help me' and he counsels her, 'Take the eight grand, Rach.'

She does, and falls over on her way out.

Two episodes in, and the audience already has a glimpse of what it will be like when a million-pound cheque is given to a contestant who needs the money. The fairytale has been told in advance. Right now, it's one mere eighth of the only previous win, but it means the world to da Costa – certainly more than a rose bowl would.

'Take the eight grand, Rach': cash creates a drama distinct from that of kudos prizes. Money means different things to different people, which is why it's vital to know more about the contestants on money quiz programmes. They become characters in a story – like *Only Fools and Horses*' Del Boy, who hopes to clear a bill of £50,000 for unpaid tax when he enters the *Millionaire*-proxy *Goldrush* (asked **In which state was President Kennedy when he was assassinated in 1963?**,[16] he answers: 'Well, he was in a terrible state. . .').

What's going on at home determines the real value of money. Take the previous chapter's David Stainer, who in 2002 said that he would trade his *Who Wants to be a Millionaire?* winnings for the *University Challenge* trophy. In 2015, as a father and husband, he looked back on the prize as a useful way of funding his subsequent studies and of finding a foothold on the London property ladder. 'If anything,' he told me, 'the more long-lasting disappointment is not having won more than I did.'

[16] Texas, as alluded to in the Garfield questions above.

By the time Stainer competed in 2001, the first million had finally been won. But it wasn't a rags-to-riches tale; it seemed more like a case of riches-to-riches.

Judith Cynthia Aline Keppel, only the third person to hear their fifteenth question and the first to try to answer it, wasn't the kind of contestant you tended to see on an ITV quiz. In fact, unless you count the fictional 'posh birds' in the channel's comedies and dramas, she wasn't the kind of person seen on ITV full stop.

But hers is an exquisite performance. She meets Tarrant's scurrilous introduction – 'as a garden designer, Judith's ambition is to let Alan Titchmarsh mess about in her shrubbery' – with polite near-laughter, and emits nothing rowdier than an occasional 'wow' as her winnings pile up. After her Phone-a-Friend gets her to £125,000 by completing **the stage direction from *The Winter's Tale* 'Exit, pursued by a . . .',**[17] she chirrups, 'Oh, bless you, Gillie, thanks so much.' Her response to being asked for the patron saint of Spain is 'I'm sorry, but I'd like to do Saint James,' one of many apologies, as if she knows that the programme expects someone who knows the answer to a £500,000 question to jump up and punch the air like Fred Housego didn't. (She also, as Boris Johnson put it, managed to, 'submit without complaint to the Labrador lickings of Chris Tarrant'.)

And when she considers the prospect of one of the programme's horrifying prize-drops, she reflects that '£32,000 is still very nice.' No 'take the thirty-two grand, Jude' advice for this contestant, just an 'I've been very lucky' at the penultimate hurdle.

Everyone watching at home already knew that Keppel was going to take the jackpot: the tale was in the *Sun*, allegedly

17 Again, the answer is bear.

'leaked' by an audience member. Richard Wilson thought that Keppel's victory was 'ever so slightly suspicious'; it went out the same evening that his BBC character Victor Meldrew died in *One Foot in the Grave* and beat it in the ratings game 14 million to 11 million. (Meldrew's demise had also been 'leaked'.)

Viewers and reviewers reckoned there might be something in Wilson's suspicions: Keppel had been given no questions on sport, say, or soap operas. Saints and Shakespeare for six-figure sums; even her Fastest Finger First (**putting the prime ministers Eden, Douglas-Home, Macmillan and Churchill in chronological order**[18]) seemed tailor-made for a contestant with a friend called Gillian, aunts whom she hadn't told about the show because she 'was afraid they might disapprove' and a vicar who bade his congregation, 'Let us all pray for easy questions for dear Judith'. It was also impossible to dislike her.

The relevant TV watchdog was asked to investigate, and cleared ITV of jiggery-pokery. Others remarked that a fix was hardly necessary for Keppel to perform so well. A life of culture and travel, they said, made the last few questions simply easier than they would be for regular punters. When it was reported that Keppel was a cousin to Camilla Parker Bowles, she was dubbed 'Camillionaire' and some purported to trace her lineage, via an Arnold Joost Van Keppel, to the king who appeared in her clinching question:

Which king was married to Eleanor of Aquitaine?[19]

    A: Henry I   B: Henry II
    C: Richard I   D: Henry V

During her deliberations, Keppel told Tarrant: 'I saw her tomb, funnily enough, in France this summer.'

Who Wants to be a Millionaire? was a programme which, deeply unusually, didn't hold auditions, at least in its British infancy. As producer Colman Hutchinson told it, 'Ten people turned up on the day: we knew their names, where they came from, and that was it.'

And who benefited to the tune of a million? Keppel was the first. The sixth and final was the daunting Ingram Wilcox, one of the two civil servants beaten by Housego in 1980. Between came Robert Kempe Brydges, who prompted the terse BBC headline 'Fourth Millionaire "is Millionaire" ', following reports that the former company director already had a million (or two). A neighbour mused that 'gambling on the tricky questions must be a lot easier when you're already worth millions – I suppose £16,000 must seem like loose change to him,' and the show replied, 'We'd love a penniless bin-man as our next winner, but it never happens.' In fact, it seemed that the underdogs tended to have better luck on *Mastermind* and *University Challenge*.

The public had decided that while the working and the middle class might now appear on the same programme, in quiz it still paid to be well off.

And the final scores tell us that . . .

16. Winning isn't everything
Not all quiz champions are winners

A mystery neurological condition cut short the teaching career in Brunei of Anthony Burgess: he was stretchered from the classroom, flown to London and warned never to return to the Tropics. He was astonished by the post-rationing country he returned to, especially by such American concoctions as the big-money quiz. So he lambasted it in a novel.

One Hand Clapping (1961) takes its title from the unanswerable question 'Two hands clap and there is a sound; what is the sound of one hand?', **one of the kōans of which religion?**[1] Using a vocabulary of under a thousand words ('TV', 'baked beans', 'big'), Janet Shirley tells the tale of her husband, Howard, an honourable salesman with a photographic memory. Howard enters *Over and Over*, a quiz hosted by Laddie O'Neill. (A 'sort of American or Irishman, you couldn't be sure which, with a very pointy sort of face', Laddie is modelled on *Double Your Money*'s Hughie Green.)

[1] Zen Buddhism.

But contestant and quiz are not a good match; Howard answers in far more detail than the show requires. Asked **what three sisters wrote books under the name of Bell?**,[2] he gives the Haworth sisters' pseudonyms and their dates of birth and death, forcing the out-of-his-depth Laddie to mumble, 'I haven't got all that written down here.'

Well, of course he doesn't. *Over and Over* doesn't 'do' context. (And neither, usually, do the smarter quizzes: Robert Robinson expected the *Ask the Family* families in 1972 to know **which of the sisters was known as (a) Acton Bell (b) Currer Bell and (c) Ellis Bell**[3] and then of course moved straight on.) It's about regurgitating discrete informational nuggets, and Howard happens to be very good at it; when he took his GCE, the examiners presumed that he had cribbed his answers. 'Howard seemed to have all these interests,' remarks Janet, 'but that was really just his photographic brain.'

When he wins the jackpot and becomes mildly famous, Howard tells a reporter for the *Daily Window* about his memory; the reporter replies that he *had* thought that Howard was 'somebody who loves books': 'I see now that you're not. Just a knack, that's all. A sort of trick. A kind of deformity, I suppose you could call it.'

Howard might be a symptom of a meaningless world, but at least he and Janet have their winnings to keep them happy, right? If you're planning to read it, skip the rest of this paragraph. Howard and Janet begin a life of luxury, but Howard feels that he has denigrated the various writers he gave as quiz answers. Ruminating 'the vulgarity and silliness and the brutishness and nastiness' of the world, he offers Janet what he has become convinced is a wonderful birthday present: a suicide

[3] (a) Anne; (b) Charlotte; (c) Emily.
[2] Charlotte, Emily and Anne Brontë.

pact with barbiturates. Janet reneges and kills Howard with a coal hammer.

Ouch. It's a comic exaggeration, but in real life, too, the winners of the period would not always be what you'd call lucky.

The diary entry for 24 August 1948 by Mrs Jane Caffrey of Wakefield, Rhode Island, begins: 'Took kids to beach in the morning. Very hot. Jim and I went to clambake in the afternoon at Willow Dell. Asked a few people to house for late afternoon. Jim won $24,000 jackpot on *Sing It Again* program. Everybody excited.'

It's just what millions dreamed might one day be in their own journal. Following the clambake, Jane's ex-cop husband, James, received a call from CBS telling him that his telephone number had been selected as one the quiz would call, and so to 'be sure not to use your phone between eight o'clock and nine o'clock'. He presumed it was a prank from the guys at the garage he used but, just in case, plugged in the radio set near to the telephone.

The phone didn't ring until seven minutes to nine: a friend with a dinner invitation. While James was yelling, 'Can't talk! Can't talk!', an electrical storm in Springfield, Missouri cut off a contestant just as she seemed ready to claim the prize. Two minutes later, CBS got through to the Caffreys.

Sing It Again presented its questions in musical form, culminating in the Phantom Voice of some unnamed celebrity. The one James found himself invited to identify was **the movie mogul whose company had merged with Metro Pictures and Goldwyn Pictures in 1924,**[4] and he got it right.

[4] Louis B. Mayer.

As soon as the call was ended, the phone began to ring again – long-forgotten colleagues, press queries, a helpful stranger from New York who claimed the victory was because of her prayers – and didn't stop until after 4 a.m. That night, the family dog Whisky died on the front lawn. James blamed that ominous event on the night's excitement.

In the morning, the Caffreys picked up the Sunday papers (in which they featured) and went to the beach to escape. They were mobbed. James had to recount the previous evening so many times that he concocted a little speech: 'Oh, it won't be quite twenty-four thousand, I'm afraid. That's a radio figure, you know. And don't forget, those tax boys will be after me. Still, I was pretty lucky, I guess.'

He was right that it wasn't $24,000. The jackpot came in the form of various goods and one service – having Mr Caffrey's portrait painted. As that day's *Providence Journal* reported, 'The winner, James Caffrey of Providence Avenue, Wakefield . . . was worried by just one thing – where is he going to store 7,500 cans of soup, one of the major items in the all-inclusive prize.'

And he was right about the tax. The IRS wanted a return on the items as if they *were* real money, and the suppliers told Caffrey that they were forbidden from offering a cash alternative – so, to avoid their stroke of luck making them into people who had a lot of soup and even more substantial debts, the Caffreys spent the next few months trying to offload the prizes.

They took out some warehouse space, but it was filled almost immediately by the cans. Caffrey took his new 'two-thousand-dollar ring' to a local jeweller, who thought that it might fetch $1,200 if the Caffreys could think of somewhere to sell it. Caffrey tried hawking to the boys at the Narragansett racetrack, but their girlfriends preferred 'more conservative' merchandise than the gaudy prize: 'That's the kind of stuff they used to give them in the old gangster days.'

For months, Caffrey balanced his regular job with his new one as an 'abysmally depressed' salesman of second-hand goods – and, with ninety dollars here for the Venetian blinds and $112.32 there for the set of five dozen sheets and pillow-cases, he eventually amassed enough for the tax bill. He gave the soup to his church, to distribute among the hungry.

Not quite the promise or premise of 'That could be me.' It was some consolation to Caffrey, though, to see himself played on the big screen by another James (**one who had starred in movies including *It's a Wonderful World* and *It's a Wonderful Life*[5]**) in a 1950 fast-turnaround comedy called *The Jackpot*, which follows the Caffreys' tale astonishingly faithfully.

Intellectuals' novels and screwball movies alike drew on a public awareness that winning might involve losing. And, to this day, when the winner *does* take home cash, there are often still taxes to pay: one recurring tale is of the contestant who spends what they think they have won before the episode is aired and the prize (minus tax) paid. Such levies are hardly unreasonable, but, if you've been poorly advised, they can be unexpected. Another recurrer is the tale of the champion who, like the lottery winner, is ruined by sudden wealth. Take Marlene Grabherr, the first female winner of *Wer Wird Millionär?*, who became a Millionär in 2001 by answering this question:

Which of the Bee Gees are twins?[6]

A: Robin and Barry   B: Maurice and Robin
C: Barry and Maurice   D: Andy and Robin

5 James Stewart.
6 Robin and Maurice ('Welche beiden Gibb-Brüder der Popband The Bee Gees sind Zwillinge?').

And then, she said, she found herself besieged by demands from her siblings for lavish holidays and luxury cars; she loaned her winnings away until she could no longer afford a dentist, and died from an oral tumour. Equally grim was the fictional fate of Tony Hancock in a 1958 episode of *Hancock's Half Hour*, where his so-called friends mercilessly blackmail him after he wins £4,000 on, effectively, *Take Your Pick*. (**What did 'Take Your Pick' and 'Michael Miles' become rhyming slang for?**[7]) You can almost hear those BBC bosses who worried about the ruinous effects of giving away even a few quid muttering, 'Well, I did tell you so.'

Not that there needs to be money for a winner to lose. In her gently harrowing 2009 documentary *I Won University Challenge*, Alisa Pomeroy talks to former contestants: not the ones who are now household names (such as **the actor whose roles include Harry Potter's Professor Sprout and the Cadbury's Caramel bunny**[8] and **the newsreader who wore a burqa to report from Afghanistan**[9]), but a collection of unsung former champions.

One interviewee reckons that the public's admiration for brainboxes is qualified: 'There's a sense that it's important that *someone* knows things like this. It's like the Statue of Liberty: you don't want to see it all the time, but it's important to know it's there.' Another says of his job as a postman: 'I was certainly capable of a lot more than just delivering bits of paper . . . If you've got a brain, you really ought to be using it.' Asked, 'Do you think you would have achieved more conventionally if you weren't as bright?', he answers with a firm: 'Yeah.'

[9] John Simpson (Magdalene, Cambridge, 1965; he returned to present the 1996 trophy).

[8] Miriam Margolyes (Newnham, Cambridge, 1963; she reckons that she beat Kenneth Tynan by two years to be the first to say the f-word on British television, albeit unnoticed, when she got an answer wrong).

[7] 'Thick'; 'piles'.

The impression is of a tough quiz giving young people the false impression that, once they leave university, something in the outside world will value or even care much about the knowledge they've amassed. In our day jobs, most of us are specialists to the point of routine; we soak up general knowledge the rest of the time, but it's hard to find uses for it.

That goes double for half the population. Speaking as a woman, and also as a temp, another interviewee explains that she doesn't tell her present-day colleagues about her quiz victory or other intellectual achievements 'because I don't want people edging away'. She recalls her mother's proverbial advice to anyone who finds themselves in the position of being both female and visibly intelligent: 'a whistling woman, a crowing hen – no good either to God or men'.

Those exams which begat quiz established an educational legacy which assigned home-ec and good manners for the girls, saving general knowledge for the boys, and it has taken decades for women to find a foothold in quiz. Have things changed? In some ways. In 2009, the day after Oxford's Corpus Christi captain Gail Trimble took the trophy, her brother received a Facebook message from the pornographic magazine *Nuts* asking for her email address because 'we want her to do a tasteful shoot'.

But winning need not always be a story of debt, death, degradation or dashed dreams. Now is perhaps a good moment to remember that there are hundreds of thousands of contented contestants who have gone home with a rotary iron, a waffle iron, or even a simple steam iron.

And at the very top of the quiz tree, there are some jolly tales. It depends how you measure it, but Ken Jennings is, for my money, America's top quiz contestant – partly for his 2004 record-breaking winning streak on *Jeopardy!*, but equally for the affable way he has before or since demolished any (human) opponent. Words like 'geek' and 'nerd' are slippery: sometimes, they mean someone who's unattractive; other times, the 'geek' is merely someone who isn't much fussed by fashion. In other words, a normal person, however anomalous normal people are on television outside of quiz. Anyway, Jennings is of the second type: a sensibly shirted, soberly barbered Mormon.

Over a run of seventy-four episodes of *Jeopardy!*, he won two and a half million dollars, and has since added to that in special editions. In his book *Brainiac*, Jennings, then aged thirty, describes the extraordinary experience of spending 182 days going back and forth between his Salt Lake City home (where he had spent a month watching the show standing up, using his son's ring-stacking toy as a makeshift podium for buzzer practice) and the Los Angeles studios (with the real buzzers).

It's extraordinary not least because of the show's confidentiality contract, which forbids contestants telling anyone how any show has gone until after it has been broadcast, long after recording. Eventually, Jennings had to confide in the boss at his computer-science job to secure an uncanny number of days off: the bogus ailments they concocted must have made his colleagues think of him as a human petri dish rather than a human Wikipedia. He won so many games that he was still playing by the time his first episode aired, leading to farcical cover stories to explain why he was leaving town with such regularity. 'This must be what it feels like,' he wrote endearingly, 'to be a secret agent, or Spider-Man.'

Watching his marathon has something in common with seeing Michael Larson take *Press Your Luck* to the cleaners, except that what makes Jennings remarkable is the absence of sharp practice, and his reign lasts nearly two days of solid screen-time (which took five months to broadcast). It seems for the period as if *Jeopardy!* has changed format entirely: it's now a programme where each episode sees two new contestants walk in, compete with someone who apparently remembers everything, then duly lose and leave. Somewhere around the forty-episode mark, host Alex Trebek quips, 'I know you now like we've been living together': by now, they've ditched the section where the contestants give little anecdotes about their lives and, instead, Trebek offers things like, 'So, Ken, is there anything you'd like to ask me? I've run out of stuff . . .' and Jennings replies ' . . . Um, what did you have for breakfast this morning, Alex?' before getting back to the business of politely vanquishing all-comers.

On and on it goes. Viewers nickname the other contestants 'kennon fodder' as Jennings nails Final Jeopardy questions including **Twentieth-century Vice-presidents: aptly, his middle name contained the word 'rich';**[10] **Theatrical Premières: the 'Playboy Riots' took place in this world capital in 1907;**[11] and **Famous Names: the last thing visitors see in the exhibit area of the Salem Witch Museum is a huge photo of this politician.**[12] For every thirteen questions he's asked, Jennings gets twelve right.

Unseen by us, those other contestants become resigned to their fate. 'It's no great sin to lose to Ken Jennings,' one mutters in the green room, promptly going into the studio and losing to Ken Jennings. This attitude infuriates the Californian estate agent Nancy Zerg, who repeatedly announces, 'Someone's got

10 Who is Nelson Aldrich Rockefeller?
11 What is Dublin? (following a performance of J. M. Synge's *The Playboy of the Western World*).
12 Who is Senator Joseph McCarthy?

to beat him sometime. It might as well be me.' And she gets lucky: the final question goes to just her and Jennings: 'Business and Industry: Most of this firm's 70,000 seasonal white-collar employees work only four months a year.'

Zerg writes down her answer immediately and stands, shoulders heaving, a smile tentatively preparing itself on her face as the beige-shirted Jennings blinks blankly at the board. The moment feels to him 'surreal and wrong', like an exam-anxiety dream.

When the time's up, Trebek takes her answer first. As soon as Jennings hears it, he knows that it's right, that it puts her one dollar in the lead and that his effort ('What is FedEx?') is utterly wrong. Before Trebek has finished giving the scores, the gasping audience rises atypically to its feet as Jennings, grinning, goes to shake Zerg's hand; it develops into a chaste cuddle, then Jennings breaks off to join the applause. 'You are indeed,' intones Trebek, 'a giant killer.'

And Jennings? 'Now, at long last, I know the end of the story and can go home to my family.' He's also relieved that the answer ('What is H&R Block?') is one that he won't kick himself over: H&R Block may be a hugely successful 'tax-preparation company', but Jennings has always filed his own returns.

It's also a deliciously ironic question. For one thing, Jennings says that, as soon as he heard Zerg's answer, he knew that he had lost not on some abstruse minutia but on 'the humanizingly easy question' that millions of viewers would know.

For another, the press were already trying to suss what Jennings's federal and state tax bill would be. (They didn't know that he was also to pay a tithe to his church.) H&R Block shrewdly and publicly offered Jennings free financial services for life.

Jennings in fact did what you would expect a bookworm to do: he borrowed a book from his local library on how to avoid being one of the 75 per cent of windfall-recipients who is out of money within five years. 'I don't want to be one of these lottery winners you see bankrupt on TV a few years later, having already lost it all,' he told the press. 'Some has already gone to charity, and I plan to do a lot more of that.' For a moment, America had to deal with the idea of a millionaire giving a charitable donation for reasons other than a tax break.

'Maybe now,' he also hoped, 'I can stop being Ken Jennings, nerd folk icon, and just be Ken Jennings, nerd, like I was before.' Happily, he didn't. Not quite. Jennings again did exactly what you'd hope he might: he wrote a bunch of factual books, starting with the witty *Brainiac* and continuing with a set of *Junior Genius* guides to ancient Egypt, maps, geography and the like.

That, pretty much, is how quiz ought to work.

Had Jennings won that seventy-fifth show, he would have tied for the obscure record of Most Consecutive TV Quiz Wins with the title-holder Ian Lygo (inevitably, a civil servant), who kept winning the hostless UK show *100%* until the producers announced that they had 'had a letter or two from people saying, "I switch on and if he's still here, unfortunately I switch off,"' and that they had summarily decided to change the rules to cap the number of wins to a number which, coincidentally, was the one Lygo was about to reach.

The professionals

Not long back, the very idea of taking quiz seriously was regarded as iffy. For most of its life, Radio 4's *Brain of Britain* was hosted by *Ask the Family*'s Robert Robinson and when, in 1987, he introduced the retired Kodak production manager Peter Richardson as 'a professional quizzer', the waspish disgust in his clipped tones was palpable.

But Robinson had – uncharacteristically – missed the *mot juste* in 'professional'. It was not then possible to survive on quiz alone: for Richardson, it was less of a living, more of a ferociously serious pursuit, and his apparent sin was to have really gone for it. Starting with Radio 2's *Treble Chance* in 1972, he established his winning methods: he learned that the programme's topical questions were compiled using the *Daily Telegraph* and took that newspaper for three months before taking the prize. He worked out the precise moment to buzz in on the typical *Sale of the Century* question – just before he recalled the answer – and was so sure of winning that show's final that he hired an estate car to take home his booty, into which he duly loaded a hi-fi, some gold . . . everything, in fact, except the Mini he also won.

Grands here, ten grands there: when Richardson entered *The Krypton Factor*, which inventively mixed physical and mental challenges, viewers saw him simply walk the obstacle course, and the show changed its rules to prevent contestants winning through knowledge alone. Had he restricted himself to Radio 2 and ITV and avoided the smarter quizzes, Richardson would probably never have offended Robinson's sensitive nose. But he had the further temerity to enter such programmes as *Mastermind* (where he was a semi-finalist in 1977 with the Fiction of J. R. R. Tolkien) and *Brain of Britain*, without the 'at least we got £30' attitude of a Lord Quinton.

Ten years later, not much had changed. In 1997, Magnus Magnusson wrote this, not of Richardson, but of his only rival in the Mastermind Club's competitions:

Certainly, he takes major competitions very seriously, and wins them with astonishing regularity; but he thinks the use of terms like 'semi-professional' or 'professional' misleading or inappropriate (unless they are used humorously) because they imply some degree of ability to make a living by 'quizzing', which simply cannot be done in this country.

Magnusson was talking of Kevin Ashman. In Ashman, Britain has its quiz king: more unassuming than Richardson – more, in fact, like Ken Jennings.

Ashman's journey has not been unlike Richardson's (he uniquely won *Brain of Britain* while still a reigning Mastermind, say), but it had a different destination.

There is only so far you can go as a winner while retaining a day job: when Ashman won a holiday to the Canaries in 1993 on Sky's adaptation of *Trivial Pursuit*, he realized that civil servants are only allowed to take a specified amount of holidays, whether they've won them on various quiz programmes or not, and was given the cash equivalent.

But add one more decade, and the possibilities for 'professional' quizzers had changed, as had Ashman's work/life balance. In 2003, the BBC tried out a new show, where members of the public competed against a super-team of quiz champions.

The Beeb had tried variations on this theme as early as 1945, with the Home Service's *Quiz-masters Quizzed!*, and champions of existing quizzes later vied with each other in programmes with names like *Supermind* and *Masterbrain*. *Eggheads* has been the most enduring, and would hardly have been worth the name if it didn't have Ashman in its near-unbeatable team.

And now, making a living from quizzing simply *can* be done in this country. Ashman is no longer a civil servant: like Ken Jennings, quiz has allowed him to give up the day job (and the night job of setting *Brain of Britain* questions). ITV's *The Chase* provides similar gigs for another set of champs.

Alongside Ashman in the *Eggheads* resident team is someone who appeared in an earlier chapter – Judith Keppel – and someone who might have. The 1983 Mastermind, Chris Hughes, was a kind of pre-Housego Housego: instead of a taxi, he drove a tube train on **the line which goes between Cockfosters and Heathrow.**[13] It seemed to be Hughes that Bill Bryson had in mind when he described *Mastermind* as an example of something unique to the United Kingdom: 'I have never been able to decide whether that is deeply impressive or just appalling – whether this is a country where engine drivers know about Tintoretto and Leibniz, or a country where people who know about Tintoretto and Leibniz end up driving engines. All I know is that it exists more here than anywhere else.'

Unlike Housego, Hughes's attempts to 'professionalize' his win were stymied by his employers, who figured that if he was so clever, they should hang on to him and get him trained up in those computers which they figured might become important. Come *Eggheads*, though, Hughes and Keppel could play together in a professional super-team.

It's Ashman who the 'civilian' teams fear the most, though, and Ashman who the audience warms to the most: he is, rightly, known to and respected by millions. This is especially the case in his favourite subject. At primary school, Ashman was taught a lot less history than he would have liked, so he effectively set his own syllabus at home. By secondary school, he already knew much of what they intended to teach him, and he hasn't stopped reading since. *Eggheads* contestants learned quickly not to choose Ashman as their opponent in history rounds, after years

13 The Piccadilly line.

of him correctly and effortlessly answering multiple-choice questions such as . . .

Which Dorset village gives its name to the martyrs, the six farm labourers who in 1834 were sentenced to seven years' transportation to Australia for organizing an early form of trade union: is it Bridport, Tolpuddle or Lulworth?[14]

. . . which prompted a 'Strangely enough, I made a point of going there just a few months ago to have a look at the museum'; and, very occasionally, the awkward sudden-death deciders . . .

Which historian and geographer of Greek descent wrote the forty-seven-book _Historical Sketches_ at the beginning of the first century?[15]

. . . which prompted an uncharacteristically blank moment from Ashman, swiftly followed by 'I don't know this one. Or at least, candidates are wandering about. I will try . . .' followed by the correct answer.

Come 2014, Ashman's paramountcy in history has become a running gag. So when a contestant faced with history chooses Ashman as his opponent, we get suppressed giggles and a sense of occasion.

The host, Jeremy Vine, coaxes from Ashman the number of times he has lost a history round 'since the beginning of _Egg-heads_, ten years ago' (it's actually zero) and the number of history _questions_ he has got wrong in that decade ('Same,' admits Ashman, breezily adding, 'It'll happen.') As the questions come, Vine ratchets up the tension ('He may weaken!' 'Will lightning strike here?') until the last, which Ashman

15 Strabo.
14 Tolpuddle.

needs to answer correctly to avoid elimination: 'Historically, Kevin, **what item of clothing was a mandilion: a cap, a shoe or a jacket?**'[16]

'Ah,' says Ashman, immediately knowing that he doesn't know and sending a warning that something unusual is going to happen.

I'm far from alone in that I tend to zone out of the contestants' out-loud reasoning on *Eggheads*, but this time I'm riveted. 'I'll rule out cap,' he begins. OK. But why? Do the linguistics seem wrong? Does he know caps better than he knows foot- and outer-wear? Is it merely a hunch? We can only guess (much like anyone asked a question about a mandilion).

The giggles are gone. The other Eggheads twitch and fidget. Ashman tries aloud the expression 'mandilion . . . jacket' to see how it sounds. Nothing grabs him. He ponders the word itself again, trying to find a way in. 'It looks like something that could be ceremonial . . .' and then the answer drops: 'I'll try shoe.' He shrugs with the grace of a champion sportsman who knows that he is not unbeatable. 'I really don't know.'

Boom.

What's striking about the moment that follows is the distance between Vine's fitting excitement at the creation of '*Eggheads* history' and Ashman's lovable impassivity.

It's a cracking piece of television, but for me it's more: it's a moment that shows us where quiz had reached. We see a civil servant (well, of course – civil servants are rivalled only by teachers for the profession most seen outside the big-money quiz programmes) who has devoted his life to general knowledge. He's honed his chops on both strands of British quiz, furthered his reputation in the world of league quiz, all the

16 A jacket.

while learning the lists. And now he's on a team with a Millionaire and a former train driver, in a format which has combined the worlds of kudos quiz (the Eggheads) and money shows (the challengers play for cash). *Who Wants to be a Millionaire?* is a month from ending in the UK, but the BBC has found one of those compromises it was seeking in the 1950s, where the champions play 'for something which money can't buy, the Eggheads' reputation', having made quiz into much more than a hobby. And the end of Ashman's history streak shows that chance will always provide an upset, eventually.

17. Slight difference of opinion here, Jim

Accusations and recriminations

Sometimes, the answer to a question comes from, um, somewhere other than your memory. And sometimes, you have the opportunity to make out that you knew it all along.

Nine per cent of quizzers, for example, have pretended that they knew the answer in a TV or radio quiz once they've heard the right one being given. One in ten have looked up an answer when playing an online quiz. And in pub quizzes, the sharp practice is even sharper. Eleven per cent of us have used a phone in a pub quiz. Around the same number have done the following: given an ambiguous answer hoping for the benefit of the doubt (10%); eavesdropped on another team (11%); audibly discussed a wrong answer to stymie another team (12%). And more than one in four (27%) have used another team's answer after accidentally (they claim) overhearing or seeing it.

Small wonder that these things can get heated. In 2005, a BBC report described a Bristol pub quiz where a dispute over a single question was described by one contestant as 'a

Wild West-style brawl' and resulted in mass arrests – since those taken to the cells included the host, the quiz continued there.

At least brawls are over quickly. A question at the King's Arms in Bedford in 2002 spawned a legal dispute that wasn't resolved for over two years. The long-serving host, Tony Barclay, finished each quiz night with a jackpot challenge. On the fateful evening, for a pot which had accumulated over sixteen weeks, teams had to write down the names of the first five presenters of the BBC's lottery programme.

This question is not pub quiz's finest hour, and it would be easy to imagine the conversations among the contestants, even if they hadn't become part of the court evidence. **The first 'proper' lottery host**[1] is a clear enough answer (though do you include her co-host, Gordon Kennedy?) – then it gets hazy around stand-ins, or hosts who had a run of two or three weeks. And what about Noel Edmonds, who hosted just the launch edition?

One team had a query: were they only looking for *regular* presenters? Then two bad things happened. Barclay said, 'Yes, just regular presenters' – but didn't check that this still fitted his answer sheet. The other bad thing was that Dave Crane, who by his reckoning had been to over a thousand pub-quiz nights, pricked up his ears.

He insisted that Barclay confirm the new wording. (Another contestant told the local paper that Crane's three-man team No Fear were nicknamed No Fun by the other teams because of their habit of disputing answers.) Crane duly crossed out Noel Edmonds's name and added Phillip Schofield's. 'As a team,' he later insisted in court, 'we knew with 100 per cent certainty

[1] Anthea Turner.

that Noel Edmonds had only presented the first edition of the National Lottery as a celebrity guest.'

'Schofield' was not in the answer then read out by Barclay. 'Edmonds' was. Crane remonstrated, but this was the era before smartphones could settle such things on the fly. No Fear were denied the jackpot, but they did have the moral high ground – at least for a moment.

Grouching over a dodgy question is part and parcel of pub quiz. Less typical is what happened the next day. Unlike most pub-quiz teams, No Fear had a public website, where Crane published a special new post headed 'Read a True Account of What Happened When Tony Barclay Ripped Us Off', which accused Barclay of being a cheat and a fraudster and warned punters to stay away from his quiz nights. For good measure, he also contacted the Fraud Squad.

If, rather than defaming Barclay, Crane had merely castigated him for a dodgy question, that might have been the end of it. But an ugly spiral began: Barclay asked Crane to remove the libellous post; Crane refused; Barclay's solicitors asked Crane to remove the post; Barclay asked Crane to pay the solicitors' fees; Crane refused, and so the courts got involved (that's 'courts' plural: Northampton, Bedford and Luton county courts, the High Court and merrily back to Luton County Court). Throughout, Crane insisted that this was a case not of an honest mistake but of being swindled. It's a warning to any host that workings on some question or other might someday end up as Exhibit A. Noel Edmonds was never called as a witness, but at times it seemed like he might be.

In the final trial, Judge John Hamilton seemed nonplussed. 'I doubt,' he pronounced, 'that very often a question in a pub quiz can have led to a full-scale defamation case two years later' – a fair comment, perhaps, but one which underestimates the tenacity of the ardent pub-quizzer. He called Crane's plea of justification 'clearly preposterous' and instructed him to pay £5,000 damages and £12,500 legal fees.

The jackpot prize would have been £210. But it was never about the money.

When it *is* about the money, there's even more pressure on the questions. Compare the original *Fifteen to One* (where contestants hoped to win an archaeological artefact and host William G. Stewart adjudicated on not-quite-wrong answers) to its revamp (where the worthy winner takes home £40,000 and Sandi Toksvig is, accordingly, much stricter about matching answers to what's on the card).

(Stewart could be strict when he had to be, though: contestant Trevor Montague decided that the rule debarring former contestants from reappearing didn't apply to him and reappeared with slicked-back hair and an earring as the apparently Italian 'Steve Romana'. After his 'Montague' shows were repeated on Challenge, this one went to court too, and 'Romana' had to return the Greek vase he had swagged.)

Fifteen to One has confrontation built into its rules, but it has always been a fair and decent quiz. When the millennium started, other shows decided that dispensing with decency might prove attention grabbingly innovative. 'We broke every single rule,' insisted Anne Robinson when she took her show to America, unnecessarily adding, '*The Weakest Link* has not left a television rule in place.' What she meant was that she was rude to the contestants.

It's true that there was novelty in witnessing a host seething with contempt because a contestant had failed to identify **the creature which has knobbly knees and turned-out toes and a poisonous wart at the end of his nose.**[2]

2 A gruffalo (from the book by Julia Donaldson and Axel Scheffler).

While it may have been directly influenced by *Big Brother*, *The Weakest Link* (bad working title: *Money Chain*) was positively genteel compared to, say, *Truth or Consequences*, the 1940s American show which took the carnival aspect further, offering $15 for correct answers and penalties for wrong guesses, such as lying on a sheet next to a female seal and imitating the mating call of the male. A 1955 op-ed in the *Picture Post* reckoned that cruel quiz was 'in keeping with our times. We do not destroy those who have lost. We make them eat a bowl of jelly with chopsticks.'

The Robinson vehicle was, though, successful. Five years in, it was named as the TV programme with the second-most international versions (96, behind *Who Wants to be a Millionaire?*'s 106), and it began a mini-era of nasty quiz – *The Enemy Within*, *Dog Eat Dog*, *King of the Castle*, *Greed*, *Divided*, *Shafted* and the rest – which dabbled with various combinations of hostility and rudeness, even when the host didn't seem like their heart was really in the abuse (Ulrika Jonsson).

Following *The Weakest Link*'s American launch, Fox even tried a show called *The Chamber*, whose contestants ostentatiously signed a release form before answering questions from 'torture chambers' where they were covered in ice, blasted with hot air, and so on. It went out in the same month that the Red Cross went into Guantanamo Bay. Six episodes of *The Chamber* were recorded; three were broadcast.

Happily, the fad fizzled. The most successful quizzes of the 2010s have gone many miles in the other direction: in *Pointless*, the hosts gallantly pretend to believe that some atrocious guesses might be right, while the boffins who defend *The Chase*'s jackpot feign belligerence in a tone which is closer to panto, and all the better for that.

*

After His Honour Geoffrey Rivlin QC gave his summing-up in the case of R *v.* Ingram, C., Ingram, D. and Whittock, T., he called the jury back. They were no longer to discuss the verdict, as one of them had apparently been overheard in a nearby pub gabbling excitedly about the trial. He was in dereliction of his civic responsibilities, but his exhilaration was understandable. This was not ordinary jury duty. It was also no ordinary trial in that the evidence – in the sense of the facts presented in the courtroom – seemed to have no bearing on the outcome.

The defendants were Charles Ingram, his wife, Diana, and another *Who Wants to be a Millionaire?* contestant, Tecwen Whittock; they were charged with 'dishonestly procuring Christopher Tarrant to sign a cheque', and the cheque had been made out for, naturally, a million pounds.

And so the jury got to see something that no member of the public had, but that everyone had talked about: a recording of the third time Tarrant wrote such a cheque, a year and a half before. Not only that, but they saw material that is routinely edited out of a broadcast show, including Tarrant's scurrilous banter. And they got to play along. It was as much fun as you could have in Southwark Crown Court, for everyone except Whittock and the Ingrams. It was also unusual for another reason: everyone already knew the story.

Though Ingram's run to the top was not broadcast, the nation was very familiar with him: the events of 10 September 2001, when Tarrant handed over the cheque, made a welcome diversion from stories about the following day and its aftermath. The press had a new Charles and Diana to play with. Unlike Judith Keppel, they didn't have any apparent connections to royalty, but they, too, were seen as broadly 'posh': Ingram was Major Charles Ingram.

A cheat is one thing: a cheating senior officer, though – that gets your attention. Pundits and the public marvelled at the apparent audacity: to pull off a million-pound sting right in front of the cameras!

For the jury, it was like a lo-tech heist movie: the prosecution case was that a crime had probably been committed, and the job was to work backwards and figure out how.

Operation Durban, as the police investigation was termed, had wondered whether Ingram was wearing a vibrating pager on each limb: left arm for option A, right arm for B, and so on. There was no evidence for it, but perhaps the Ingrams had scrapped this ruse and replaced it with another, where an accomplice was giving hints in the form of *coughs*: one cough for A, two coughs for B . . . ? And – audacity again – might this this accomplice have been Tecwen Whittock, sitting metres away in Millionaire's Row, hoping to be the next contestant? Such entertaining lines of enquiry had found their way into the *Sun* and, from there, into media around the world.

The Ingrams' role was less entertaining: they had only to insist on their innocence. The major also needed to rebut the impression that he couldn't have got the answers without help: he gave evidence sporting a tiny Mensa badge.

Sometimes he came across as trying too hard. In his penultimate question, he had been asked to choose the city which was redeveloped by Baron Haussmann and had changed his mind to Paris at the last moment. In court, Ingram gave this account of his reasoning:

> I knew that Paris was a planned city. The centre of Paris was cleared of slums during the nineteenth century, and it was rebuilt into districts and boulevards. Prominent in my mind was the economic reason. In the middle of the nineteenth century, France was coming out of the revolutionary period and it was decided, I think by Napoleon III, that . . .

If a defendant gave that testimony nowadays, you'd wonder if he'd swallowed a page of Wikipedia. Ingram's circumstantial problem was that while an innocent man might give this account, so, too, would a guilty man who'd had time to look it up. The court heard the recording of the question, with a cough highlighted before Ingram gave the answer.

This was a key piece of evidence; it also prompted an outbreak of laughter so loud that Judge Rivlin had to intervene with a threat to send everyone out.

But His Honour couldn't stem the relentless jollity. At times, he was part of it: in one among many diversions, a lawyer asked Chris Tarrant why TV's waiting-around spaces are called green rooms. Tarrant didn't know, but Judge Rivlin interjected, 'I can tell you that I do know that, my wife being a musician. I'll tell you later.' The rest of the court booed, as if the judge were going to an ad break at a tense moment, so he relented and **revealed his answer.**[3]

The jurors got to play along with the real quiz questions, too: prosecuting counsel asked for the tape to be stopped during Ingram's final question . . .

A number one followed by one hundred zeros is known by what name?[4]

A: Googol

B: Megatron

C: Gigabit

D: Nanomole

. . . so that the jury could guess the answer. Another interjection from Judge Rivlin: 'Do you pay up if they get it right?'

---

[3] 'There are two reasons. The first because it is behind the scenes and at one point there was a strain of green paint which was very cheap. Another reason given is because the artists say it is the time when they are about to go on stage and they are turning green.

[4] Googol (following Google's initial public offering in 2004, the number which inspired its name became much more widely known as users googled 'Why is it called Google?').

Other questions – of a 'making-of'-*Millionaire* kind, which fans had pondered for years – were answered, too. Yes, said Tarrant, the cheque props were actual cashable cheques, and he had been happy to hand the major his. No, he didn't know the right answers, unless he already happened to. What about his habit of going to breaks? His screen, he explained, which displayed a handy reminder of how much a contestant stood to lose, might flash up 'Break Available' or 'Break Now': 'Sometimes,' he said, 'it's quite fun to make them sweat a bit – and sometimes not. That is something I control.'

The court also learned about a subculture that few had encountered: the aspiring contestants who did a lot more than simply ring the entry line and hope to be chosen.

Diana Ingram, in fact, had been a contestant in April of the same year and left with £32,000, after getting this one wrong:

Who wrote the nonsense poem, 'The Hunting of the Snark'?[5]

    A: GK Chesterton   B: Hilaire Belloc
    C: Edward Lear   D: Lewis Carroll

And a few months before *that*, her brother Adrian Pollock had also dropped back to £32,000 on his own question eleven:

In the USA and Canada, Labor Day is celebrated in which month?[6]

    A: May   B: July
    C: September   D: November

Sister and brother, it became clear, thought about the programme *a lot*. They had assembled their tips and theories into

[6] May.
[5] Lewis Carroll (accept Charles Dodgson).

a book, *Millionaire: An Insider's Guide*. After Charles's win was announced, a publisher had added him as an author and accepted the manuscript; it was never to appear.

So what were their tips? Pollock had more to offer would-be Millionaires than advising them to simply ring the number as often as their phone bill could handle. He studied the programme website to discern, from its timeline of when people called most often, which calls were more likely to land him in the studio. It seemed to work for him. Hurdle one cleared.

But his Fastest Finger First let him down. And so, like Ken Jennings, Pollock concocted a gismo at home, from six pounds' worth of basic kit, and practised. Eventually, playing the real thing, he got a question so simple that it all came down to speed . . .

Starting with the smallest, put the answers to these sums in their correct order.[7]

A: Half of 10
B: Third of 9
C: Quarter of 8
D: Fifth of 5

. . . and 7.1 seconds later, he claimed the hot seat. Tarrant mentioned his previous appearances and observed that he had not stumbled 'through lack of trying'.

Most viewers didn't give that a second thought, but the devoted demi-monde of aspiring contestants was intrigued. Four visits to Millionaire's Row must mean you know some secret.

Fatefully, one of them was Tecwen Whittock, who used the electoral roll to work out where to find Pollock. And since Pollock was trying to help Diana get on the show, the pair then

7 D, C, B, A: Fifth of 5 (1); Quarter of 8 (2); Third of 9 (3); Half of 10 (5).

shared tips. (One of their stranger theories was that when you called, you should crudely disguise your accent using a kind of robot voice, in case the show had regional quotas.) The relationship continued: Pollock lent Whittock his Fastest Finger First doodad. More fatefully still, Whittock did manage to get on – not during Diana's run, but during Charles's.

For the prosecution, some evidence that Whittock (the alleged code-cougher) and Charles (the alleged beneficiary) had spoken would have been helpful. Proof that they had then hatched a plan would have been a smoking gun. But perhaps they didn't need a smoking gun. The court heard about the contact between Whittock and Pollock, and later between Whittock and Diana. It might not have been illegal, but it was surely evidence that these were Odd People Who Loved a Quiz Show Too Much. Nowadays, such tactics would be discussed in a Facebook group of super-fans. And one thing these super-fans would do is post YouTube compilations of Chris Tarrant's body language.

Among the many talents Tarrant brought to *Who Wants to be a Millionaire?* was inscrutability. Contestants just couldn't read him. When he asked if you were sure, did that mean he knew the answer himself, so you should change your guess? What did it mean when he leaned in to you? Leaned back from you? Did he want certain contestants to win?

Yes, he told the court. Quite often, he said, he found himself 'thinking, "Please, please, please give me your final answer, I know you're right" – but I keep that strange face.' More secrets! Wait, though: tell us more about that face: 'I have developed a strange, impassioned face that hopefully does not give them a clue to whether they are right or wrong . . . When the money gets up to serious amounts, and certainly when you get up to £64,000 and up to one million, it is absolutely essential. I am very, very aware exactly what I am thinking.'

The court had seen that face many times. Judge Rivlin went so far as to wryly suggest ('I think I know what the witness means') that in his own line of work, he had to use the same face. In case of doubt, Tarrant announced, 'Well, it's like this,' and over-knitted his brows for the benefit of a delighted courtroom.

This did, in fact, relate to the case; the major had spent what seemed like a decade answering his tenth question.

Who had a hit UK album with *Born to Do It*, released in 2000?[8]

A: Coldplay   B: Toploader

C: A1   D: Craig David

50:50 offered Ingram A1 and Craig David, and left him none the wiser. The case against him was that his inane babbling was to solicit a Whittock cough after either 'A1' or 'Craig David'; his defence was that, since Tarrant was a DJ, he had, like other contestants, been hoping for an inadvertent Tarrant cue (like the audience gasp when he considered A1 as a final answer). Or even an advertent cue: 'I just felt he was willing me not to go for A1.'

So the jury found themselves having to seriously ponder a contestant's state of mind when Tarrant says, 'It's up to you – I can't influence your judgement at all.'

For the prosecution, this was beside the point. Charles's prevarication was seeking a signal all right. But it was all about the coughs. If the jury learned a lot about the making of *Who Wants to be a Millionaire?*, they learned more than they could ever have dreamed about coughing.

The theory that had a single cough meaning option A and four coughs D had been abandoned – the recording didn't back it up. So, what if it there *had* been a coughing code, but maybe

[8] Craig David.

one where it was nigh on impossible to tell what was really going on? Perhaps a gentle cough might signify something like 'Go with what you've just said' and an indignant cough 'What, are you crazy? Abort!'

If this was the plan, Whittock (who went home with £1,000 when he got his turn) was a woeful choice of conspirator. He brought to the court a doctor's note – or rather, the defence brought a professor of respiratory medicine with the news that Whittock had a triple-whammy: dust allergy, hay fever and asthma, for which he carried a mini-apothecary of cures and salves. Nerves alone, the court was told, could trigger in Whittock involuntary coughs. Nobody could deny that Whittock was a cougher.

And there had certainly been a lot of coughs in the Elstree studio that night. Many were Whittock's – others were from the audience, perhaps triggered by their own nerves, maybe by Whittock's coughs. The court itself suffered ripples of coughing, especially when coughing was part of the evidence, which was often. Before Judge Rivlin's summing-up, there was so much coughing that he announced that he had 'wondered whether it was safe to hear a coughing case in March' and took an early adjournment.

A courtroom lost to reflex coughing while considering pre-meditated coughing: the absurdity was lost on no one – and this was the real challenge for the prosecution. There were coughs during Charles's deliberations, but then there were coughs everywhere, so their job was to eliminate any reasonable doubt that most of the coughs around the correct answers were Whittock's, and that Whittock coughed more often when the correct answer was mentioned than the rest of the time.

All they could do was to play the jury recordings, which drew their attention to what were termed 'particular coughs', and hope that a conspiratorial pattern might seem to emerge. A sound expert called as a witness conceded that 'forensic analysis of coughing is relatively uncharted territory', adding, 'We are ploughing a virgin furrow here.' A police 'source' later told the *Telegraph*, 'I've never thought that we've been able to find every piece of the jigsaw.' Still, once you've been told to listen for it, hearing an amplified cough after the laughing-stock Ingram mused something daft like, 'I think it's a hat,' was deeply funny.

And that was enough.

Having got past Southwark's own coughing pandemic, Judge Rivlin gave the jury his summing-up. 'Do not be over-critical and over-analytical,' he told them. 'This was, after all, a game show – although the stakes proved to be very high.'

So the jury (minus the ejected blabbermouth) retired to give their final answer. A successful quiz contestant sometimes has to set aside reasonable doubt to get to an answer. Here, there was little doubt what they would come back with.

But the first time they returned, their verdict was puzzling. They had heard evidence that Whittock and Diana had been in contact but none suggesting that Whittock and Charles had. However, a majority found Charles and Whittock guilty; Diana, they couldn't agree on. When the official history of Southwark Crown Court's many fraud trials is written, this will probably not be recorded as the best example of a jury having understood a case. Perhaps if the Ingrams had been tried in a Scottish court, they would have got **the third verdict available there**,[9] where the defendant comes across as guilty but the evidence isn't top-notch.

They were sent back out, and came back twenty minutes later with a 'guilty' for Diana, too. Sentencing time. This was 'a

[9] Not proven.

most unusual case', said Judge Rivlin. 'I am not at all sure,' he added, 'it was sheer greed that motivated this offence': 'I am sure all three of you were besotted with quiz programmes and the ambition to be successful on a major television show. It was this which caused you to wonder whether you could beat and, it has to be said, cheat the system.'

And the punishment? 'Thank your lucky stars that you are not going to prison' (which infuriated the press). Referring to the Ingrams' three daughters, Judge Rivlin said, 'There's no way I'm going to deprive these children of their parents.' So their eighteen-month sentences were suspended for two years and they were fined £15,000 each, plus £20,000 costs. For Whittock, a suspended twelve-month sentence, a £10,000 fine and £7,500 costs. The million-pound cheque had, of course, been cancelled. Financial and professional ruin were, judged the judge, punishment enough.

And the fun was over. It had been an expensive party. Some estimated the cost of the trial at half a million pounds; others, inevitably, at a million. And some wondered whether public money – or the police – need have been involved at all in a case of alleged cheating in a private game. Instead of R *v.* Ingram, C. &c, could this not have been a civil matter between the Ingrams and the show? In their contract, contestants agreed that 'the Company may refuse to pay winnings or reclaim all sums paid to Show Players in the event of a reasonable suspicion of his/her fraud, dishonesty, or non-entitlement to participate in the Competition under the Rules'.

As the dust was settling, Stephen Glover wrote in the *Daily Mail*, 'The proper thing to do in these circumstances would surely have been for Celador to withhold the £1 million which was not rightfully Major Ingram's and invite him to sue for the prize in the civil courts at his own expense if he was so inclined.'

During the trial, in one of Southwark's many corridors, the journalist Jon Ronson put the same thought to one of the arresting officers. 'This trial,' he was told, 'is about protecting the integrity of the *Millionaire* format.'

It's unlikely that a civil case would have caught the public imagination in the same way. The trial operated as pre-production for Celador's enormously entertaining documentary *Major Fraud*, where the Ingram questions were broadcast for the first time, less than a fortnight after the verdict. Almost 17 million people watched, and the first advert was for Benylin cough mixture.

Also paying attention was an Indian diplomat. The trial gave Vikas Swarup an idea for a novel. 'If a British army major can be accused of cheating,' he figured, 'then an ignorant tiffin boy from the world's biggest slum can definitely be accused of cheating.' And so he wrote *Q&A*, which begins with the line, 'I have been arrested. For winning a quiz show' and which was adapted as the fourth movie from Celador Films, *Slumdog Millionaire*. There had been talk of adapting the Ingrams' tale for the big screen. *Slumdog Millionaire* is the opposite of what that would have been: you root for the contestant, not for the big show, and the underdog millionaire literally makes a song and dance of his eventual victory. It's a testament to the sheer narrative powers of the prosecution in the Ingrams case that they managed to persuade a real-life jury to go the other way.

18. You can't win them all

The shame of being wrong

> And don't forget, it's not the winning that counts: it's the not doing so badly you make a total pillock of yourself.
>
> Lee in 'Pointless', *Not Going Out*

Britain loves to laugh at wrong answers. The wrongest are gathered into Facebook posts, YouTube channels, newspaper articles and entire TV programmes. Here are some from *The Weakest Link*:

Thirteen is known as a '*what* dozen'?[1] Half.

What G is a boneless corset?[2] G-string.

Which royal family member was on the two-hundredth show of *A Question of Sport*?[3] Ricky Tomlinson.

Of what is botany the study?[4] Bottoms.

What is the full first name of presenter Dec, of Ant and Dec fame?[5] Anthony.

5 Declan.
4 Plants.
3 Princess Anne.
2 Girdle.
1 Baker's dozen.

We guffaw at the sheer imbecility of the contestant who, we imagine, imagines that Kew's Botanical Gardens showcases bottoms from around the world. We even borrow some of the sounds of quiz – 'quack quack oops', 'bzzt wrong' or even the sound of a buzzer (something like 'nnh-nnnnk') – and use them in conversation when charmlessly correcting friends and family on matters factual.

We don't tend to imagine how long it would take any of us – with audiences in the studio and at home waiting for our answer, with those 4,000-lux lights beating on us, with our larynxes sucking downwards any remaining fluid from our pharynxes, leaving our tongues flaying with all the purpose of a beached porpoise – to say something preposterous. Ten minutes? Five? One? Psychologists might describe the experience using the 'Yerkes–Dodson law', according to which a little stress can up your game, but a little more and anyone who's trying to perform 'on demand' in front of others very soon finds themselves fluffing things they would otherwise find a doddle.

In the moment, the quiz contestant's brain often, and reasonably, tells the mouth that 'don't know' or 'pass' will guarantee zero points, while *any words whatsoever* increase the chances of scoring to at least something. So let's hear it for the wild, wildly wrong guessers! Let them not be inhibited by the risk of appearing in some future collection of humiliating gaffes. After all, any fluffs uttered by the apparently infallible host will be re-recorded at the end; it's seldom those of the benighted contestants.

At least most unlucky guessers tend to remain nameless. For others, the indignity is so personal and so prolonged that they become hapless news items, named as well as shamed. This happens more often with the kudos quiz programmes. Failing to answer harder questions might be easier to do, but the very act of entering a tough quiz is to set yourself up, and so, it seems, there is further to fall.

Mastermind goes out of its way to minimize the chances of ignominy: making the questions in the final a little less terrifying, say, or the decision in the 1980s to tailor a couple of general-knowledge questions to each contender, to let them play to their strengths and maintain their confidence.

Another *Mastermind* tradition is advising applicants not to choose as their specialized subject something from their line of work. The idea here is that those who have suffered the bad luck of a terrible night can maintain integrity and dignity when back in the workplace.

This advice was not followed by grammar-school art teacher Arfor Wyn Hughes.

By 1989, he had spent, in his words, 'twelve or fourteen years' building and imparting his knowledge of art, in particular of Impressionism and Post-Impressionism. He was a long-standing fan of the show, and read four books a week. As a scion of the Stockport and District Pub Quiz League, his general knowledge should have been fine.

So why should he choose any specialized subject other than the one he knows the best? He considers the Life and Works of Henri de Toulouse-Lautrec, but that's been done before, so he goes for the broader Impressionist Painting and Post-Impressionist Painting 1830–1914. 'It'll be,' he tells himself, 'a piece of cake.'

Still, once he is accepted on to the show, he mugs up, to shorten the odds of losing the odd point on some name, title or date, until he's happy that what's in his memory will tide him 'through any questions that could be thrown at me'.

He arrives at the Great Hall at the University of Lancaster

for the first episode of the eighteenth series in the standard male-contender costume of a suit minus jacket but plus crested tie. He is fairly happy and assuredly confident, and remains so during the afternoon's rehearsal, which rattles through some old sets of general-knowledge questions and which he wins by four points. This will all be fine.

The audience in place, the lights dip and the theme tune 'Approaching Menace' – or, as Hughes later terms it, 'that dreadful music' – is piped in. Something changes. He actually feels his confidence leave his body.

Somewhere in Hughes's consciousness, Magnus Magnusson welcomes the applicants who will shortly be upon 'our faithful old Black Chair, which has been with us, man and boy, chair and stool, for all these seventeen years'.

Throughout this introduction, the other three contenders sit with their hands in tidy laps; at the end of the row, the art teacher has already crossed both arms and both legs, and closed both eyes for good measure. That ambience, created of Bill Wright's memories of his Gestapo interrogation rooms, does something similar to Hughes:

Mr Hughes, you have two minutes on Impressionist and Post-Impressionist Painting between those dates . . .

The millions who will be watching at home won't expect to get many of the specialized-subject questions right, but they will expect the contenders to, and some of them should have a fair chance at the first one, which is really only there to let the contender settle into that chair, answer without even thinking and get in the right mood for more challenging stuff. Hughes steels himself.

'Now,' continues Magnusson, '**in April 1874** . . .' (even if you're still a little nervy, this is a sportingly phrased opener,

247

with the key information at the end) '. . . **which critic coined the term "Impressionist?"** '[6]

It's all over before the reply comes.

Hughes offers 'Vauxcelles'. In some ways, this is not a bad answer: Louis Vauxcelles, they say, coined 'Fauvism' and 'Cubism'. In more important ways, it's a terrible one. He didn't coin 'Impressionism'. The answer is wrong. More importantly, it punches Hughes square in the brain. It seems impossible to him that anyone with a grasp of the Impressionists might forget where the word 'Impressionists' came from, but he has to accept that he has managed it.

Hughes has a little extra time to get past this – in the answer, Magnusson gives one of his trademark manglings of the French tongue, followed by a correction – but in the time it has taken for Hughes to get focused, more questions have somehow been asked.

Here's one you could guess without having ever heard of Claude Monet: **In what distressing circumstances did Monet paint a portrait of his wife Camille in 1879?**[7]

Usually on *Mastermind*, the zooming-in camera captures facial expressions of intense frustration, followed by relief and a shifting of bottom, poise returning. Hughes is frozen throughout. When he sees it later, he will describe himself as 'a bump on a log'. He stares.

Halfway through eternity, he is asked for **the name of the dwarf in Cézanne's painting submitted to the Salon in 1870.**[8] All he can think of to say is 'Who's Cézanne?' That he doesn't actually do so is scant comfort.

[8] Cézanne's friend and fellow artist Achille Emperaire.

[7] She was on her deathbed.

[6] Louis Leroy, in *Le Charivari*. He did not intend the term as a compliment.

As each question comes in, he's thinking about the previous one and why he hadn't managed to give an answer which he knew he knew. And if you've totally missed the question, and all you know is that it's about Impressionist Painting and Post-Impressionist Painting 1830–1914, you can't even proffer a better-than-nothing guess. What would *you* say? 'Monet'? 'Manet'? '1840'? 'Impressionist'?

The only word you can say is 'pass'. And the next time, 'pass' again. And so saying 'pass' takes a grip on Hughes. Magnusson will later describe the phenomenon to him as 'a pass spiral'.

Still they come: **In Gauguin's painting entitled *Ia Orana Maria* or *Ave Maria*, in what unusual pose does he show the Christ child?**[9] Hughes would have been better off if his specialized subject were the Second Law of Thermodynamics.

He isn't aware how many times he's passed. Every *Mastermind* contendor knows that 'the number of passes' will count against them, but Hughes hasn't got there yet. He hasn't realized how badly he's done.

There's a hint of awareness in his slump as the *peep-peep-peep* indicates the end of the round, and the ghost of a grimace at his score of five, but the general-knowledge doesn't go much better. Magnusson tactfully announces his score as quickly as possible while remaining audible – 'And-in-fourth-place-with-twelve-points-is-Arfor-Wyn-Hughes' – then draws breath as if changing subject – 'In third place with twenty-two points . . .' The runner-up has twenty-six points; the winner twenty-eight.

It's not until a 'charming young girl' from the BBC asks him backstage how it feels to have done so badly that the penny drops.

[9] On Mary's shoulder (not to mention as a Tahitian).

In a flash of self-awareness, Hughes recalls watching *Mastermind* from his armchair, thinking, 'Why on earth are those people on this programme? They don't know anything!' and he suddenly sees that it was a disaster, and one that hasn't yet been broadcast. For the audience at home, not privy to all the answers he nearly gave, Arfor Wyn Hughes will be the epitome of 'those people'. Typically of a teacher, he feels that he has not just let himself down, he has let the audience down, and he has let Magnusson down. Then Magnusson is there, putting an arm around him – 'Never mind, Arfor' – and repeating the words he has given to abler performers: It's only a bloody game.

On the first Sunday evening of the new year, the first episode of series eighteen is broadcast. Mrs Hughes tells Arfor that she has invited some friends, so as not to make it too sombre a viewing. But this is not to be an intimate disgrace. In fact, *chez* Hughes is host to a horde of friends, neighbours, the Stockport and District Pub Quiz League, a Spanish couple, a photographer from the local press and a collection of helium balloons bearing the word 'PASS'.

Term starts.

The children are merciless. In the corridors, there are no words: just unbroken voices humming 'Approaching Menace'. Some of the pupils have seen his humiliation; everyone has heard about it. Lessons become impracticable. Any question he puts to a class – **What colour do you get when you mix blue and yellow paint?**[10] – is met with the same, sniggered, four-letter word.

Kids can be cruel; so, too, can teachers. Hughes's colleagues begin to refer to him using **the three-word nickname of the**

10 Green.

much-derided sportsman who had recently become the first to represent Great Britain in ski-jumping at the Olympics.[11] And that is the end of the teaching career of Arfor Wyn Hughes. At the end of the next school year, he again takes the only option available to him – early retirement, the professional equivalent of 'pass'. Poignantly echoing the pre-*Mastermind* lives of Fred Housego and his namesake Chris, he drives a bus and then a taxi.

And, in fact, despite what the crowing newspaper coverage insists, Hughes does not even have the iffy distinction of being the worst *Mastermind* contender, before or since – but choosing his professional interest as his specialized subject has made him legendary. This is neither perch-toppling (Hughes was not the director of the National Gallery) nor *schadenfreude* (he's a likable Welshman who, in Magnusson's words, 'deserves some sort of accolade as the most sporting loser we ever had on the programme'). It's just a sad story.

But it has a semi-happy ending.

In 2003, shortly after the conclusion of R *v.* Ingram &c, William G. Stewart opens his final episode of *Fifteen to One*. He has asked, he says, 350,000 questions (though not necessarily 350,000 different questions) to 33,975 contestants over the course of 2,265 shows. And in the last one, the finalists include, placed ninth in the entire series so far, one Arfor Hughes.

Now, this isn't the Bollywood version. Hughes doesn't become the last-ever series champion. He's knocked out, but not until the second round – and for crying out loud, this is *Fifteen to One*. It's serious quiz. Thirteen years later, he shows that those DUNCE and DISASTERMIND headlines were wrong; the pupils and teachers were wrong. It *was* nerves

---

11 Eddie the Eagle (after Michael Edwards).

in the Great Hall. Hughes can quiz. 'The scar,' he says, 'has healed.'

In 1964, *University Challenge* hosted a special match pitching the tutors of New College, Oxford, against their students. Peter Mullings, the show's director, recalled how it went:

> The dons would hear the question and they would say to themselves: 'This is what the question is asking.'
> Then they would think: 'This is what the answer is. Let us press a buzzer, and then we will say the answer,' not realizing that by the time they'd done this the [students] had already answered and were halfway through their bonuses.'

These academics, who lost 250:50, were not also-rans. They included the celebrated A. J. Ayer, author of *The Meaning of Life and Other Essays*, *The Central Questions of Philosophy* and, notably . . .

. . . *The Problem of Knowledge*.

Join us next time

19. I'm feeling lucky
The future of quiz

One topic that quizzes tend to avoid is the future. It's almost always impossible to give reliable answers. Still . . .

What will the quiz of tomorrow look like?

Compared to other early radio and TV, quiz was positively interactive. You could play along; you could even apply to play for real. And, since then, we've been given many opportunities to cut out the middle-man of broadcast and quiz from pubs and homes. After Trivial Pursuit saved the board game from the threat of video games, computers themselves began to offer quiz.

The earliest specimens were humble (*Brain Storm*, 1984's 'ultimate quiz for the Apple II computer', boasted 720 questions) but made the most of the available processing power to produce something more than on-screen exams marked by an automaton. *Triple Brain Trust*, for example, pioneered the practice of not punishing contestants for questions which were spelled not-quite correctly. Others emulated the familiar devices of television quiz.

Bob Brainbank, 'host' of the prophetically titled *Millionwaire*, had an assistant called Donna Diskdrive. When Bob asked Donna to 'say hello', instead of giving contestants an eighties-style twirl she would make the user's drive audibly whirr. Bob also asked contestants where they were from, aping the banter at the top of a real-money quiz, and offered replies like 'Nice hospital there.' Soon, machines branded with the logos of actual TV quizzes were giving out money in pubs. For the Trivial Pursuit console, someone had to type in each of the questions from the cards of the Genus edition; other games concocted fresh challenges.

And it didn't take long for some people to see the opportunity in this new kind of device: like a fruit machine, it offered cash; unlike a fruit machine, you could beat it time and again if you knew enough, through having good general knowledge, topped up with the answers for any given game. And so, during the golden age of UK quiz machines, there were about a hundred people who contrived to earn up to £1,000 a week by touring pubs, hotels and snooker halls answering questions on *Adders and Ladders*, *Barquest*, *Give Us a Break*, and the rest.

For the devoted fact-collector, this was not just lucrative: it was a deeply pleasant, if furtive, form of self-employment: a working day which demanded that you visit a pub, buy a half of lager or cola, check the machine's high-score table to see whether it had recently been cleared out by another professional, answer questions (remembering which games had inaccurate answers) and take a tax-free £5, £10 or £20 before moving on (remembering to make notes of any new questions, new answers, new locations) and repeating. Some would play a pair of adjacent machines simultaneously for fun (and coins).

The professionals didn't apply for television quizzes: for one thing, the prizes were less impressive; for another, publicans weary of the *clunk-clunk* of pound coins emanating from their machines tended to safeguard their cut of the takings by barring players who looked like they might be too good.

The manufacturers entered a game of cat-and-mouse but,

even when the volume of questions in a game rose from 4,000 to 75,000, the professionals kept up. Eventually, the machines deployed the trick used in Trivial Pursuit: the 'stoppers', jackpot-denying questions which asked for arbitrary numerical answers like the attendance at some football match or other, effectively turning the machines from games of skill into lotteries.

The stoppers successfully stymied the pros, but they also made the games less enjoyable for normal members of the public – and quizzes which are no fun and which give no prizes are not popular. Goodbye, then, to the quiz machine – but not to the machine that does quiz. Those screens on which we have watched quiz are now two-way. We routinely expect more interactivity than yelling those answers that we think the contestants really should have got.

You Don't Know Jack is a computer quiz which shows what's possible: its 'host', Cookie Masterson, is programmed with so many responses that you feel that 'he' is actually reacting to your answers and performance, and the questions are assembled with wit and immense care – unlike most quiz apps and sites, it never feels like it's been churned out by combining online lists of facts with some question marks.

Its 'dollar' prizes, though, aren't real. And that is the ingredient missing in digital quizzes. Certainly, someone will devise a format which is native to its device (tablet, smart TV, whatever) rather than being a TV effigy, which makes encounters into events – and which offers real money. That person will become about as wealthy as **the Lydian king who was defeated by Cyrus the Great in 546BCE.**[1]

---

1 Croesus (accept Kροῖσος).

Will we compete against machines?

We already are. In an earlier technological epoch, IBM answered the question of whether computers can play chess. They *really* can, and we've learned that their ability to work through the possibilities offered by a chessboard and its pieces makes them much better than us.

Quiz, though, is different – especially on the buzzer. Working out what a question is asking for and feeling the penny drop is a more allusive business, less susceptible to sheer computational power. Quiz questions tend to be asked in natural language, one of the holy grails of artificial intelligence.

And so IBM has returned, this time with a machine that quizzes: it's called Watson and it appeared on *Jeopardy!* in 2011 armed with fifteen terabytes of data, including all of Wikipedia, in a showdown with Ken Jennings and another champion.

Its limits were revealed by questions like the one from the category Double Meanings which asked for **The word which fits both definitions: 'Stylish elegance, or students who all graduated in the same year'**[2]. Watson poignantly offered, 'What is "chic"?', and humans rejoiced that there was still something that we can do better – until Watson won all three matches.

Jennings remained upbeat. 'My puny human brain,' he wrote, 'just a few bucks' worth of water, salts, and proteins, hung in there just fine against a jillion-dollar supercomputer.' Watson, meanwhile, has quietly moved on to such natural-language projects as trying to work out how we're feeling from what we're saying. (Personally, creeped out and nervous.)

[2] What is class?

Will quiz questions be different?

Watson's invincibility suggests a future division of intellectual labour. Since machines are so much better than us at storing and retrieving information, perhaps we should leave them to it and concentrate on what they *can't* do: making connections and assembling that information into pleasing combinations. Isn't storing dry facts now much like remembering, as some stubbornly do, pi to a hundred decimal places: something we need not bother with?

The first era of quiz tested us on what we could remember from the stock of general knowledge – that is, from the kind of data that computers now regularly store. Trivia, you might say. The next era could test us on the kind of allusive, meaningful connections that only people can make.

Put another way, quiz could get much harder. I managed, via friends of friends, to see a copy of a quiz which amuses British intelligence employees every Christmas. It is as hard as you would expect. Here's an example of a question which invites you to combine disparate pieces of general knowledge:

A perjurer (a), a chief clerk (b), a great one (c), some Japanese gentlemen (d) and one who wasn't asked (e) are all tragically associated with an awful place (f). How is this?[3]

You can't even cheat here: you can merely free-associate your way to some likely parts and hope that they might reveal the whole.

And cheating gives us another push to change the way we ask questions. On the American *Who Wants to be a Millionaire?*, the phone-a-friend lifeline was removed in 2010 because too many friends were googling the answers. Host Meredith Vieira explained, 'The game is really not about that – it's about what's inside somebody's head.'

The same goes for pub quiz. Where cheats were once obliged to feign a loo break in order to find ten pence and phone a friend who had a copy of the *Guinness Book of Hit Singles*, they can now feign replying to an urgent text message and phone Google – and, as we saw above, 11 per cent of us do just that.

Down the years, I've experimented with ways of making questions Google-proof. At first, I tried to use technology against itself, putting lines of celebrated movie dialogue through various languages of translation software and back to English, ending up with the likes of, 'No, Christ - this is an imp!' and 'Where we shall be, we are not wanting thoroughfares' and asking contestants to **name the films.**[4]

Computer translation is now too deft to create pleasingly garbled phrases, so I do a similar job myself by providing 'Just the Gist' of the content of a pop song:

> **A man confesses a murder to his parent. He later pleads impecunity and seeks clemency in vain. He is resigned to his fate.**[5]
> **A refuse collector tries to strike a balance between tonight's merriment and tomorrow's punctuality.**[6]

6. 'Get Me to the Church on Time.'

5. 'Bohemian Rhapsody.'

the Future ('Where we're going, we don't need roads').

4. *Monty Python's Life of Brian* ('He's not the messiah, he's a very naughty boy') and *Back to*

The technology in a contestant's pocket is also catching up. Everyday apps will identify the songs in a music round and the famous faces in a picture round; I've tried playing the former at the wrong speed and blurring the latter, but it's only a matter of time until those tricks likewise fail.

What's the point of knowing things?

A concerned psychologist told the *Observer* in 2000 that the 'entire concept of intelligence is being reassessed, with the ability to absorb and retrieve nuggets of information being prized above and beyond the ability to question and assess'. He added, 'It's not too extreme to compare quiz shows to a cancer: they're virulent, contagious and dangerous.'

Gosh. Well, certainly, information needs context. The fan of quiz who stores away **The name of the Eliot poem from which Evelyn Waugh took the title of his novel *A Handful of Dust*[7]** but does not read either poem or novel is being intellectually short-changed. Then, so, too, is the reader of either work who is lacking in general knowledge.

A Handful of Dust is an astonishing tale, but Waugh introduces its lead character in a way that presumes the reader's acquired knowledge includes an awareness of **the architectural movement characterized by All Souls College, Strawberry Hill and the Palace of Westminster[8]** and its relation to Anglo-Catholicism. As for the Eliot poem, good luck making sense of that if you don't get a decent score on these stinkers:

Which eastern religious figure wrote the discourse known as the Fire Sermon?[9]

9 The Buddha.
8 Gothic Revival (accept neo-Gothic, etc.).
7 *The Waste Land.* ('I will show you fear in a handful of dust.').

Which pioneering work of anthropology was published in two volumes in 1890 by Sir James Frazer?[10]

Which Shakespearean character's crazed and final spoken words are 'Good-night, ladies; good-night, sweet ladies; good-night, good-night'?[11]

Where can you find the man with three staves, the Wheel and the Hanged Man?[12]

Which animal's cry is rendered in French as 'Cocorico'?[13]

Of course, you might know all of the above, and everything else that Eliot refers to, and still fail to understand his poem. But it's unlikely that they're *all* mere nuggets of information to you, and the reader with a well-stocked memory will certainly enjoy the poem more than the one who has to keep breaking off to look things up.

Looking things up. An increasingly critical skill, but do we really want to forget about remembering and to subcontract the business of knowing to machines? While we remain in the Google age, this is not so much delegation as entrusting our human experience to an advertising corporation. If you don't know the dots, how can you connect them? Google co-founder Larry Page described the future of knowledge like this: 'Eventually you'll have the implant, where if you think about a fact, it will just tell you the answer.'

This is a vision where the quizzes of the future begin with an instruction for all contestants to deactivate their implants. It's also one in which retrieving information from your own memory seems quaint, archaic – even brave.

13 The cockerel.
12 In a Tarot deck.
11 Ophelia (Hamlet).
Magic and Religion).
10 The Golden Bough: A Study in Comparative Religion (accept The Golden Bough: A Study in

So the answer to the question above is: no. We do not want to forget about quizzes of straight knowledge, however humiliatingly we are bested by the Watsons.

And while Google-proof questions are enormously rewarding to set and fun to answer, it's cheering that we do still also want to quiz in a way that asks us to do such unadorned mental feats as, say, naming **the United Kingdom prime ministers from the *General Knowledge Bee* on 19 April 1938 to the successful *Who Wants to be a Millionaire?* pitch of 4 April 1998.**[14]

Our ever-more specialized working lives, the never-ending acceleration of available information and the near-ubiquity of 'search' pressure us to know only what we need to in the moment and to forget it straight away.

Homo sapiens – people who know. Quiz is one of the few ways in which we celebrate the activity that we named our species after: knowing not just a little, but as much as we can. We would do well not to forget this.

Besides, the best nugget to know about 'The Waste Land' (apologies if you haven't answered that one yet) is that, like most of the quizzes mentioned above, it had **an utterly preposterous working title.**[15]

[15] 'He Do the Police in Different Voices', itself a borrowing from *Our Mutual Friend*.

[14] Neville Chamberlain, Winston Churchill, Clement Attlee, Anthony Eden, Harold Macmillan, Alec Douglas-Home, Harold Wilson, Edward Heath, James Callaghan, Margaret Thatcher, John Major, Tony Blair.

Closing credits

20. DUM-dum-dum-DAH
Quiz music

A final word about the unsung people who give TV quizzes their personalities: the composers of the theme tunes which often become recognizable within a beat, which we hear more frequently than **the UK's top-three best-selling singles**[1] and which sometimes contain erudite nuggets appropriate to their medium – like the four-note quotation from Beethoven's *Fifth* in Ed Welch's *Blockbusters* theme, which can be heard just as the composer appears in the hexagons of the title sequence.

Quite often, the composers didn't even mean for their music to be used to introduce quiz; many themes come from 'library music', pieces which are created for a one-off fee and can wallow unnoticed in those libraries for years.

As it happened, when Bill Wright asked the BBC Gramophone Library to offer something with foreboding for *Mastermind*, the first piece he listened to was the one he chose: Neil Richardson's 'Approaching Menace', which had previously been used, by spooky coincidence, in a 1969 BBC radio drama about prisoners of war.

Library music can pay off in other ways: being the creator

[1] 'Bohemian Rhapsody' (again), 'Do They Know It's Christmas?' and the best-seller, 'Candle in the Wind' (1997).

of a piece of ubiquitous aural furniture endows enormous professional kudos. Richardson, who would go on to conduct the score for *Four Weddings and a Funeral*, attended that final final in Orkney and remarked there that 'Approaching Menace' had 'kept me in whisky for twenty-five years'.

Others are specially written, some even incorporating the programme's title. I'm thinking especially here of that daytime intra-Europe competition *Going for Gold* and the immortal lines of its theme song: 'Everyone's trying/Trying to be the best that they can/When they're going for/Going for gold'. Its composer, Hans Zimmer, likewise later moved into cinema, a shift from soft rock to elaborate orchestration which he says would have been impossible without quiz: 'If you want to be an electronic whizz-kid synthesizer composer there's nothing worse than when the electricity gets cut off, which kept happening to me frequently in those days for non-payment of bills. And *Going for Gold*, God bless them, they kept me alive!'

No more playing catch-up for Hans, who has since scored **a film series based on a nautical theme-park ride,[2] a 1997 musical with songs by Tim Rice and Elton John[3] and the film which was offered to Russell Crowe with the words, 'It's a $100m film, you're being directed by Ridley Scott and you play a Roman general.'[4]**

2 *Pirates of the Caribbean.*
3 *The Lion King.*
4 *Gladiator.*

Resources
and thanks

Citations are mentioned in the notes. The resources I found most useful and which are most recommended for further reading are below, in no particular order.

The best book on an individual quiz is Magnus Magnusson's *I've Started So I'll Finish: The Story of* Mastermind; there is some wonderful background between the questions in Peter Gwyn's University Challenge: *The First Forty Years* and the Trivial Pursuit characters can be seen in all their glory in Louise Bernikow's *Esquire* piece from March 1983, 'Trivia Inc.'.

Brainiac by the *Jeopardy!* champion Ken Jennings is a compelling memoir which also details the origin and development of the American love of trivia.

Most of the King William College questions can be found in various collections, most recently, *The World's Most Difficult Quiz* and its sequel.

J. Kent Anderson's *Television Fraud* is a thorough and compelling dredge through the 1950s scandals, and Thomas A. DeLong's *Quiz Craze: America's Infatuation with Game Shows* is a fascinating portrait of early American quiz.

The history of knowledge can be found in various forms in Peter Burke's *A Social History of Knowledge II*, Ann M. Blair's

Too Much to Know and, indeed, Charles Van Doren's *A History of Knowledge*.

So many thanks to my editor, Helen Conford, and to my agent, Andrew Gordon, for making this book possible, and also to:

Those with whom I've discussed and created quiz: Debi Allen, Chris Cadenne, Mark Chappell, Keith Chegwin, Emma Cook, Victoria Coren Mitchell, Andrew Davies, Thomas Eaton, James Harkin, Jenny Hawker, John Henderson, David Lea, Siân Lloyd, Sara Low, Daniel Maier, Philip Marlow, Richard Osman, Daniel Peake, Sue Perkins, Huw Rhys, Hugh Rycroft, Jeremy Salsby, Jo Street, Chris Stuart, Guy Turner, Mike Turner, Chris Vallance, Jack Waley-Cohen, Giles Wilson and, of course, Shaun Pye.

Those who have enabled me to find and assemble material: everyone at BBC Archive, Sean Blanchflower, the staff of the Bodleian Library, Ben Caudell, Pat Cullen, Thomas Eaton, Kathryn Friedlander, Bamber Gascoigne, Jon Harvey, Kathryn Johnson, Jackie Jones, the staff at the National Archives, Frank Passic, Tom Provan, the Quiz Discussion Group on Facebook, Daniel Radcliffe, Richard Rogan, Martin Smith, Bene't Steinberg, Bill Thompson, Colin Whorlow and, of course, my mum.

Those who have seen the innards of the book before publication: Emma Bal, Jeff Bowman, Derek Caudwell, Sarah Day, David Evans, Rebecca Lee, Ingrid Matts, Shoaib Rokadiya, David Stainer, Claudia Toia, Sean Walsh and, of course, Alexander Hamilton.

Those with whom I have quizzed, including The Littlest Hobos, Happy Team, and of course, Loaf.

And 'welcome back': Lucy and Raphael.

Notes

Introduction: My **poll** was of 2,037 adults, conducted online by YouGov between 6 and 8 May 2016. The figures were weighted and are representative of all GB adults (aged 18+). The findings are remarkably similar to those from earlier polls (by the turn of the millennium, one in ten Britons described themselves as 'quizaholics', and over eight in ten said that they 'like' or 'really like' to quiz): see 'Q: Why Do We Love Quizzes?', *Observer*, 5 November 2000, and YouGov's entry for 'Quizzes (Activity)'.

1. **Mighty contests rise**: The **chapter title** is from Pope's *Rape of the Lock* ('What dire offence from am'rous causes springs/What mighty contests rise from trivial things'), which is quoted on the box of the original Genus edition. The **Trivial Pursuit story** is told in: Ken Jennings's wonderful *Brainiac: Adventures in the Curious, Competitive, Compulsive World of Trivia Buffs* and also 'Pac-Man for Smart People', *Time*, 3 September 1984; 'How Two Nerja Hacks Made a Billion from Trivial Pursuit', *Olive Press*, 24 June 2010; 'Trivia is Earning Trio Millions', *Sydney Morning Herald*, 16 December 1984; 'Issues Pursued in Copyright Lawsuit are Not Trivial', *The New York Times*, 13 November 1984; 'Trivial Lawsuit', *Notre Dame & St Mary's Observer*, 9 November 1984; 'The Decline of Trivial Pursuit', *Slate*, 13 April 2005; Chris Haney's obituary in the *Guardian*, 30 June 2010; Elizabeth Sudmeier's paper 'Factually Elite: Trivial Pursuit, Education and the 1980s'; Tim Walsh's *Timeless Toys: Classic Toys and the Playmakers Who Created Them*; Richard C. Levy & Ronald O. Weingartner's *The Toy and Game Inventor's Handbook: Everything You Need to Know to Pitch, License and Cash-in on Your Ideas*; and especially in Louise Bernikow's lengthy piece in *Esquire*, March 1983 (vol. 103, no. 3), 'Trivia Inc.: It's a Simple Board Game, but for Its Founders the Prize was Joy, Sorrow and a Multimillion-dollar Conglomerate', to which anyone interested in the game's genesis owes endless debt. (One version of the origin

myth starts the story at a Scrabble board with a couple of tiles missing and surrounded by beer bottles, but others wonder whether this was concocted once the new game was supported by the makers of the old.) There is a list of **Trivial Pursuit mistakes** in the post 'Trivial Pursuit – Original Genus Edition Updates and Corrections' at the *Trivia Why's* blog, and the **fictional bra history** is *Bust Up: The Uplifting Tale of Otto Titzling and the Development of the Bra* by Wallace Reyburn, who also wrote *Flushed with Pride: The Story of Thomas Crapper*. Alongside '**mongie**', another example of dated language comes in the TP question 'What black was nominated for vice-president at the 1968 Democratic National Convention?'; I've only seen a photo of the front of the card and presume the answer is Julian Bond, who was proposed but not actually nominated. The **plagiarism case** was initiated in October 1984 and initially dismissed on 22 March 1985, and **the findings of the 1987 appeal** are in the admirably readable 'Worth *v*. Selchow & Righter Company' (827 F. 2d 569). Unknown to almost everyone, *Columbo*'s art department had had to choose a name when designing his badge prop, and went for 'Frank', but it passed unnoticed in the blink of a few frames. 'Frank' was never seen in the credits nor heard in dialogue – much less 'Philip'. There is more on **mountweazels** in 'Not a Word', *New Yorker*, 29 August 2005; *The Oxford Handbook of the Word*; 'On Google's Bing Sting', *The New York Times*, 2 February 2011; and episode 7 of series 1 of the BBC's *Map Man*. In tribute to Worth, there's a mountweazel in this chapter.

2. Quite a quiz: The **etymology** of 'quiz' is discussed throughout the OED, and in the *Oxford Dictionaries* article 'What is the Origin of the Word "Quiz"?' **Richard Daly**'s propensity for duelling is described in a hilarious passage in the memoirs of the Irish politician Jonah Barrington, *Personal Sketches of His Own Times*; other hijinks are related in Benjamin Smart's *Walker Remodelled: A New Critical Pronouncing Dictionary of the English Language*; Frank Thorpe Porter's *Gleanings and Reminiscences*; and John C. Greene's *Theatre in Dublin, 1745–1820: A Calendar of Performances*. **Stephen Fry** cites '*Qui es?*' in the *Daily Telegraph/QI* Christmas 2008 Quiz, published on 18 December that year. The listings of the **early BBC bees, quizzes and teasers** are all available to browse via genome.ch.bbc.co.uk at the Radio Times Archive. The **parliamentary uses of catchphrases** are – Blair: Debate on the Address, 6 December 2000; Burridge: Queen's Speech Debate (2nd Day), 28 May 2015; Foot: Airfields (Food Productions) Orders of the Day, 4 March 1954, all courtesy of the best public record, *They Work for You*. It should also be noted that 'Give 'em the money, Barney' had been used in a pensions debate in 1949, but Earl Winterton appealed to the Speaker for protection, believing that he had been called 'barmy'. After a protracted exchange, Labour's Charles Simmons noted, 'It is apparent that the noble Lord fails to listen to the most human programme broadcast by the BBC.' There is a chapter on the **Central African Republic** in Alexander Armstrong & Richard Osman's *The 100 Most Pointless Things in the World*.

    3. Ask me another: The **Imperial Examination** is described in Ichisada Miyazaki's *China's Examination Hell: The Civil Service Examinations of Imperial China*. The **Bentham bangings-on** are in *Constitutional Code* and *Official Aptitude Maximized; Expense Minimized*, and the sorry story of **Charles Guiteau** is told in Kenneth D. Ackerman's *Dark Horse: The Surprise Election and Political Murder of President James A. Garfield*. Christopher Stray's description of **the jester** is from episode 1 of the BBC Radio 4 programme *Turn Over Your Papers . . . Now!*, 12 November 2007, and the **broader context for the coming of exams** is fascinatingly told in John Roach's *Public Examinations in England 1850–1900*, which both sounds like and would make for a wonderful *Mastermind* specialized subject. The University of **Cambridge Local Examinations Syndicate** is now Cambridge Assessment and tells more of this story at cambridgeassessment.org.uk and in *Examining the World: A History of the University of Cambridge Local Examinations Syndicate*. The **Harvard hopes** are from episode 3 of *Turn Over Your Papers . . . Now!*, 26 November 2007. **Freud**'s claims are in Chapter 5D of *The Interpretation of Dreams*; in A. A. Brill's translation, he goes on to assert, 'We have had increasing confirmation of the fact that the anxiety-dream of examination occurs when the dreamer is anticipating a responsible task on the following day, with the possibility of disgrace.' John **Dunton's remarks** are from the splendidly titled *The Life and Errors of John Dunton, Written by Himself, Together with the Lives and Characters of a Thousand Persons Now Living in London, &c.*, and **D'Israeli**'s can be found in *Calamities and Quarrels of Authors*. The birth of *Ask Me Another!* is recalled in fraternity magazine *The Diamond of Psi Upsilon* (vol. 15, issue 4), and the **development of trivia**, including Robert L. Ripley as well as Dunton, Southwick, Esty and Spafford, is described in more and entertaining detail in *Brainiac: Adventures in the*

Curious, Competitive, Compulsive World of Trivia Buffs, by *Jeopardy!* champion Ken Jennings, to which I am indebted. The crossword fad of 1925 is described in my own *Two Girls, One on Each Knee: The Puzzling, Playful World of the Crossword*. The odd attempt was made by radio to cash in on the Amherst japes of *Ask Me Another!*, which fizzled, and a similar false start in quiz was *The Time Questionnaire*, a current-affairs Q&A promoting the then-new *Time* magazine. **Criticism of *Ask Me Another!*** can be found in the *Time* piece 'Education: Ask Me Another Monday' (14 February 1927), and the **praise of Van Doren** can be found in, for example, the Society pages of the *Miami Daily News*, 20 February 1927. The recollections of **S. P. B. Mais's grandson** Sebastian Shakespeare are from his sobering *Evening Standard* piece 'Being a Writer is a Poor Choice of Job', 4 March 2009.

4. **Starters for ten**: The first episode of ***Quiz Ball*** was broadcast on 22 December 1966 on BBC1; it has since been preserved for the nation by Richard Osman and the BBC Archive and can be found within iPlayer. The **history of spelling bees** is told in James Maguire's *American Bee: The National Spelling Bee and the Culture of Word Nerds*. College Bowl is described in Thomas A. DeLong's *Quiz Craze: America's Infatuation with Game Shows*; Ray Broadus Browne & Pat Browne's *The Guide to United States Popular Culture*; and David Babe's *Television Game Show Hosts: Biographies of Thirty-two Stars*. The Paxman aside is from his introduction to Peter Gwyn's *University Challenge: The First Forty Years*. *Mastermind*'s origins can be found in Magnus Magnusson's *I've Started, So I'll Finish: The Story of Mastermind*; James Rampton's 2011 *Independent* series Long Runners; and at the BBC's *Mastermind* pages. The genesis of *Pointless* is described in the *Guardian* piece 'Pointless: Alexander Armstrong and Richard Osman on TV's Favourite Quiz', 4 June 2013, and the *Jeopardy!* legend features in Ken Jennings's article for the March 2014 edition of the *Smithsonian Magazine*, 'How Merv Griffin Came Up with that Weird Question/Answer Format for *Jeopardy!*' and in Merv Griffin's autobiography, *Merv: Making the Good Life Last*; Griffin is addressed like this by Dorothy in episode 17 of season 7 of *The Golden Girls*, 'Questions and Answers' (1992): 'You're the most beloved man in America. You are bright, you are charming – you are the anti-Trump.'

5. **Who wants to know?**: The **early days of American radio** are described in John Dunnin's *On the Air: The Encyclopedia of Old-time*

Radio; Donna L Halper's paper '1922 Exercise and Expertise: Radio Broadcasting Promotes Health Education'; and especially Thomas A. DeLong's *Quiz Craze: America's Infatuation with Game Shows*. There is a table showing **the number of feathers on various birds** and a discussion of chicken counts in Wetmore, Alexander (1936): 'The Number of Contour Feathers in Passeriform and Related Birds', *Auk*, vol. 53, no. 2. The Mark **Goodson** quote is from Barry Norman's documentary, *Come On Down!*, BBC1, 23 August 1985. There is more on **Hughie Green** in volume one of Bernard Sendall's *Independent Television in Britain*. Bob **Monkhouse's snooker gag** was in the episode of *Bob's Full House* broadcast on 19 December 1987, also preserved at iPlayer, and the *'very* **wrong'** *University Challenge* answer was in the second quarter-final of series 13, BBC2, 11 February 2013. **The 'gravitas' issue** is discussed in Su Holmes's Edinburgh University Press book *The Quiz Show*. Shane **O'Doherty** appeared on *Who Wants to be a Millionaire?* on RTÉ on 17 June 2001 and, more briefly, on 1 July. Michael **Palin** is part of *The Making of QI*, BBC2, 10 September 2011, and Bamber **Gascoigne recalled his prep** in conversation with me and in *University Challenge: The Story So Far*, BBC2, 27 December 2008.

6. What are the chances of that?: Jade **Goody**'s tour de force was broadcast on BBC2, 4 May 2006. There is much on **luck versus merit** in Roger Callois's book on play, *Les Jeux et les hommes: le masque et le vertige*, and **call-TV practices** (which incorporated ambiguous and baffling questions as well as easy ones) are outlined in *You and Yours*, BBC Radio 4, 10 October 2006, and in the House of Commons Culture, Media & Sport Committee's *Call TV Quiz Shows Third Report of Session 2006–07*, 25 January 2007. The *$64,000 Question* **producers** speak in the PBS *American Experience* documentary of 2000, 'The Quiz Show Scandal'. Arthur **Chu**'s tactics are discussed in *Jeopardy!* champ Ken Jennings's piece 'Arthur Chu is Playing *Jeopardy!* the Right Way', *Salon*, 10 February 2014; 'Bad Boy of *Jeopardy!*, Arthur Chu, Refuses to Apologize – Should He?'; *Wall Street Journal*, 6 February 2014; 'Controversial *Jeopardy!* Champ Arthur Chu Tells His Story', *AV Club*, 24 February 2014; and 'Our Interview with *Jeopardy!* Champion Arthur Chu', *Mental Floss*, 1 February 2014. The quotes about Michael **Larson** are from James P. Taylor Jr's wonderful 2003 documentary *Big Bucks: The Press Your Luck Scandal* and David Babe's *Television Game Show Hosts: Biographies of Thirty-two Stars*.

7. **Well done if you got that at home**: Bamber **Gascoigne** was talking to the BBC in part one of *University Challenge: Class of 2014*, BBC2, 7 July 2014. The transformation of **College Bowl** is related in 'Total Recall', *The New York Times*, 4 April 1999, and the Associated Press piece '*College Bowl* Returns to TV Tonight', 23 May 1984; the more recent scene is described in 'The Super Bowl of the Mind', *Slate*, 3 May 2012. The **Chicago Open starter** was from a batch edited by Austin Brownlow, Andrew Hart, Ike Jose, Gautam & Gaurav Kandlikar and Jacob Reed uploaded to hsquizbowl.org, the Quizbowl Research Center; the **QLL bonuses** were set by Atletico/Piccadilly B./Sunset Desserts and Amoebas. Chomsky discusses '**colourless green ideas** sleep furiously' in *Syntactic Structures*. The **sheep** description of the General Knowledge Paper is from a 1934 article in the *Rangoon Gazette*. The **fruit-themed** questions are from set 15 of the 2004–05 GKP and the **musical** questions are from set 9 in the 1983–4 paper, both reproduced in *The World's Most Difficult Quiz: The King William's College General Knowledge Papers*; the **Red Sea** set is in the 1954 collection *General Knowledge Papers 1905– 53 Prepared for King William's College Isle of Man*, and the history of the **General Knowledge Paper** can be found in those books, *The World's Most Difficult Quiz 2: More King William's College General Knowledge Papers*, the 1982 collection which eschews the word 'quiz', *The King William's College Tests: Thirty of the Most Confoundingly Difficult Tests Ever Set* and the *Guardian* piece 'I Like to Irritate', 24 December 2004. The **angry** *Times* piece is headed 'General Ignorance', 19 December 1933. The **short, sharp shock** question is from the 26 October 2015 episode of Radio 4's *RBQ*, and the **Dalmatians** question from 21 July 2014. The **Egyptian hieroglyphs** were introduced to *Only Connect* in the first episode of series 4, BBC4, 6 September 2010, and the cartoon which inspired them was 'Rarely Correct' by Stephen 'Friz' Frizzle. The **answer's in the clue** question was set by the programme's original question editor David J. Bodycombe for the final of the sixth series (BBC4, 17 December 2012), and the **Abba** question by his successor (me) for the start of series 12 (BBC2, 13 July 2015). The **April Fool** *Mastermind* was broadcast on BBC1 on 1 April 1987.

8. **Everything you always wanted to know**: The **description of Mycroft Holmes** is from 'The Bruce-Partington Plans' in *His Last Bow*, and the massively selective account of some of the achievements of **Thomas Young** is drawn from Andrew Robinson's *The Last Man Who*

Knew Everything: Thomas Young, the Anonymous Polymath Who Proved Newton Wrong, Explained How We See, Cured the Sick and Deciphered the Rosetta Stone. The Tom **Lehrer** couplet is from 'The Elements'. The **way we used to organize knowledge** is described in Richard Yeo's *Encyclopaedic Visions: Scientific Dictionaries and Enlightenment Culture*; Andrew Brown's *A Brief History of Encyclopaedias: From Pliny to Wikipedia*; and Peter Burke's *A Social History of Knowledge: From Gutenberg to Diderot*; and, more especially, his *A Social History of Knowledge II: From the Encyclopaedia to Wikipedia*, the titles of two of which suggest that all informational roads currently end at Wikipedia. **Homer Simpson's model of cognitive neuroscience** is from *The Simpsons*, series 5, episode 22, 'Secrets of a Successful Marriage': he cites as evidence the wine-making course that made him forget how to drive; the article mentioned is by Maria Wimber, Arjen Alink, Ian Charest, Nikolaus Kriegeskorte and Michael C. Anderson (*Nature Neuroscience* 18, 582–9 (2015)). The **interviews with the champions** are 'Quizzing with Kevin Ashman' in the *Financial Times*, 29 May 2015; 'Winning Mastermind' in *Pass*, the quarterly magazine of the Mastermind Club, 2012:2; and 'Quiz Rivals Have No Answer to *Times* World Champion' in *The Times*, 13 June 2015. **David Elias** is interviewed at the programme pages for Channel 4's *Grand Slam*.

9. Buzz before you think: The data on **'true or false' questions** are from William Poundstone's *Rock Breaks Scissors: A Practical Guide to Outguessing and Outwitting Almost Everybody*, and there is some similar analysis, specifically of quiz-show strategies, in John Haigh's *Taking Chances: Winning with Probability*. The effect of **the pub near Granada Studios** (not the Rovers Return) is described in *University Challenge: The Story So Far*, BBC2, 27 December 2008, and (along with other mind-alterers) in Peter Gwyn's *University Challenge: The First Forty Years*. The ***Times/Mastermind* exchanges** are from 2 and 5 January 1974, and the **Derren Brown japes** are in episode 1 of series 2 of *Trick or Treat*, Channel 4, 2 May 2008. The **Humphrys/Paxman showdown** was on the *Today* programme, BBC Radio 4, 21 September 2012. The **Joan Crawford-fancier** is quoted in 'Dentist Pursues Trivia Prize, Carries Day', *Wall Street Journal*, 9 May 1984; the ***Two Pints* advice** is from episode 5 of series 9, 'Stot or Pronk', BBC3, 27 February 2005, and *How Old was Lolita?* is by Alan Saperstein. **Ralph Morley's moment of bravery** is in the first quarter-final of the 2013/14 series, BBC2, 13 January 2014. The **over-confidence effect** is explored in the work of Sarah C.

Lichtenstein and Baruch Fischhoff, and the **multiple-choice research** is in Ludy T. Benjamin, Timothy A. Cavell & William R. Shallenberger III's 'Staying with Initial Answers on Objective Tests: Is It a Myth?' in *Teaching of Psychology*, 11 (3), 133–41. The *Who Wants to be a Millionaire?* **data** are from James Surowiecki's *The Wisdom of Crowds*, and the **kamikaze moment** is related in Peter Lee's memoir *Yes Chris – Final Answer*. Peter Richardson's **advice on buzzer technique** is quoted in Magnus Magnusson's *I've Started, So I'll Finish: The Story of Mastermind*, and Roger Tilling was speaking in part 2 of *University Challenge: Class of 2014*, BBC2, 1 September 2014.

10. **Good question!**: 'Paddington Hits the Jackpot' is in the collection *Paddington at Large*. Magnus Magnusson recalls **running out of questions** in *I've Started, So I'll Finish: The Story of Mastermind*, and describes how the contestant, Nancy Wilkinson, 'asked, very sweetly, if I would like *her* to ask *me* some questions!' (before winning the final). **'Inherent interest'** is discussed by executive producer Peter Gwyn in part 2 of *University Challenge: Class of 2014*, BBC2, 1 September 2014; David Briggs's concept of **'shoutability'** is described in Chris Tarrant's *Millionaire Moments: The Story of Who Wants to be a Millionaire?*; and Neville Cohen and Janet Barker are visible again as Folio Quiz. The **story of *Treasure Hunt*** is told in volume three of Adam Nedeff's magisterial *This Day in Game Show History: 365 Commemorations and Celebrations*. The **Durie 'winge'** is from 'A Question of Science', *New Scientist*, 15 August 1985. The **description of Lindemann** is from 'The Most Powerful Scientist Ever: Winston Churchill's Personal Technocrat', *Scientific American*, 6 August 2010. **Snow's Rede Lecture** was delivered on 7 May 1959 at Cambridge's Senate House and adapted into the book *The Two Cultures and the Scientific Revolution*; it inspired the **Flanders and Swann** song 'First and Second Law', which is on *At the Drop of Another Hat*. The **cricket question** was written by quiz-show supremo Hugh Rycroft and asked in episode 15 of series 10 of *Only Connect*. Marcus **Berkmann** was talking to Simon Fanshawe in *Next Question Please!*, 5 September 2007, and runs a quiz company called Brain Men; Thomas **Eaton** featured in a July 2015 adaptation of Joanna Biggs's book *All Day Long: A Portrait of Britain at Work*, and the **QI facts** are related in *The Making of QI*, BBC2, 10 September 2011.

11. **We're just checking that for you**: Theodore Bikel recalls the **'Edelweiss'** story in *Theo: An Autobiography*. The **Congo confusion** is in

episode 6 of series 1 of *After You've Gone*, 'Let's Get Quizzical'. David **Elias** gives a compelling account of setting for *University Challenge* as part of Sean Blanchflower's wonderful UC site at blanchflower.org, and the *Britannica* '**scissors**' are mentioned in Robert Kerr's *Memoirs of the Life, Writings and Correspondence of W. Smellie*.

12. **What do points make?**: Michael **Davies** was talking to Elizabeth Farnsworth on the PBS *Newshour* feature 'TV's Final Answer?', 19 January 2000. The **anti-prize letters** can be found in the FCC's Boxes 3877–8 (Docket 9113), as cited in Jason Mittell's 'Before the Scandals: The Radio Precedents of the Quiz Show Genre' (in Michele Hilmes & Jason Loviglio's *Radio Reader: Essays in the Cultural History of Radio*). Richard **Hoggart** was cross-examining an ITV mogul giving oral evidence to the Pilkington Committee (PRO HO244/40), and Lord **Airedale** was speaking on the Cable and Broadcasting Bill, 27 February 1984 (Hansard, vol. 448, cc 1111–43). The **BBC memos** are from 3 July 1930 and 9 July 1930 (Control Board Minutes); the first and others among the BBC quotations are from Su Holmes's detailed academic study *The Quiz Show*; the second and others from volumes two and four of Asa Briggs's *History of Broadcasting in the United Kingdom*; and some of the American quotes are from Thomas A. DeLong's indefatigable *Quiz Craze: America's Infatuation with Game Shows*. The **Symington's Soups competition** is described in the 13 September 2002 *Times Educational Supplement* piece 'We ask the Questions', by *Sale of the Century* and *Top of the Form* setter David Self. Dan **Golenpaul** was interviewed in 1964 for the Columbia Center for Oral History (NXCP88-A1824). *Confound the Experts!* was first broadcast on the Regional Programme London on 2 April 1939; Wilfred **Pickles** was talking to the *Yorkshire Evening News* (30 January 1950, also cited in Holmes's *The Quiz Show*); and the Richard **Bacon** sketch is from episode 6 of series 4 of *John Finnemore's Souvenir Programme*, Radio 4, 20 November 2014. Cecil **McGivern**'s thoughts are from 29 November 1954 (also via Holmes). Louis **Barfe** has much more on the era in his splendid *Turned Out Nice Again: The Story of British Light Entertainment*. The exchange about **whether ITV had too many prize programmes** is from February 1956 (Independent Television Authority file 5004), and the debate is described in much more detail in volume one of Bernard Sendall's *Independent Television in Britain*. The likening of quiz to **girls and wrestling** is cited in Peter Black's *The Mirror in the Corner: People's Television*. The **Supreme Court** case was

347 U. S. 284, and the debate is described in, again, Jason Mittell's 'Before the Scandals', in the *Time* piece 'Radio: Goodbye, Easy Money', 16 August 1948, and *The New York Times* article 'Giveaways to Get Court Aid', 20 September 1949. Not everyone caught on fast to *The $64 Question*'s change of fortunes: as late as 1957, the quiz-sceptic Richard Hoggart, who we met above, was still using the old version of the phrase: a passage in his *The Uses of Literacy* decries popular culture's predilection for stories in which the little man makes it in life against the odds: to suggest that 'all the time he had the sixty-four-dollar answer but did not know it' was, thought Hoggart, 'a lie'.

13. Say it ain't so, Charles: The **quiz scandals** were widely covered at the time and are examined in compelling detail in J. Kent Anderson's *Television Fraud: The History and Implications of the Quiz Show Scandals* and the PBS American Experience documentary *The Quiz Show Scandal*. The **Dotto contestant** was talking to the (London) *Times* for the 28 August 1958 piece 'US Inquiry into Quiz Shows', and **Van Doren's account of his recruitment** is in the affecting *New Yorker* piece 'All the Answers', 28 July 2008. The culture of **UN interpreters** is described in Lynn Visson's 'Diary', *London Review of Books*, vol. 35, no. 21. The *Time* **piece**, 'Television: The $60 Million Question', is from 22 April 1957, and **Van Doren's lengthy *Life* article**, 'Junk Wins TV Quiz Shows', is from 23 September 1957. John Steinbeck's **'On all levels it is rigged, Adlai'** can be found in *John Steinbeck: A Life in Letters*.

14. Here's what you could have won: The **British *Twenty One* imprudence** is described in Bernard Sendall's *Independent Television in Britain: Origin and Foundation, 1946–62* and *The Times* piece 'ITA to Consider Precautions for Quiz Programmes', 18 February 1959; the Pharos piece is from the 7 November 1958 edition of the *Spectator*. The **NUT submission** is in 'Memorandum of Evidence to the Pilkington Commission on Broadcasting', National Archives file ED 147/559, and the **survey data** are from Harry Henry's *Public Opinion and the Pilkington Committee*, conducted by the Thompson Organisation in 1964. Tony **Green** was speaking on ITV's fiftieth-anniversary *Gameshow Marathon*, 22 October 2005, and the **'rotary ironer'** is from Bill Lewis's 'TV Games: People as Performers' in *Television Mythologies: Stars, Shows and Signs* (ed. Len Masterman). The **prescient *Times* tycoon** editorial is from Valentine's Day 1985. The ***Who Wants to be a Millionaire?* story** is told in Peter Bazalgette's *Billion Dollar Game: How Three Men Risked It All and*

Changed the Face of TV; the judgement in the 2004 case 'Celador Productions Ltd *v.* Melville' (neutral citation no: [2004] EWHC 2362 (CH)); Albert & Justin Malbon's *Understanding the Global TV Format*, 'Life's a Pitch', *Campaign*, 7 January 2015; John Plunkett's *Guardian* piece '*Who Wants to be a Millionaire* – the Quiz Show That Said No to Simon Cowell', 6 December 2013; and Brian Viner's *Independent* piece 'Three Wise Men, a Star and a Miracle', 19 July 2000. The **market research** was carried out in July 1996 by Catherine Gammon for the Qualitative Consultancy with the company's director, Allison Parke, and presented in August. And for phonoaestheticians, there's more on **the euphony of 'cellar door'** in Cyrus Lauron Hooper's 1903 novel *Gee-Boy* and George Jean Nathan's 1935 collection *Passing Judgments*. Bob **Holness**'s comments are from 'Beeb Axe Quiz', *Daily Record*, 14 June 2002. Robert **Thompson** was talking on the above-mentioned PBS *Newshour* feature 'TV's Final Answer?', 19 January 2000. The **recent Tarrant** quotes are from a *Telegraph* profile, 4 November 2013, and ' "*Who Wants to be a Millionaire* is over because Contestants No Longer Take Risks," Says Chris Tarrant', *Mirror*, 19 December 2013; the **Lanchester** is from a footnote in 'The Robots are Coming', *London Review of Books*, vol. 37, no. 5 (the prize ladder had by then disposed of the classic £64,000 prize and instead included £50,000 and £75,000); and there is some early work on risk-aversion in the show in the fascinating Warwick University Economic Research Paper (no. 719) by Data Roger Hartley, Gauthier Lanot & Ian Walker, 'Who Really Wants to be a Millionaire: Estimates of Risk Aversion from Game Show Data'. '**Knowledge Its Own End**' is a chapter heading in Cardinal Newman's *The Idea of a University*. There is plenty more on the **University Challenge trophy** at blanchflower.org/uc. The *Antiques Roadshow* in question was from Tredegar House, BBC1, 23 November 2014, and the **Magnusson quote** is from his *I've Started, So I'll Finish: The Story of Mastermind*. The **Bjortomt/Stainer exchange** is in 'I Thought I Knew Everything – but I Soon Discovered "Everything" is a Big Word', *Guardian*, 29 January 2002, and Fred **Housego** was talking to Bradley Walsh in episode 2 of *Come on Down!: The Game Show Story*, ITV1, 17 August 2014.

15. Knowledge is power, and vice versa: The documented **history of pub quiz** and quiz league is patchy, but a tale can be pieced together by browsing local newspapers from the 1940s at the British Newspaper Archive, and Nick Pearce of Durham University has begun the scholarship on the topic with his 2012 event Understanding the Pub Quiz, a podcast of which is at the Economic and Social Research Council website. The Sharon **Burns** profiles include the February 1988 *Director* magazine feature 'Who is the Woman behind All Those Pub Competitions?' and the presciently titled April 1991 *Woman's Realm* piece 'Who Wants to be a Millionaire? They do!' *The Uncommon Reader* was first published in 2006 in the *London Review of Books*, vol. 29, no. 5. The *Top of the Form* **story** is told in *The Top of the Form Story*, BBC4, 25 March 2008, and Hugh Grant recalls his appearance during *Inside the Actors Studio*, Bravo, 12 May 2002. **'Natural Born Quizzers'** was the fifth instalment in *Coogan's Run*, BBC2, 15 December 1995, and its quiz was called *Top of the Class*. The **'Trotsky' intervention** is described in *University Challenge: The Story So Far*, BBC2, 27 December 2008; Peter Gwyn's *University Challenge: The First Forty Years*; and Aaronovitch's *Times* piece 'When Che and Marx were the Real Buzz Words on *University Challenge*', 24 April 2013. Manchester teams are now trained rigorously by the indefatigable Stephen Pearson. Clive **James** gives a detailed account of Pembroke's travails in his autobiographical *May Week was in June*. **'Bambi'** was broadcast on BBC2 on 8 May 1984, and Alexei Sayle refers to 'Bambi' as 'the moment resembling Oliver Cromwell's suppression of the Levellers' in the *Guardian* piece 'I'm Still Full of Hate', 22 January 2013. Stephen **Fry** recalls his visit to Granadaland in more detail in *Fry: A Memoir* and says of losing the final (a best-of-three): 'Nothing will ever put it right. Nothing, I tell you.' Robin **Carmody** writes at the WordPress blog *High Functioning Human*, and the *Not the Nine o'Clock News* **sketch** is from episode 3 of series 4, '*Hi Se Seo an Nuacht ag a Naoi Chlog*'. The Cecil **Corker** quotes are from an interview at *Off the Telly*, 'Fill the Stage with Flags!', October 2005, and the *Ask the Family* entry at the magnificent online encyclopaedia UK *Gameshows*. The **quotes from the Quintons** are in the lengthy *Mail* piece 'What Happened to Britain's Brainiest Families?', 18 October 1997. Patricia **Owtram**'s letter was published on 7 April 2005 and followed up on 17 April with the piece 'Dumber and Dumberer'. Her letter ended: 'If the BBC was going to take someone's idea, make it over, use excerpts from it, repeat selected programmes, and devote airtime to knocking them down, it might have been a courtesy to tell the deviser that this was going to happen.' **Dick and Dom**, meanwhile, are quoted in the self-slamming BBC piece 'Dick and Dom Slam BBC over Quiz', 24 November 2005.

The musical question is from the episode broadcast at 6.50 p.m. on BBC1, 9 January 1978, and the current-affairs one from April 2005. The **Kirkbride and Fuller** quotes are from the *Telegraph* piece 'Is Mastermind Dumbing Down? Pass', 6 August 2004. Irene **Thomas** evokes a bygone era of quiz in her autobiography *The Bandsman's Daughter*. The **Housego quotes** are from 'What Happened Next?', *Observer*, 9 February 2003, and episode 2 of *Come on Down!: The Game Show Story*, ITV1, 17 August 2014. Eleanor A. Maguire's paper on **cabbies' hippocampi** was written with David G. Gadian, Ingrid S. Johnsrude, Catriona D. Good, John Ashburner, Richard S. J. Frackowiak, & Christopher D. Frith for the *Proceedings of the National Academy of Sciences of the United States of America*, vol. 97, no. 8, pp. 4398–403; I am indebted to Kathryn Friedlander for pointing me at E. A. Maguire, K. Woollett & H. J. Spiers's 'London Taxi Drivers and Bus Drivers: A Structural MRI and Neuropsychological Analysis' in *Hippocampus*, 2006;16 (12), 1091–101, which posits that complex spatial representation 'might come at a cost to new spatial memories and gray matter volume in the anterior hippocampus'. William G. **Stewart** was talking to the *Stoke Sentinel* for the piece 'Game Shows: Haven't They All Done Well?', 23 May 1998. **Del Boy** enters Jonathan Ross's *Goldrush* (ITV scuppered plans for a Tarrant cameo with *Millionaire* trappings) in the Christmas 2001 episode of *Only Fools and Horses*, 'If They Could See Us Now . . . !' The **Keppel performance** is summarized on the 2001 DVD *Who Wants to be a Millionaire? Magic Moments and More*, back from the days when people might buy a disc of clips from a quiz programme (as an extra, not available to those who bought the compilation on videotape), and now, of course, in less edited form on YouTube, with more detail in Tarrant's largely accurate book *Millionaire Moments: The Story of Who Wants to be a Millionaire?* Boris **Johnson** interviewed Keppel for the *Spectator* piece 'The Wrong Sort of Millionaire', 2 December 2000. Colman **Hutchinson** spoke about the show in the 'Masters of Entertainment' seminar at the Entertainment Masterclass/Medienbord seminar, 13 August 2007, and the other millionaires are described in Neil Wilkes's *Digital Spy* story 'Fourth Contestant Wins *Millionaire*' and the BBC piece 'Fourth Millionaire "is Millionaire"', both 27 September 2001.

16. Winning isn't everything: As Andrew Biswell's *The Real Life of Anthony Burgess* and his introduction to the 2013 edition of *One Hand Clapping* describe, Burgess's novel was written under the pseudonym

Joseph Kell, which avoided flooding the market with a glut of Burgesses and allowed Burgess himself to review his own work. The **Caffrey** edition of *Sing It Again* was broadcast by CBS at 8 p.m. on 28 August 1948, and the outcome is described in 'Quiz Programs Most Popular', *Nebraska State Journal*, 5 September 1948, and in fascinating detail by family friend and pioneering literary journalist John McNulty in the *New Yorker*'s 'A Reporter at Large' series, 19 February 1949, as well as in an interview with James **Stewart** in 'New Film to Give Push to Movies, Radio Feud', *Paris News*, 7 July 1950. The sorry tale of Marlene **Grabherr** is told in, among other places, '*Günther Jauchs erste Millionärin starb in Armut*', *Die Welt*, 14 October 2014, and the *Hancock's Half Hour* episode is 'The Prize Money', BBC Light Programme, May 1958. *I Won University Challenge* was made by Alisa Pomeroy for episode 3 of series 2 of the BBC's peerless *Wonderland* strand, BBC2, 5 November 2009; one interviewee gave a more upbeat account of his victory at the time in the *Guardian* piece 'Question Time', 4 April 2003. Gail **Trimble** related her brother's response ('Seriously, mate, would you give your sister's contact details to *Nuts*?') in the *Guardian* article '*University Challenge* Star Gail Trimble Adapts to Public Eye', 24 February 2009. (Corpus later lost the title because team member Sam Kay contravened the programme's rule that 'students taking part must be registered at their university or college for the duration of the recording of the series'; Manchester said they were 'saddened to have been awarded the trophy under such circumstances'.) The **end of Jennings's** *Jeopardy!* **odyssey** is told in his *Brainiac: Adventures in the Curious, Competitive, Compulsive World of Trivia Buffs*, and in Nancy Zerg's Associated Press interview '*Jeopardy!* Streak Comes to End', 1 December 2004. (There's also a horrendously mercantile take in the same day's *Bloomberg* piece '*Jeopardy!* Winner, Tax Loser'.) The sample **Final Jeopardy questions** are from 24 November, 9 November and 7 October 2004. He lost on 30 November, and all the questions can be found at the splendid J! Archive site. The Ian **Lygo** story was told on *Five News*, 14 December 1998, and Peter **Richardson**'s varied life is described in the 2012:2 edition of the Mastermind Club's 'Pass' newsletter. The **Magnusson** quote is taken from, again, his *I've Started, So I'll Finish: The Story of Mastermind*. Bill **Bryson**'s indecision is from his *Notes from a Small Island: Journey through Britain*, and the **mandilion** episode of *Eggheads* was on BBC2 on 6 January 2014.

17. **Slight difference of opinion here, Jim:** The **sharp-practice stats** are from the poll I commissioned and mentioned in the introduction

(with 'quizzers' being the 81% of us who watch, listen or take part in quizzes). The **Bristol brawl** is described in Denise Winterman's tremendous *BBC News Magazine* piece 'Not Just a Trivia Matter', 13 January 2005. The **Noël Edmonds legal saga** was reported widely; the best coverage was local, in particular the *Bedford Times and Citizen* piece 'Pub Quiz Master Wins Libel Damages', 11 January 2005. Anne **Robinson's thoughts on rule-breaking** are from Michael Tuft's compelling documentary *Annie Goes to Hollywood*, BBC1, 9 May 2001, and the show's backstory is described in Archie Bland's *Independent* piece 'What's It Like to Face Anne Robinson on the Cult Quiz Show?', 24 March 2012. The **jelly/chopsticks** thought is from Victor Anant's *Picture Post* piece 'The "Give-Away" Shows: Who is Really Paying?', 10 December 1955. The data on **international versions** are from the BBC News piece '*Millionaire* Dominates Global TV', 12 April 2005. The tale of **the Ingram/Whittock trial** is taken from the many contemporaneous newspaper reports; more colour is given in the 'Phoning a Friend' chapter of Jon Ronson's *Lost at Sea: The Jon Ronson Mysteries* (Ronson followed this up in the 2006 *Guardian* piece 'Are the *Millionaire* Three Innocent?'), and in *Bad Show: The Quiz, the Cough, the Millionaire Major* by investigative journalist Bob Woffinden. The *Telegraph* **'source'** is quoted in the piece 'Did a Careless Whisper Betray the Million-pound Conspiracy?', 8 April 2003, and the Stephen **Glover** piece, 'Why This Trial Should Never Have Happened', is from the same day. *Millionaire: A Major Fraud* was broadcast as an edition of the *Tonight with Trevor McDonald* series thirteen days later, and the **Swarup** quote is taken from 'I'm the Luckiest Novelist in the World', *Guardian*, 16 January 2009.

18. **You can't win them all**: '**Pointless**' is episode 5 of series 7 of *Not Going Out*, BBC1, 21 November 2014. Arfor Wyn **Hughes** discusses his ordeal in the 'Disastermind' segment of *TV Hell*, BBC2, 31 August 1992, and in episode 3 of *Come on Down!: The Game Show Story*, ITV1, 24 August 2014, and Magnusson discusses him in *I've Started, So I'll Finish: The Story of Mastermind*. His episode was broadcast on BBC1 on 7 January 1990 and the New College **dons-against-students** game is described in Peter Gwyn's *University Challenge: The First Forty Years*.

19. **I'm feeling lucky**: *You Don't Know Jack* has existed in pretty much whichever format people have been using from CD-ROM to apps and social media. **Watson's workings** are described at the IBM site; in 'The Robot Will See You Now', *Atlantic*, March 2013; 'IBM's Watson

Can Sense Sadness in Your Writing', *Engadget*, 22 January 2016; and 'IBM Watson: The Inside Story of How the *Jeopardy!*-winning Supercomputer was Born, and What It Wants to Do Next', *TechRepublic*, 10 September 2013. **Jennings's remarks** are from 'My Puny Human Brain', *Slate*, 16 February 2011. I've mentioned some of the ungoogleable questions before in a piece for the ***BBC** News Magazine*, 'Can Pub Quizzes Survive in the Smartphone Era?', 1 June 2011. The *Observer* **piece** is Amelia Hill's 'Q: Why Do We Love Quizzes?', 5 November 2000, and Larry **Page's vision of the future** was given to Steven Levy in 2004 and recorded in his book *In the Plex: How Google Thinks, Works and Shapes Our Lives*.

20. **DUM-dum-dum-DAH**: The **prisoner-of-war drama** was Eric Williams's *The Wooden Horse*, Radio 4, 20 October 1969, and Hans Zimmer recalls *Going for Gold* in the *Empire* magazine piece 'Empire Meets . . . Hans Zimmer from *Going for Gold* to Man of Steel'.

Index